MW01632233

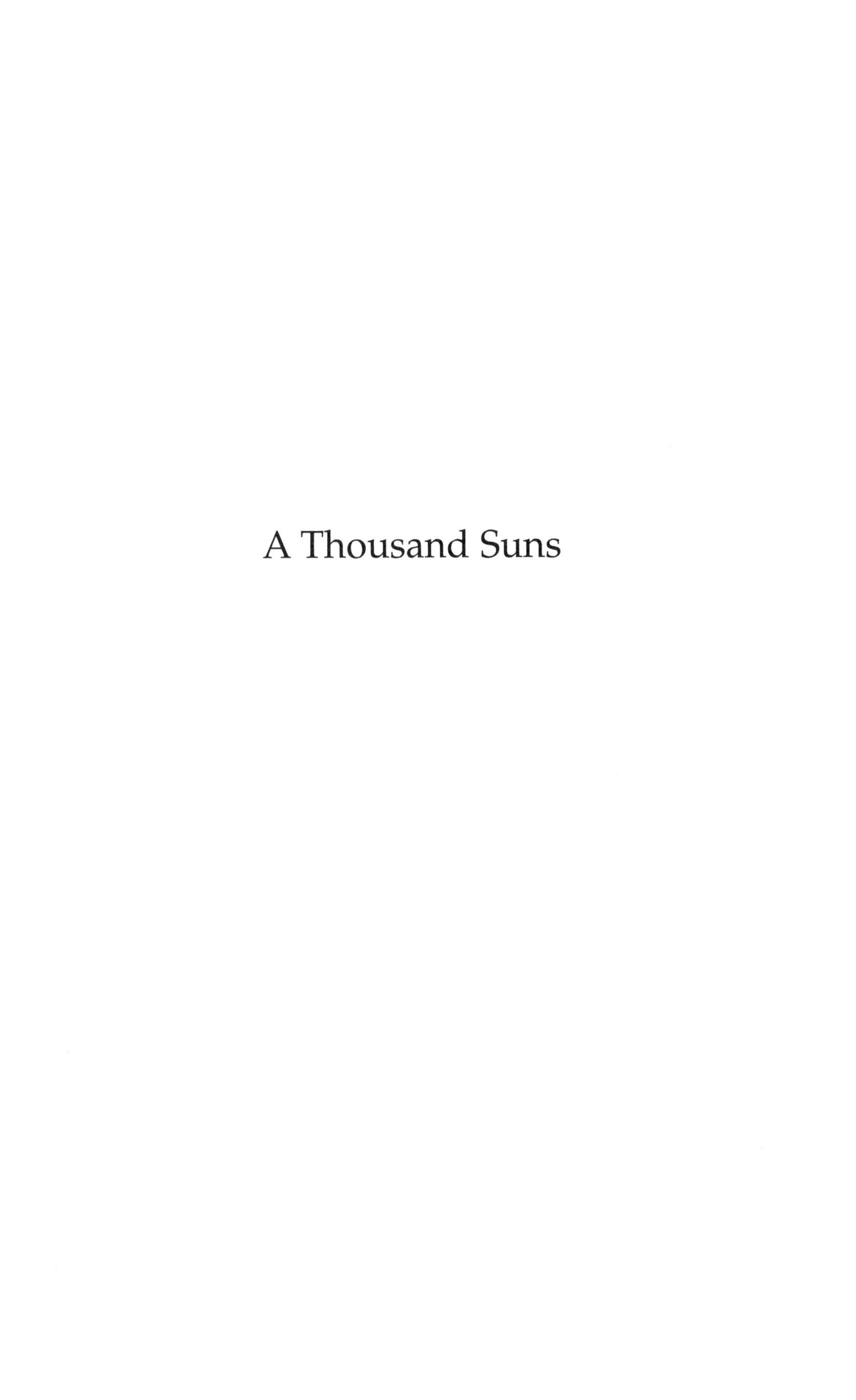

A Thousand Suns

A Thousand Suns

Designing Your Future with Vedic Astrology

Linda Johnsen

Yes International Publishers
Saint Paul, Minnesota

Cover photo from the Hubble telescope was processed by the
Space Science Institute for NASA

Library of Congress Cataloging-in-Publication Data
Johnsen, Linda, 1954 -
A thousand suns: designing your future with Vedic astrology / Linda Johnsen.
p. cm.
Includes bibliographical references.
ISBN 0-936663-35-9
1. Hindu astrology. I. Title.
BF1714.H5 J665 2003
133.5'9445—dc22 2003024433

Yes International Publishers
1317 Summit Avenue, Saint Paul, MN 55105
651-645-6808
www.yespublishers.com

For the Jyotir Vidya
with reverence and awe

Acknowledgments

Fifteen years ago scarcely anyone in the Western world had heard of Vedic astrology. I was living in an ashram in Pennsylvania while I completed a graduate degree in Eastern Studies, yet even there I heard nothing more than faint rumors that the Hindus had a secret science of the stars. India's yogis and pandits were graciously teaching us yoga and meditation, but were reluctant to reveal the more esoteric systems of their tradition.

In the nid 1980s the silence was finally broken. Sri R. Santhanam and Sri Poputal M. Padia agreed to teach a Western astrologer named James Braha. Braha's classic book, *Ancient Hindu Astrology for the Modern Western Astrologer,* introduced the world to Jyotish, one of the six sacred sciences of india's wisdom tradition.

Today I don't believe there's a major city in the Western world where Vedic astrology isn't practiced. its phenomenal growth in the United States is due in part to the enthusiastic efforts of the American Council of Vedic Astrology. I had the pleasure of serving on the ACVA Board and editing its journal for four years. I'd like to express my appreciation to Dennis Harness, David Frawley, Jim Kelleher, and the rest of the ACVA team who've done so much to create the wonderful sense of community we Vedic astrologers here in the U.S. enjoy.

Another important reason for Hyotish's current popularity has been the unstinting support of *The Mountain Astrologer,* the finest astrology magazine in the world. Thanks so much to Tem Tarriktar, Kate Sholly, Nan Geary, janette deProsse, linda Puffer, and the rest of the staff at TMA who always make room for a Vedic article! I don't think readers have any idea how much work it takes to put out a magazine ike TMA. Having served as Vedic Astrology Editor there for eight years, I can personally attest to the exceptional integrity, commitment, and amazing good humor of TMA's talented staff.

Though I've studied with a number of excellent teachers, most of whose views are represented in this book on one page or another, I owe a special debt of gratitude to Hart deFouw and the lineage of his mentor, K.L. Mantriji. Hart is the finest teacher of Jyotish in the West today. Sutdying with him has been a remarkable privilege. Thanks also to Aletha deFouw, the anchor of the Vedic Vidya Institute.

Where would any of us be without our support group? Here in the San Francisco Bay Area I've been extraordinarily fortunate to share my astrological explorations with fellow Jyotish enthusiasts Bette Timm, Martha Betz, K.C. Chamberlain, Christine Earl, Ariella ben David, Danielle Williams, Bill Edwards, Grace, Eric Nelson, Steven Highburger, Hank Friedman, Brilla Hall, Jennifer Clayton, and Brian Conrad. Needless to say the gretest measure of support comes from my husband Johnathan Brown, whose adventures, reflected in his astonishing horoscope, have provided material for more than a few of my articles on astrology! Johnathan, incidently, created the star charts and Christine Earl helped design the cover for this book.

Many, many thanks to my good friends at Yes International Publishers in Saint Paul. They are people who publish books because they love knowledge and serve spirit. I hope they publish a thousand more!

And finally I must acknowledge my most profound indebtedness to the great souls who taught me the upayas: Shree Maa, Swami Satyananda, Ammachi, and the masters in the lineage of Bengali Baba, especially Swami Rama, who always insisted that no matter what the stars say, "*You* are the architect of your destiny."

I bow again and again to Lord Ganesh, commander of the constallations, to Lord Varuna, king of the night sky, to Lord Brihaspati, who governs my mind and heart, and to Shri Parashara, the master himself, the embodiment of the science of light.

Contents

Part 1
The Sages and the Sacred Sky

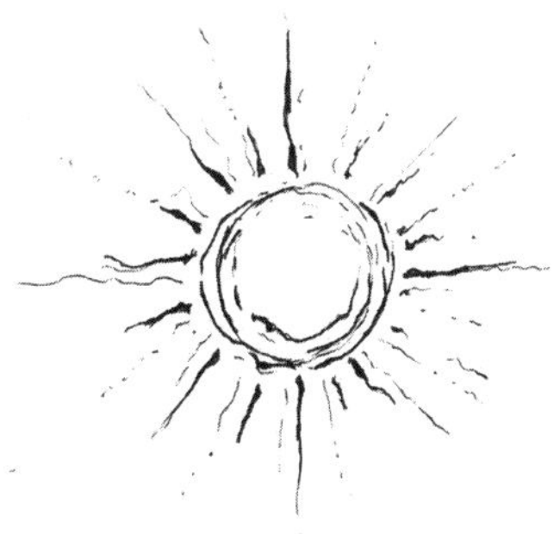

The divine manifests itself in many forms.
It appears as the planets to bestow on us
the results of our previous actions.
In this way it teaches us to renounce our evil tendencies
and to do only good.
Brihat Parashara Hora Shastra 2.3-4

Whatever we do is reflected in the whole,
in the one universal mind,
and returns to us with the same intensity.
Ammachi

Astrology is the eye of wisdom.
Without eyesight, a man cannot find his way.
Prashna Marga 1.12

1

Entering the Universe of Vedic Astrology

Donald Walters first stumbled across the *Book of Bhrigu* when Raja Mrigendra Singh invited him to visit an astrologer in the tiny Punjabi town of Barnala. The local astrologer owned a book written by a sage named Bhrigu thousands of years ago, which had been copied and recopied over the generations. In it was inscribed the destiny of every human being who ever lived, Singh insisted.

Walters was a disciple of Paramahansa Yogananda, one of the first Hindu masters to bring yoga to the West. Through Yogananda, he had learned to appreciate the wisdom of India's mystical traditions. But this claim was so outrageous, the normally open-minded Walters had trouble politely concealing his skepticism. Still, the next day he climbed into the raja's car for the sixty mile drive to Barnala. In an unassuming home on Gaushala Road, Walters met Pandit Bhagat Ram, keeper of the *Book of Bhrigu.*

The book, it turned out, was a huge mass of brittle sheets on which North Indian-style horoscopes and their delineations had been painstakingly printed by hand. Stacks of pages were pressed between wooden boards and carefully wrapped in cloth. Humble and sincere, the pandit disappeared into his library, emerging two minutes later with the appropriate horoscope for Walters. It described Walters' "previous incarnation" in Persia, as well as his present life as "a teacher lecturing on spirituality in a foreign country." Oddly, it explicitly stated that his name was "Kriyananda"—a rare name in India. Stunned, Walters passed the page to his friends in the room, asking them to verify the Sanskrit. They confirmed that the pandit had read the page correctly. Walters, whose monastic name was indeed Kriyananda, and whose lifework was teaching meditation in America, wandered out of the house in a daze.

A few months later Walters was back. This time he was prepared to conduct some serious research. If the pandit was a fraud, Walters was determined not to be fooled a second time.

In a few moments Bhagat Ram brought out a new reading in which the ancient sage Bhrigu began by saying he would not review Walters' past lives since that had already been covered in the previous reading. This time Bhrigu claimed his client's name was "James" (Walters' baptismal name) and that he had been born in "Rumanake" (close—Walters was born in Rumania) but was presently living in "Amerika."

Could the pandit somehow have made inquiries into Walters' life and produced a fraudulent reading? Walters had to know. He obtained permission to take the reading with him to Delhi, where several scholars independently verified the Sanskrit translation. At the Indian National Archives, laboratory technicians used chemical analysis to certify that the page had been produced over a century previously, the last time the *Book of Bhrigu* was recopied.

In the reading Bhrigu offered several specific predictions for Donald Walters, most of which soon came to pass. In addition Bhrigu offered some intimate information about Walters' family members; facts which Walters was able to substantiate when he returned to the U.S. The ancient sage also counseled Walters on several important issues—the very concerns Walters had been wrestling with the day he consulted Bhrigu.

This sounds like science fiction doesn't it? An astrologer giving accurate readings for clients who will come to him more than a thousand years after his death? You and I are rational people; we know the *Book of Bhrigu* couldn't possibly exist. Yet any one of us can take the bus to Barnala in the Punjab—and there it is. I sit here with a photocopy of Walters' palm leaf reading before me, which with my fledgling Sanskrit I can transliterate for you. Yes, Bhrigu spelled the name of Walters' adopted country "Amerika" even though George Washington and Thomas Jefferson would not be born till centuries after the prediction was written.

As my husband, a physics major and veteran traveler to South Asia, likes to say, "Don't think of India as another country. Think of it as another planet. In India, everything is different. Even the laws of physics. Things that should happen, don't. Things that can't happen, do." I'm not so sure the laws of physics are actually different in India, but the understanding of these laws is definitely not the same. Perhaps that's the reason things which seem miraculous to our Western minds are taken completely for granted in a culture where so many saints and yogis cultivate higher states of awareness.

I first went to India not to study Vedic astrology but to learn about India's ancient Goddess tradition and its allied tantric sciences. But when I made a disparaging remark about astrology to a tantric yogi, he looked at me in astonishment. "How can you understand tantra unless you know astrology?" he demanded. He told me the following story about his own guru's encounter with the *Book of Bhrigu.*

This tantric's spiritual master, Bhole Baba, was a remarkable adept who had lived in the Himalayas for much of his life, doing advanced spiritual practices. While passing through the Punjab he decided to test the local Bhrigu pandit. Disguising himself as an Indian businessman, he stopped by the Bhrigu library. The pandit disappeared into his stacks to find the appropriate reading for the incognito mystic. Moments later he came running out, the horoscope he had just read clutched in his hand, and threw himself to the floor in full prostration before the saint. "Either you are an enlightened master," he cried, "or all my work here is meaningless."

One of my professors in graduate school, where I studied Indian philosophy, confirmed that his own Bhrigu reading had discussed his past and future incarnations. It had gone on to correctly describe his caste and unorthodox lifestyle in this life, along with offering miscellaneous correct details like the first syllables in the names of his wife and children. This was from an astrology reading that had been prepared for him centuries before he was born.

How can this be possible? As we take a closer look at Indian astrology, at least some of the mystery begins to peel away. First, not only Bhrigu but many other sages of the Hindu tradition founded schools of astrology. There are over 150 predictive compendiums like the *Book of Bhrigu* scattered throughout the Indian subcontinent. They're called *Nadi Granthas* which means "knowledge which unties knots in the flow of destiny." These voluminous texts were probably not prepared by a single sage, but by the seer's many apprentices. Evidently, part of their training as astrologers involved preparing predictions for future generations of clients! Traditions something like this continue today. Recently two American women who studied astrology in southwest India told me that their teacher required them to sit down at dawn, consider the positions of the planets throughout the day ahead, and then write out a list of questions his clients would ask him that day, as well as the correct answers. (Don't believe this is possible? I'll show you how it's done in Chapter 7.)

Here's another important reality check. The *Nadi Granthas* don't really contain readings for every human being who ever lived. In fact, they contain a limited number of delineations for particular souls "destined" to receive a reading. Therefore not everyone who consults the *Book of Bhrigu* or any of its numerous counterparts will find a reading waiting there for them. I also hasten to add that although the delineations are often amazingly accurate, they are not infallible. Whether this reflects a breakdown in the principles of Indian predictive astrology, the free will of a client acting to "break" from the destiny foreseen by sages like Bhrigu, or the incompetence of the particular student preparing the reading, I can't say.

If you're wondering how an astrologer who lived and died ages ago could come up with the names of future clients such as Kriyananda, here's the secret. In Indian astrology certain Sanskrit syllables are associated with particular stars and constellations. Therefore a random mix of syllables that would have been meaningless to the astrologer at the time (such as A-me-ri-ka) might nevertheless have been "spelled out" by the positions of the planets during a reading done centuries ago.

Astrology in India

I should add that the *Nadi Granthas* are only one small branch of the enormous, prolific tree of Hindu astrology. The vast majority of Indian astrologers work with other aspects of the tradition, including reading horoscopes based on the moment of your birth. Typically a *janma kundali* (birth wheel) is drawn up by hand, along with up to nineteen subcharts and extra tables delineating planetary strengths, in order to give what the Indians consider a complete reading. In an era before computers, the amount of calculation this entailed was staggering.

People in India take these readings very seriously. I remember suffering through all the indignities visitors from the West are initiated into in that magical land: struggling with the monkeys trying to tear my underwear off the clothesline on the roof of my Benares hotel, feeling the heat of incredulous stares as I unwittingly climbed aboard the all male rather than the all female compartment of a Madras train, and continually swilling massive doses of urgently needed anti-diarrheals. Then one day I happened to turn to the "personals" column in a Delhi newspaper. "Engineer seeks light complexioned bride. Send horoscope." "Doctor looking for wife. Biodata required." I thought of tipsy men sidling up to single women in American bars and asking, "Hey baby, what's your sign?" In India that question is taken very seriously. If you're looking for a husband or wife, be prepared to show your horoscope.

In fact, one of the most common jobs Hindu astrologers do is check for relationship compatibility. In India it's the parents' responsibility to have the horoscope of their son or daughter's prospective mate thoroughly scrutinized before marriage arrangements are finalized. If the couple's charts are seriously incompatible, the proposed union is canceled. This aspect of astrology is so deeply embedded in Hindu culture that even some professional Indians abroad, like the Hindu software engineers my husband works with in Silicon Valley, defer to the astrologer's judgment in the selection of a marriage partner. If this seems improbable to you, consider that generally they haven't yet met the husband or wife their parents have chosen for them back in India. Under these circumstances, no wonder they consider it prudent to arrange an astrological pre-screening.

Astrologers are also frequently employed to determine auspicious dates for religious ceremonies, important events like moving into a new house, and for the inauguration of enterprises such as opening a new shop. There are especially astrologically potent times for everything you can image, from first putting on a new necklace, to launching a course of study or cursing a neighbor. When the Indians gained independence in 1947, astrologers were immediately consulted to set the "time of birth" for the new nation.

Indian astrology is also used for answering straightforward questions. "I lost my expensive silver bangle. Where is it?" "My brothers fight constantly. What can be done?" "Will I make a profit from this financial arrangement?" "Can my business partner be trusted?" "My mother is extremely ill. Will she recover?" The astrologer casts a chart for the moment the client poses the question, and reads the possibilities inherent in that moment of time. "Venus is pre-eminent in the chart; you will find your jewelry. Check again the southeastern portion of your husband's place of business." "Jupiter and Mars adversely aspect one another. There will be no peace between your brothers." "Mercury is crossing the Ascendant. This business venture will be very profitable for you. However the Moon's north node is in the 12th house. Take care you do not squander your earnings."

In the United States educated people often sneer at "pseudo sciences" like astrology, while religious leaders rail against it as "superstition." In India, however, astrology is a hallowed part of the indigenous spiritual tradition, and orthodox brahmins (the Hindu priestly caste) are required to learn basic astrological principles in order to properly schedule rituals and festivals. Courses in astrological science are even taught in Indian universities. India's leading astrologers conduct lively debates on the future of the country and its numerous celebrities in newspapers and popular magazines. These articles are followed with great relish by large segments of the population.

Many Hindus also check the newspapers daily for their horoscopes. In India you don't look up your Sun sign, however. Traditional Hindus are more interested in which of the 27 Vedic Moon signs you were born under. You'll learn about your Vedic Moon sign in Chapter 6.

If you simply name the date, time and place you were born, a well-trained Indian astrologer can tell you what constellation was rising over the eastern horizon at that moment, and approximately where the Sun, Mercury, Venus, Mars, Jupiter and Saturn were placed in the sky. This is not as hard as you might think, incidentally. Hindus have been recognized as superb mathematicians from antiquity, and formulas for quickly calculating planetary positions were widely known.

What's difficult to calculate however, is the position of the Moon, since it moves through the zodiac so quickly. So from time immemorial Hindus have given their children names corresponding to whichever of the 27 constellations the Moon was traveling through when they were born. This way astrologers with no access to published planetary tables instantly know where in the birth chart to place a person's Moon. Imagine growing up in a culture where astrology is so important that your name is assigned based on the position of the Moon.

Astrology continues to play a significant role in people's lives in South Asia even today. Because it throws light on the dark and mysterious landscape of the future, astrology is called *Jyotir Vidya,* "the science of light," or *Jyotish* for short. The astrologer is called a *jyotishi,* "light bringer" and *daivajna,* "one who knows the divine will." To practice Jyotish is a sacred calling. Traditional jyotishis often spend hours a day in prayer and meditation, aligning themselves with divine purpose as it reveals itself in the movement of the stars, so that they can more meaningfully guide their clients.

Jyotish is usually called Vedic astrology in the West because it is rooted in the Vedas, India's oldest and holiest scriptures composed more than 5000 years ago. Veda comes from the Sanskrit root *vid,* meaning "knowledge." *Vid* is also the source of our English words wit, wisdom, and Druid. Brahmin priests in India use Jyotish to find the most propitious dates for chanting the *Veda's* sacred hymns and performing Vedic rites.

Cycles of Destiny

My own first encounter with Vedic astrology occurred when I asked James Braha, author of the classic *Ancient Hindu Astrology for the Modern Western Astrologer,* to do a reading for me. James' reading, done over the phone from out of state, was so specific and accurate that I seriously wondered whether he had secretly called up some of my friends to ask about me. Now that I've studied the system he used, I can easily see that Braha didn't need to conduct a private investigation. All he had to do was glance at my Vedic birth chart and compare it with my planetary cycles. Mercury is associated with education in my horoscope, and sure enough during my Mercury period I was in college. In my chart the shadow planet Ketu represents spirituality, and during my Ketu period I had moved into an ashram to devote myself to spiritual practice. As Ketu gave way to the Venus cycle (Venus governs both marriage and material luxuries), I left the ashram, got married, and bought a car, furniture and a stereo system. I knew absolutely nothing about Vedic astrology at the time, yet every major event in my life was unfolding right on schedule according to principles outlined in this ancient science.

Western astrologers tend to see the birth chart as a psychological map, a mythologically-based key to the human psyche. They use their clients' birth charts primarily as an entry to personality and compatibility issues, often downplaying the use of a horoscope as a predictive tool. If your Sun is in Virgo, your Western astrologer may tell you you're detail oriented and are compatible with people born in water signs like Cancer or Scorpio. She's much less likely to tell you that next March you need to be particularly careful about your health, or that you'll probably marry two years from now and have your first child the following January.

Vedic astrology, however, has a strongly predictive focus. For thousands of years clients have gone to Indian astrologers wanting to know when they would get married, if they would meet with professional success, the most auspicious time to start a new business, what health problems loomed in the future, whether their children would do well. For thousands of years in an unbroken tradition, Vedic astrologers observed the positions of the planets and carefully correlated their data with events in the lives of their clients. Today there exists more astrological literature in Sanskrit and the other Indian languages than in the astrological traditions of all other cultures combined.

In ancient India qualification standards for anyone wishing to become an astrologer were extremely high. Astrological schools, without exception, were founded by men and women who were not only astronomers, scholars or priests, but also yogic adepts. The fathers of Indian astrology, like Bhrigu, Parashara and Jaimini, are still universally hailed as spiritual masters. They understood that looking into destiny is not a frivolous affair, and that it requires more than ordinary intelligence and insight to guide a client to break free from the yoke of a particular chain of destiny, such as a string of unsuccessful relationships.

Nearly two thousand years ago an astrological adept named Varaha Mihira insisted that the serious student of astrology must possess not only intellectual brilliance but the highest ethical principles, advanced command of meditative states, excellent communication skills, profound compassion and a thorough knowledge of "occult" techniques such as mantra science, rituals and the reading of omens.

Until recently, Hindu astrologers did not specify payment for their readings, but worked on a donation basis. They cultivated a sense of contentment with whatever offering their clients might make, whether it was a purse filled with gold or a cup of grain. Srila Bhaktivedanta Prabhupad, a spiritual leader who rose to international prominence in the 1960s, fondly remembered the astrologers who appeared outside his home when he was a boy. "They were honored as very respectable guests. When we were children, such brahmins would visit householders like humble beggars, and people would derive great benefit. The greatest benefit was that a householder could save a great deal of money from being spent on doctor bills because the brahmins, aside from explaining the past, present and future, could ordinarily cure all kinds of diseases simply by giving instructions and some medicine."

Astrology, Prabhupad added, is "a system by which anyone can immediately get information about what he was in the past and what he is going to be in the future. Thus the highest knowledge was easily available even to the poorest man in society. The brahmin would give him all the benefit of his knowledge without asking remuneration, and the poor man, in return, would offer a handful of rice, or anything he had in his possession. In a perfect human society, perfect knowledge in any science—medical, astrological, ecclesiastical and so on—is available even to the poorest man, with no anxiety over payment."

Astrologers originally performed their work as a spiritual service, not as a means of enriching themselves, and many of them cheerfully remained quite poor. They would not dream of beginning a reading without a chant invoking the grace of God and acknowledging the insight and altruism of their teachers. Every ancient and medieval astrological treatise in India opens with a prayer.

In addition, Vedic astrology has always had a strong esoteric component. Advanced astrologers were taught to move beyond the birth chart to contact the planets within. In fact, the most important prayer in the Hindu tradition, the Gayatri mantra, is specially formulated to align oneself with one's "inner Sun." The prayer, roughly translated, says, "We bow to the inner Sun, the most splendid light in all the worlds. Please illuminate our minds."

The original astrologers were not only spiritual prodigies but also formidable astronomers. Vedic texts more than five thousand years old reveal knowledge of previous pole stars (Polaris has been the North Star for only a short period of time by the standards of the immensely ancient Vedic civilization) and the precession of the equinoxes. Incredibly, Indian astronomers had even correctly worked out the speed of light centuries before Western physicists. It was probably the combination of intuitive insight developed through yoga practice, superb astronomical and mathematical skills, and a database of thousands of years of observations of human behavior in relation to stellar movement, that led Vedic astrologers to create an astronomical predictive system so precise that a student of the sage Bhrigu could sit down and write a remarkably accurate delineation for a person who would not be born for another thousand years. Tapping into the cycles of destiny, a long-departed Indian astrologer could discern the tide of fate that would carry Donald Walters from a foreign land called "Amerika" to the tiny town of Barnala for a startling lesson in Vedic astrology.

Invitation to the Stars

The Vedic system will have an enormous impact on the way astrology is practiced in the West in the twenty-first century. In northern California where I live, astrologers who are not trained in the Hindu system now specifically identify themselves as "Western" astrologers in their ads to avoid receiving numerous calls asking for a Vedic reading.

Needless to say, as we are confronted with the predictive accuracy of the Vedic chart, challenging philosophical issues materialize in the most disconcerting manner. Questions about past lives and predestination have to be addressed. Our role in creating our own triumphs and tragedies has to be acknowledged. When we start seeing ourselves as spiritual beings who arrive on Earth with a purpose to fulfill—and as souls whose inner light is reflected in heaven—our understanding of ourselves will be forced to widen.

As you scan through the following pages you will be entering a new universe, one in which karma and reincarnation—twin abstract theories on which the Vedic horoscope is based—suddenly become objective realities. It's a whole new field of experience that may rattle the core of your current beliefs.

But yoga—the mystical science at the root of Vedic astrology—is not about belief. It's about testing the claims and experiencing the results for yourself. India's ancient yogis saw the soul as an eternal sojourner in the cycles of destiny, and beyond. They articulated their insights in invaluable texts describing different forms of yoga, different paths to divine awareness, including the path we today call astrology. They bequeathed their knowledge to humanity in an effort to help the rest of us find our way from the bondage of karma to the freedom of a life lived consciously in spirit.

You are about to enter a universe in which the laws of physics are different: where things which we tell ourselves can't happen, do.

Try Vedic astrology on your own chart. You'll never be able to look at the world the same way again. Like Galileo when he first aimed his telescope at Jupiter and discovered its moons, your universe is about to expand.

2

Return to the Source: Ancient Indian Astrology

It was the first century of the Christian era and Apollonius of Tyana was on his way to India. If you had lived in the Roman Empire then, it's unlikely you would have heard of Jesus Christ, who wouldn't become widely known for another century or two. But you would definitely have heard about Apollonius, the most famous sage of his era. Emperors Nerva and Titus both sought his blessing before assuming command of the empire. Emperor Septeminus Severus ranked Apollonius among the greatest men of antiquity, along with Alexander the Great and Orpheus. Emperor Lucius Aurelian, during his bloody campaign in Asia Minor, spared the city of Tyana out of respect for the great sage who had been born there.

Apollonius, a physician practicing medicine at a temple of Aesclepius in eastern Turkey, had often heard that the Indians possessed advanced spiritual sciences. He believed that if he could learn these techniques, he would be much better equipped to help the patients who flocked to him for healing.

In the 3rd century Hellenistic classic, *The Life of Apollonius of Tyana,* Flavius Philostratus documents Apollonius' studies in an ashram in the Himalayan foothills where his Indian gurus taught him the secrets of *Surya Vidya,* the science of the Sun. "The living universe loves itself more intensely than any human lover can love someone separate from himself, with a passion that knits all of life together in one harmonious whole. Its size is immense, and it governs itself with many hands." Among these governing hands, the Indians explained, are the stars and planets.

Apollonius was fascinated with astrology but his teachers warned him, "Before one can accurately foresee the future, he must purify himself physically and mentally. Only someone who understands himself can grasp the workings of destiny." According to Philostratus, Apollonius devoted most of his stay in India to studying Vedic astrology, and went on to write a four-volume textbook in Greek explaining its principles. This important book, *Divination by the Stars,* is mentioned by numbers of ancient authorities, though tragically in the 4th century all of Apollonius' books were destroyed by Christian fanatics.

Ironically, Apollonius' mastery of Vedic astrology got him into trouble back in Rome. His enemies charged him with black magic because of his uncannily accurate knowledge of future events. Again and again the sage explained that his foreknowledge was not the result of sorcery but of science—Vedic science. He was initiated in the mystery schools of Greece, and spent two years studying with the Magi in Babylon. He also lived for several decades among the hierophants of Egypt. Yet at the end of his long life he solemnly insisted that the greatest knowledge he had found anywhere in the world was that of the *sophoi,* "the wise," of India.

The Arabs too, though formidable astrologers in their own right, spoke of an ancient, powerful system of astrology preserved by Hindu brahmins. A thousand years after Apollonius, Al-Biruni, one of the greatest *munajjims* (Muslim astrologers) of his era, set out to learn the Vedic system. "I do not spare either trouble or money in collecting Sanskrit books ... and in procuring for myself, even from very remote places, Hindu scholars who understand them and are able to teach me." Al-Biruni's descriptions of Indian astrological practices were so detailed and accurate, they serve as an excellent introduction to the subject even today.

And now, a thousand years after Al-Biruni, you and I are about to make a mental pilgrimage to India, seeking the wisdom of the science of the Sun. But before we begin, let's take just a few minutes to learn who the astrologer-sages of ancient India actually were.

A Culture of Enlightenment

If you had lived in 2600 B.C.E., North India is where you would have wanted to be. It was home to the most advanced civilization in the world, the Indus-Sarasvati culture. It was huge, extending from eastern

Afghanistan to the west end of the Ganges. It's the wonder of modern archeology, filled with beautifully designed cities that had better sanitation than many parts of the world do today.

The most astounding thing about this culture was that unlike Sumer and Egypt, the two other major, though much smaller, civilizations flourishing at the same time (in fact unlike any other high culture in the history of the world) archeologists have been unable to find any conclusive evidence of war. Nowhere is there an image of a brutal ruler massacring his enemies or ruthlessly imposing his will on the people. (Mesopotamia and Egypt were filled with such images.) There are no swords or other weapons specifically designed for killing people, no war helmets, no shields. Not one of the human remains excavated so far has shown signs of death by violence. Thousands of years later, when the Chinese Buddhist pilgrim Faxian visited north India in the fourth century C.E., he reported that you could still travel from one end of the country to the other without fear of robbery or assault.

When Apollonius visited this area in the first century, he was astonished to discover that kings there lived in homes not much more opulent than those of the common people. When he asked the local *raja* about this, the king replied that he couldn't bear to raise taxes on his subjects, whom he saw as his children, just so he could live in luxury. Archeologists confirm that as far back as they have searched, there don't appear to be any palaces; it seems rulers lived much like the ruled. The king also explained to Apollonius that the real leaders of the country were sages, ascetics who devoted their lives to spiritual practice and spent part of their day counseling government officials, royalty and anyone else, no matter how poor, who came to them for advice.

India's ancient epics, the *Mahabharata* and the *Ramayana,* confirm the enormous impact enlightened sages had on the governance of the people. Apollonius reported he had never seen such high ethical standards and pure moral conduct anywhere else in the world.

Many of the Indian cities of 2600 B.C.E. were built along the Sarasvati River, at that time rivaling the Amazon as the largest river on Earth. Due to tectonic changes, the river vanished around 1900 B.C.E., yet to this day Sarasvati is known as the goddess of spiritual wisdom, the arts and education. This must reflect the high level of culture and literacy of the people who once lived along her river banks.

Today we think of India as a culture of poverty. We forget how recent this perception is. The ancient Sumerians imported luxury items from India by the ton, their cuneiform records show, and even borrowed Hindu accounting methods. Two thousand years later, long after the Sumerians had vanished, the Romans developed a dangerous trade deficit to India which seriously destabilized their economy. Ancient Roman trading centers have been unearthed in India.

Remember why "In fourteen hundred and ninety-two, Columbus sailed the ocean blue"? Because the backward states of northern Europe were desperate to establish trade with India and its islands, the wealthiest area in the known world. In fact, when Columbus arrived in the Americas, he mistakenly named the natives he met there "Indians." When the British consolidated control over much of India in the 18th century, they called it "the jewel in the crown" of the British empire, recognizing India as by far their most valuable conquest. It was only then that India was reduced to the state of poverty we associate with it now, after Europeans had removed almost everything of value they could find.

While the lion's share of archeology has been done in the dazzling lost cities of the north, Dravidian-speaking South India fostered its own rich culture. Walking along the gorgeous beaches of southwestern India I've tried to visualize the ancient merchants we know arrived here from Egypt, Arabia and Mesopotamia in search of spices and other Indian treasures. The South Indians also preserve a tradition of a fantastically advanced culture once centered in Sri Lanka, said to have developed an early form of flying vehicle. Unfortunately the extensive excavations needed to uncover its hidden artifacts have barely begun.

Back in the north, archeologists have uncovered evidence of typical Hindu cultural practices dating back to at least 10,000 B.C.E.—that's as far back as the last Ice Age. And thanks to the single-minded diligence of India's brahmin caste and lineages of saints and yogis, at least some of the wisdom of India's ancient high-minded culture has been preserved intact. This includes Jyotish, its system of astronomy and astrology.

Ancient Astronomers

Astronomy has always been incredibly important to the Hindu people. From time immemorial it was the brahmins' job to keep track of the passing of the year, which they marked with appropriate rituals. Time was sacred to the Hindus, who aligned themselves with its currents by participating in special rites performed at certain times of the day, of the month and of the year. They used both a twelve-fold division of the solar year, which we still know today as the twelve signs of the zodiac, as well as a 27 day month reflected in the 27 signs of the lunar zodiac still used in India today. Both systems are mentioned together in very early texts; the earliest surviving horoscopes mention both the solar sign (such as Aries or Taurus) and the lunar sign (such as Ashvini or Bharani). A 4400 year-old coin unearthed at Harappa, one of the largest ancient Indus-Sarasvati valley sites, shows a scorpion on one side, representing the solar sign Scorpio, and on the other a deer with an arrow, representing the lunar sign Mrigashira which lies exactly opposite Scorpio along the ecliptic.

The Hindus have always been superb astronomers and cosmologists. Unlike orthodox Christian and Islamic intellectuals of the West, Hindus have always recognized that the universe is billions of years old. Their description of how our Earth is destined to perish (roasted by a reddening Sun, then burnt to ashes as the Sun balloons up in size at the end of its life) matches modern Western scientific thought in detail. More than a thousand years before Copernicus, Indian astronomers like Aryabhatta taught that the Sun, not the Earth, is the center of our solar system. In the earliest surviving astronomical text, the *Surya Siddhanta,* they even mention a civilization—they called its capital city Siddha Puri—of advanced adepts on the exact opposite point of the globe from India. This would be the high culture of Central America, unknown to most Europeans till Columbus.

The Hindus were expert mathematicians who invented the decimal system and were comfortable with numbers in the quadrillions. They developed the so-called Arabic numerals (0 through 9) we use today. These mathematical skills helped immensely in tracking the orbits of the planets and calculating horoscopes.

Professor Subhash Kak of Louisiana State University recently pointed out to me a remark by a 14th century Indian scholar named Sayana. In his commentary on the *Rig Veda* Sayana writes, "With deep respect I bow to the Sun, who travels 2,202 *yojanas* in half a *nimesha*." A *yojana* is about nine American miles; a *nimesha* is 16/75 of our seconds. I'll do the math for you.

2,202 *yojanas* x 9 miles x 75 ÷ 8 *nimeshas* = 185,794 m.p.s.

Sayana is saying that sunlight travels at 186,000 miles per second. Here we have an Indian scholar who died in 1387 C.E. stating the correct figure for the speed of light, a number unknown in the West till Fizeau and Foucault rediscovered it in the mid-19th century. This reemphasizes what a mistake it is for us to underestimate the astronomical abilities of the Hindus.

Ancient Astrologers

According to Hindu tradition, astrology is a vastly ancient science. A version of Vedic astrology related to that practiced today is said to have been codified by the sage Parashara sometime before 3100 B.C.E. This is not to say that astrology as we know it now was fully developed at that time, but that the essential principles out of which our modern system grew were already recognized and applied. And yet Parashara's system, the tradition claims, represents only a small portion of the astrological knowledge of still earlier ages.

Most Western scholars dispute this account, pointing to evidence that astrology as we know it began developing in Mesopotamia quite late, perhaps 500 B.C.E., and was perfected by the Greeks who brought it to India two centuries later.

Here are the facts. The *Rig Veda* is a massive compendium of ancient hymns. It's the oldest book to survive intact into modern times. We know this huge text was composed before the disappearance of the Sarasvati River around 1900 B.C.E. because it often mentions the river in full flood. Internal evidence in the text (mostly astronomical references) push the date back to at the very latest 2500 B.C.E. Vedic tradition says the hymns were composed many centuries earlier, before the ancient Indus cities recently unearthed were even built. The sacred songs were collected, arranged into their present order, and passed on orally by the famous sage Vyasa around 3100 B.C.E.

Vyasa's father, incidentally, was none other than Parashara, the codifier of Vedic astrology himself. According to legend, Parashara was a celebrated spiritual adept and master astrologer who lived just before the beginning of the *Kali Yuga,* our present world cycle. One evening while he was sitting back in a ferry looking up at the sky, he noticed that the planets formed a pattern absolutely superb for conceiving a child who would make an immense contribution to human welfare. Mentally calculating forward nine months, the sage foresaw that on the child's birth date another even more spectacular planetary configuration would occur. Parashara immediately asked the woman sitting in the boat with him to marry him. Nine months later Vyasa, one of the most significant figures in Indian history, was born. Vyasa not only assembled the four books of the holy Veda including the *Rig Veda,* he also composed the earliest version of the epic *Mahabharata,* and collected the history and legends of ancient India into a massive encyclopedia, the first *Purana.* Thanks to Vyasa, India is the best documented high culture of antiquity.

The *Rig Veda* is a hymnal, not an astrology text, yet it's filled to brimming with astronomical references because the Vedic seers honored the stars as shining representatives of divine light. It repeatedly mentions a wheel in the sky that has 12 spokes and 360 divisions. In the Hindu tradition it presents the 12 months of the year with 360 days, the 12 signs of the zodiac composed of 30° each and the 12 houses of the horoscope.

The *Rig Veda* goes on to say, "The seven regions of the sky have seven different ministering priests. These are the seven lords of the 12 divisions." Eighteenth century Western scholars who first translated the *Rig Veda* into English were totally confused by this passage, yet anyone familiar with astrology will understand it instantly. The seven rulers are the Sun, Moon, and the five planets the ancients could see with their naked eyes (Mercury through Saturn). The 12 divisions are the 12 signs of the zodiac. The Sun and the Moon rule one sign each, Leo and Cancer. The other five planets each rule two signs each (Mars, for example, rules both Aries and Scorpio). That indeed reduces the 12 sectors of the sky into the seven mentioned here. No other interpretation makes sense.

The very first historical reference to the planet Venus in all its astrological glory occurs in the *Rig Veda.* In hymn X.123, Venus is described as the planet of romance who rises like a beautiful nymph from the waters (exactly like Aphrodite, the Greek Venus). The hymn associates the planet with a bull (to this day Venus rules Taurus, the sign of the bull) and with multi-colored clothing, which in Vedic astrology is also attributed to Venus. Incredibly, the hymn was composed by a sage named Vena, whose name may well be the source of our word "Venus."

The *Rig Veda* mentions the celestial ram (Aries) as well as the celestial bull (Taurus), the lovers (as Gemini is conceptualized in India), and the heavenly goat (Capricorn). It shouldn't surprise us to find the signs of the zodiac in the text when so many other constellations familiar to us are also explicitly mentioned, including Pegasus, Orion, the Pleiades, Aquila and more. Incidentally, the stars of the Great Bear are called the Seven Sages in India. Fascinatingly, while the Sanskrit word for sage is *rishi,* the Sanskrit word for female bear is *rikshi. Rikshi* also means "north" in Sanskrit. Of course the Great Bear is the most prominent constellation in the northern sky.

So the ancient Hindus had a sky wheel with twelve spokes, recognized most of the zodiacal constellations we know now, and even associated specific qualities (like multi-colored clothing) with particular planets. Can we be sure the ancients interpreted these astrologically?

"From the summit of the sky the stars speak. They know everything but compel no one. The wheel of time, formed with twelve spokes, spins in the heavens, maintaining order," says the *Rig Veda.* I can't imagine what else the text could mean but that while the stars know and reflect our destiny, and maintain karmic law, they never infringe on our free will. This sounds like Vedic astrology to me. The text contains hundreds of hymns for realigning ourselves with the cosmic forces when we fall out of harmony with them through our misdeeds. Hindu astrologers continue this tradition to the present day.

In the *Rig Veda* the dark-robed deity Varuna represents the night sky. He is the guardian of moral order who carries a noose with which he "yanks" evil doers. In Sanskrit the word for planet doesn't mean "wandering star" as it does in Greek. *Graha,* the Sanskrit word for planet, literally means "grabber." Clearly, from remotest antiquity the stars were seen as enforcers of karmic law. Is it any wonder that in those long gone days, when people didn't have important things to do like watch reality TV or play computer games, they set about learning the language of the stars?

Very few books exclusively about astronomy and astrology have survived from early Indian history. The ancient Indians preferred to pass on their sciences via the spoken rather than the written word, and when they did commit their knowledge to writing they used perishable materials like dried palm leaves which have long since disintegrated. The ancients did, however, find other media to speak to us through the millennia. They left universal symbols to help us understand their beliefs about the cosmos.

The most famous artifact discovered in the Indus-Sarasvati valley excavations is a seal showing a male with two large, curved horns, who is seated in a yoga posture. He is surrounded by four animals: a water buffalo, tiger, elephant and rhinoceros. These correspond to the ancient Indian constellations:

- Vrishibha—Taurus the bull to us today
- Simha—Leo the lion now
- Airavata—while some Indians depicted Scorpio as a scorpion, other saw it as the head and upturned trunk of an elephant
- Uchchhaihshravas or Paga—our Pegasus lying directly above Aquarius

These four constellations represent the quarters of time (the year) and space (the four directions). Note that in the era when the Indus culture flourished, the spring equinox occurred in Taurus, the summer solstice in Leo, the autumn equinox in Scorpio, and the winter solstice in Aquarius.

The seated figure is an ancient form of the god Shiva called *Pashupati,* "lord of the animals." The animals he rules are constellations, imagined in animal form to make their confusing arrangement in the sky easier to keep straight in one's mind. The seal is making the symbolic statement that Shiva (God) governs the entire universe, including the stars and all the creatures in it.

Our word "zodiac" comes from the Greek and literally means "circle of animals." Clearly the people of ancient India already recognized this circle of animals in the sky. And they knew that while these constellations rule our destiny, Shiva, the Supreme Being, rules the stars. Jyotish helps us find our way through life and understand our experiences as the play of karma. But it also makes us keenly aware of the all-pervading justice and grace of the Star Maker, our divine source.

3

Your Past Lives: How You Created Your Horoscope

In recent years, Vedic astrology has become the brightest star on the New Age horizon. Everyone is rushing out to have their horoscope recast according to the Hindu zodiac. The reason for the excitement is that, while Western astrology offers a brilliant analysis of personality, Hindu astrology offers specific details about your future. The *dashas* and *bhuktis* (planetary cycles) described in Indian stellar lore are said to reveal if and when you'll find your true love, make your fortune, or become enlightened.

For some people though, the idea that astrology might actually work is extremely unsettling. It seems to suggest our future is written in the stars and we're simply playing out a script that was drafted for us by unknown forces. What happens to free choice if an astrologer can correctly predict that a newborn baby is going to grow up to be a plumber or a professor? What's the point of working hard to build our business if our horoscope shows we'll go through a bankruptcy? In the West, even the suggestion that our genes (much less our horoscopes) may shape our lives makes us queasy.

In the yoga tradition, however, fate and free will are two sides of a single coin. Because of the Hindus' unswerving faith in karma and reincarnation, they believe that the destiny which controls our lives is the one we created ourselves.

Reincarnation: The Basis of Vedic Astrology

Western science claims a newborn child is influenced by two factors only, heredity and the environment. That a third factor–the child's own predispositions from its previous lives–could be an even more important component in shaping an individual's personality isn't even considered. This makes it hard to explain why an Einstein or a Mozart is born into an otherwise average family. Or why one infant seems to always radiate joy, while another glowers with rage. Or why one teenager feels inexplicably drawn to ancient Egyptian civilization, while another is obsessed with medieval French musical instruments. Or why certain people are instinctively drawn together, or repelled by each other, even though they scarcely know each other.

Western religion claims that each child represents a spanking new soul, created out of thin air by God. From this perspective the birth chart seems arbitrary, a planetary blueprint randomly assigned each new soul as it pops into existence. Some infants luck into comparatively benign charts; others are born with a tough row to hoe. There's no rhyme or reason for this. It's just the breaks.

The nature of the universe is not so random, according to the Vedic tradition. The law of cause and effect is continually at work. We are guided (some might say misguided) into the circumstances in which we find ourselves by our actions and attitudes from previous lifetimes. Karma is largely responsible for our character, our environment, and the type of people with whom we associate. Karma sends one American pilgrim to Jerusalem, another to Macchu Picchu. It propels one individual to indulge in addictive drugs and another to become a pharmacist. These karmic patterns are unmistakably reflected in our birth chart. "In the classical Hindu tradition, rebirths, karma and astrology are intertwined because that is the truth which all good astrologers can see," explains K.N. Rao, one of India's leading astrologers.

A recognition of the role of reincarnation in the twists and turns of fate was originally also central to the ancient Western wisdom tradition. According to legend, the Greek god Hermes was so delighted with a devotee named Aethalides that he offered him any boon he might wish.

"I want to live forever,"Aethalides requested.

Immortality was the one gift Hermes couldn't give. He asked

Aethalides for his second choice.

"Then let me remember all my incarnations every time I'm reborn."

Aethalides got what he wanted. In a later incarnation he became famous as Pythagoras, one of the founders of Western philosophy and science. According to his biographers, Pythagoras explained that the reason for his extensive knowledge was that he remembered everything he'd learned in his past lives.

Plato, one of the most important thinkers in Western history, was profoundly influenced by the mystery schools of his time, which taught the transmigration of the soul. According to Plato, in the after-death state we have a certain amount of freedom to select the circumstances of our next life. The events of our future life flash before our mind's eye just before we enter our new body, just as the past events of our life flash before our eyes when we exit the body.

The yoga tradition of India states there is a force called *vaishnava shakti* which acts at the moment we pass out of the womb into a new life. It wipes our mind clean of all memory of our previous existence. It's caused by the shock of the immaterial soul once again "hooking up" with a physical body. This connection, according to the yogis, is made through *prana,* the life force or breath. This is the reason astrologers calculate horoscopes from the moment the infant takes its first breath. At that instant the living energy of the universe is indelibly "stamped" on the new individual, marking his or her character with the qualities of the unique moment of time reflected in the position of the planets. You may remember that in the Bible, when the Creator fashioned Adam out of clay, he "breathed into his nostrils the breath of life" and at that moment Adam "became a living soul."

The amnesia that occurs at birth actually lasts for several years, as the soul gradually settles into its new brain and nervous system. This is the reason most people can barely remember anything that happened before the age of three or four. According to the Hermetic tradition of Egypt, our souls were so distressed at having to leave our original heavenly home to enter bodies of matter, that we ourselves asked the Divine Being to remove our recollection of the past. Otherwise the memory of losing our place in the divine world would be unbearable.

Reincarnation played a significant role in early Christianity as well. In the Bible, Jesus repeatedly affirms the existence of reincarnation

(Matthew 11:14, Matthew 17:10-13; Luke 1:17). Unfortunately, these important biblical verses are ignored by Christian leaders today.

Born Again

Our birth chart outlines the qualities we developed in past lives: cheerfulness or depression, austerity or sensuality, faith or cynicism. Even without our horoscope we sense the pressure of our past karma when we feel attracted to particular people, or afraid of things that aren't really dangerous like snakes or spiders. In a past incarnation, a snake or spider may have killed us. I've been terrified of boats since I was a small child—an embarrassing situation for a Scandinavian. (We Norwegians are supposed to be seafarers practically from birth.) I was stunned when, without knowing about my phobia, a Vedic astrologer told me I had drowned in a recent life—it was obvious in my chart.

The cycle of reincarnation is called *samsara* in India, and it can be very unpleasant if we're caught in a continuing spiral of self destructiveness. It's not that great if we've reborn in an era when the world is falling apart, like when Genghis Khan swept through Central Asia or the Black Plague decimated Europe. Advanced yogis and yoginis can enter and leave the wheel of rebirth at will, rather than being more or less helplessly caught in its twelve spokes as most of us are. By consciously transferring their awareness from their old "used" body into a new one, they can avoid the effect of vaishnava shakti, and retain their memories and identity from life to life, just as Pythagoras did.

The wheel of rebirth which carries us from life to death and back again is, of course, the zodiac. The Sanskrit word for planet is *graha,* which, as I said before, literally means "the grabber." It's the force which catches us by the scruff of the soul and forces us back into yet another physical body to deal with our leftover karma. When the cycle of a particular planet comes into play, that planet is said to "grab" us as we fall into the grasp of the karma it represents.

Graha also means crocodile, the pitiless reptile which shoots out from the water to drag its victim down into the depths and make a meal of it. Fascinatingly, in Egyptian funerary art a crocodile is often shown waiting to attack the newly deceased soul in the Hall of Judgment if the person's heart doesn't prove light as a feather, free from guilt and selfishness. Incidentally, very early Christian texts discovered at Nag

Hammadi in Egypt continually bemoan the planets' power to force us back into yet another material body.

For those of us who believe the cycle of rebirth is real, it's extremely important to study our charts closely, to carefully evaluate our strengths and liabilities, and to prepare ourselves for the planetary cycles to come. We need to divest ourselves of qualities such as anger, greed, and self-delusion which generate negative experiences in this life and the next.

Death arrives for everyone sooner or later, whether we're ready for it or not. If we're still carrying a load of unfulfilled desires and obligations, our stopover in any heavenly realm for which we may qualify will be brief. Instead of passing through the portal at the roof of the sky so familiar to yogis, shamans and mystics of the inner traditions, free to explore other dimensions of the universe, we're sent back to square one, physical existence on planet Earth. Our memories are wiped away by vaishnava shakti and it's Groundhog Day all over again. We keep repeating the grade until we finally graduate. According to the Hindu tradition, if we fail really miserably we may even be set back a grade, returning in an animal body for example.

Not only individuals reincarnate, but entire cultures can re-embody themselves. I personally feel the United States is the reincarnation of the ancient Roman Empire. Like the Romans, Americans seem to share a compulsive desire to impose their cultural values on other countries, a taste for violent entertainment, and a pragmatic, mercantile approach to progress regardless of ethics or aesthetics. The Romans ultimately failed to meet the challenges of their time and their civilization perished; Americans are being confronted with remarkably similar challenges today.

In Pakistan, in Kosovo, in the Middle East, in Ireland—nearly everywhere we turn these days—we see groups of souls harboring resentments they should have let go of centuries ago. If the Vedic view of the cosmos is correct, we and our societies keep reincarnating over and over until we get things right. Only then the planets release their grip on our destiny.

Gift of the Sages

Many of us instinctively believe in the law of karma. But few of us know what our karma is. Because we can't remember our past lives, most of us have no clue what kind of effects we set in motion in previous incarnations. We don't understand why awful things happen in our lives, and plead with God like beggars for a lucky break. We're stumbling in the dark, confused about our purpose in life and angry at the terrible injustice we see all around us. Why do evil-doers often get away with their crimes? Why aren't good people always rewarded for their selfless acts?

Seeing our confusion, ancient sages like Parashara, Jaimini and Bhrigu bestowed the great intuitive science of astrology on humankind. In India astrology is called "the eye of the Veda" because with its help we're no longer blind to the forces of karma that drive our lives and determine the circumstances we live in, as well as shaping our attitudes and relationships. The sages themselves don't need astrology because they can see directly into the heart of reality. But astrology is like a prosthetic limb for the rest of us who're confined to far more limited states of awareness. It allows us to foresee the challenges and opportunities ahead as we pass (or fail) the curricula of the cosmic university.

How is this possible? I asked K.N. Rao, one of India's foremost astrologers, to explain how Jyotish works. Rao was first trained in the subject by one of the finest astrologers in Lucknow—his mother—and was later initiated in the connection between astrology and yoga by the renowned yogi Bhaskaranand. For years Rao has taught at the world's largest and most prestigious astrological college at Bharatiya Vidya Bhavan in New Delhi.

"*Sanchita karma* is the total balance of all thoughts and actions from our previous lives," he began. "It is stored in the subtle body we carry with us from birth to birth until, at the time of liberation, it is finally completely dissolved. *Prarabdha karma* is that part of our total accumulated karma which is allotted for this birth, the events destined to occur in this lifetime. This is what is revealed in the birth chart. The degree of the Moon at birth sets the wheel of our unique destiny in motion. Things don't happen when you want them to, but when they are destined to occur.

"*Kriyamana karma* is the freedom we have to improve ourselves. We are free to create *akarma,* karma that doesn't produce karma. These are selfless actions, the fruits of which we release to God. This liquidates the karmas of the past and leads to enlightenment. But we also have the choice to produce *vikarma,* non-virtuous activities leading to bondage. Practicing astrology makes one a strong believer in moral do's and don'ts because we can see that, like a calf finding its mother in a herd, our positive and negative thoughts and actions from the past will always seek us out and produce their results. The choice to act selflessly in the service of others is the one sure freedom we enjoy within the preordained orbits of our lives.

"Jyotish is a dazzling living tradition. Its very name means the science of illumination," Rao explained. "Practiced lovingly, it takes you through all the stages of yoga, from *yama* and *niyama* (personal ethics) to *samadhi* (deep meditation), from *vedanga* (spiritual technology) to *vedanta* (spiritual wisdom). Its purpose is to destroy negativity and encourage hope. The best of astrologers are yogis even today."

Yoga and Astrology

The first time I heard of Vedic astrology was when I read Paramahansa Yogananda's spiritual classic, *Autobiography of a Yogi.* Yogananda's guru Sri Yukteshwar was a master astrologer. Having studied Yogananda's chart, Yukteshwar announced, "The stars are about to take an unfriendly interest in you!" The master went on to explain, "A child is born on that day and at that hour when the celestial rays are in mathematical harmony with his individual karma. His horoscope is a challenging portrait, revealing his unalterable past, and its probable future results."

But then Yukteshwar made a point that everyone reading this book needs to understand. "The message boldly blazoned across the heavens at the moment of birth is not meant to emphasize fate—the result of past good and evil—but to arouse man's will to escape from his universal thralldom. What he has done, he can undo. None other than himself was the instigator of the causes of whatever effects are now prevalent in his life. He can overcome any limitation, because he created it by his own actions in the first place, and because he has spiritual resources which are not subject to planetary pressure.

"The wise man defeats his planets," Yukteshwar emphasized. "There are certain mechanical features in the law of karma which can be skillfully adjusted by the fingers of wisdom."

As Yukteshwar predicted, within a month Yogananda was struck with excruciatingly painful liver disease. According to his horoscope, he would have to suffer for six months. But because Yogananda performed

KARMIC FACTORS IN VEDIC ASTROLOGY

Type of Karma	Definition	Astrological Indication
Sanchita	The total karma accrued as a result of our actions in previous lives.	A 120-year portion of our total karma is shown by the planetary placements in our birth chart *(janma kundali).*
Prarabdha	Karma from past lives destined to play out in our present incarnation.	Shown by the cycles *(dashas/bhuktis)* based on the Moon's position at our birth and by transits *(gochara)* to our natal planets.
Kriyamana	Karma we're generating through our actions in this lifetime.	May be seen in a chart for the present moment *(prashna).*
Agama	Karma we are setting in motion through our plans for the future.	Revealed in a chart for the beginning of a new project *(muhurta).*
Samhita	Collective karma created by the thoughts and actions of groups of people.	Seen in horoscopes of groups, organizations, companies, or nations *(samhita jyotish).*

the appropriate remedial measures prescribed by his guru (in this case, by wearing a special protective bangle blessed by his spiritual teacher and doing lots of spiritual practice), the symptoms subsided after three weeks.

One of the things that makes yogis like Yukteshwar so awe inspiring is their mastery of India's secret sciences including meditation and related psychic disciplines. Since Swami Vivekananda first introduced yoga to the West at the World Parliament of Religions in Chicago in 1893, yogis have begun to bring their secret sciences to the West. We in the West now have at least a beginning level understanding of mantra science and of *Svarodaya,* the science of breath. (A very watered down form of Svarodaya forms the basis of many stress reduction techniques being taught in American hospitals today.) But there are many hidden techniques the yogis have not yet initiated us in. Only very slowly as we Westerners gradually open ourselves to inner life are the *vidyas* or higher sciences introduced to us by the masters.

After a hundred years of laying the groundwork with the basic rudiments of yoga practice like hatha postures and mantra meditation, the adepts are finally allowing Vedic astrology to be taught in the West. Till recently Jyotish had been so thoroughly concealed from the Western world that many students who had been practicing yoga for years weren't aware it existed. This in spite of the fact that astrology is one of the major spiritual disciplines in the Indian tradition. But you can imagine the problem the yogis faced introducing this system to a culture that doesn't even believe in karma, much less reincarnation.

Our Next Birth Chart

No one is saying the stars cause our experiences. Our thoughts and actions in this and previous lives, not the planets, create our world. The planets simply reflect our karmas back to us like a cosmic mirror.

There's a fundamental lesson to be learned here. If our actions from past incarnations dictate our experience in this life, then our actions now are drawing the horoscope we will be born with next time. We are presently in the process of creating our future, for the rest of this life and our lives to come. Therefore we are well advised to be very careful about the karma we're generating. "Be not deceived; God is not mocked." says the Bible. "For as a man sows, so shall he reap." Yet no one can reap all their karma in just one lifetime. Look around you: you'll see criminals who flourish and wonderful people who suffer terribly. But over the course of a number of lives, the scales balance out. A physical body lasts at most a hundred years. But the soul's adventures continue indefinitely. Shree Maa of Kamakhya, one of the greatest living saints of India, puts it this way: "We don't have many different lifetimes, but one infinite, continuous life in many different bodies."

In the *Bhagavad Gita* (one of India's spiritual classics), Lord Krishna explains, "Just as a man takes off his clothes at the end of the day and puts on a fresh set of clothes the next, so the soul removes its body at the end of one lifetime and puts on another at the start of the next." The soul is on a cosmic journey that takes it through many lifetimes, and perhaps ultimately through many different worlds. Vedic astrology was a tool developed by the ancient sages to help us understand this multi-dimensional process as we grapple with the karma coming to play in our lives. Hindus call it the "divine eye" because it allows us to see behind the world our senses paint for us into the mechanics of karma, the underlying energies of consciousness that create our world.

In the next chapter we'll take a look at the specific types of information a Vedic chart provides.

4

Your Karmic Report Card: What Your Vedic Chart Reveals

Your Vedic horoscope is a summary of the karma you've accrued up to the moment of your birth. It reflects your talents and abilities, relationship skills, family dynamics, financial prospects, spiritual aptitude, health, and psychological strengths and shortcomings to the extent that you developed them in previous incarnations. If you worked hard to achieve a position of leadership in a past life, for example, the same leadership qualities may resurface in your present personality even in childhood. Your Vedic chart will reflect this.

When your Vedic astrologer calculates your natal horoscope, she gets a snapshot picture of a chunk of your sanchita karma, the karma you've accumulated during your numerous past births. She'll also calculate subcharts called *amshas* which reveal these karmas in more detail. Only a fraction of this total karma, however, can play out during the course of one lifetime. So, she will next calculate a series of planetary cycles called dashas which reveal your prarabdha karma, the karmas you'll actually experience in your present life.

Your chart may suggest a spectacular financial windfall, for example, but if the planetary cycle that supports it doesn't begin till you're 100 years old, you may have to wait till your next incarnation to experience it. Note that the Vedic chart maps the karmic currents of your life in their full complexity: a cycle that's great for making money may at the same time be problematic for marriage or health.

The Data of Destiny

The Vedic astrologer's job is to help you become more conscious of your prarabdha karma. This type of karma determines:

1. The species into which you have been born.
2. The strengths and weaknesses, attitudes and talents you bring with you into this body.
3. The circumstances and events, pleasant or unpleasant, you will undergo in this body.
4. The approximate length of time you will spend in your current body.

Your astrologer will not be more than 70% accurate. If she's 80% correct she's having an exceptionally good day. The reason even the best jyotishis make mistakes is kriyamana karma, the fresh karma you've been creating since you were born. Remember, the horoscope only reveals your karmic status up to the moment of your birth. From that point on your attitudes and behaviors in this life modify the course of your karma, for better or worse. The chart reveals the samskaras or mental and emotional tendencies packed in your karmashaya, the repository of karma you carry with you from life to life like baggage. But each time you make a conscious choice you can to some extent override the vectors of destiny that were set in motion when you took your first breath.

For this reason, Vedic astrology cannot tell you what will happen in the future. It can only suggest what might happen unless you consciously act to modify or prevent it. If you throw a stone into a pond, waves will sweep out from it in circles. But if you toss in a few more pebbles the pattern will change. In most cases, karmic currents represent a trend, not a certainty, because you're still throwing rocks in the pond.

Karmic Consciousness

According to the Vedic tradition, karma comes in three strengths. First, there's karma that's easy to change. For example, if you sign up for a course in tax law, but then decide you'd rather take a biology class, you can switch courses fairly easily.

Second, there's karma that can only be altered with substantial effort. If you graduate with a degree in law, but then decide you'd rather be a doctor, you can go back to college and get a medical credential—but it will cost you a lot of time and money. The vast majority of karma playing out in your life falls in these two categories. To a greater or lesser extent, it's subject to change.

The third type, however, is fixed karma. These are the lessons you can't get out of, the experiences you must undergo for the sake of your spiritual growth, to repay old debts or because you have the karmic credit coming to you. Some individuals, like the children of royalty, are born to wealth and fame, for example. They have to deal with the issues this karma creates whether they like it or not.

Note that whether a particular stellium of karma, such as being rich and famous, is good or bad depends entirely on your attitude. You may consider fire good if it warms you but bad if it burns you, yet fire simply is what it is. Karma is just karma, the natural consequences of your actions. Any moral judgment involved comes from you. There are planetary configurations that show a woman will almost certainly be childless. For one woman this may be devastating. For another it's a huge relief.

Only a small portion of your total karma is unalterable. There do appear to be cases where a person must go through some traumatic event like the breakup of a marriage or a serious accident or illness. Or someone may definitely be destined to enjoy exceptional good fortune such as winning a lottery, landing a lead role in a hit movie or experiencing a miraculous cure. Knowing in advance when a positive cycle is likely to occur can help place you in position to take maximum advantage of a favorable period.

There is another factor to consider, however, a completely different kind of karma that can also drastically impact your life: collective karma. If a person who is running a cycle signalling physical danger happens to live in a peace-loving culture, she may fall and break her leg on the fateful day. Another person who happens to live in a culture with a high tolerance for violence could be the victim of a mugging or assault while running the very same cycle.

It is absolutely wrong to claim that if an individual is the victim of a crime, that person karmically deserved it. Just as individuals generate karma, so do neighborhoods, organizations and nations. Group karma can override or strongly modify individual karma, particularly during collective experiences like war. This shows that nature holds us responsible not

LIKELIHOOD THAT A DESTINED EVENT WILL OCCUR

TYPE OF KARMA	DEFINITION	ASTROLOGICAL INDICATION
Adridha	Karma which can easily be changed through our own effort. Flexible karma.	Shown when only weak indications for an event are apparent in a birth chart.
Dridhadridha	Karma which we can change through considerable self-effort.	Shown when several factors in a chart point toward the same fate.
Dridha	Karma which cannot be changed through human effort. Only God can alter fixed karma.	Shown when numerous factors in a horoscope all point to the same destiny.

only for our own actions, but for the attitudes and acts of the communities of which we are members. In Vedic astrology, collective or samhita karma is read from a mundane chart such as the horoscope of a corporation or a country.

Family life–the most basic form of group karma–is strongly reflected in a Vedic chart. In India the extended family system is still the norm, and families are very close. Family karma is considered to be so delicately intertwined that you can pick out the broad details of family members' lives in your chart. I have definitely found this to be true. Major events in my husband's life are reflected in my chart. So are my father's profession, my mother's health status, and even my brother's romantic life.

When a new baby or marriage partner enters the family, the entire group dynamic can change in surprising ways. For example, some infants are born with great financial karma which they're destined to enjoy in early childhood. Sure enough, you'll see that shortly after the baby is born the parents suddenly experience dramatic financial gains. Indian matchmakers actually look for prospective husbands or wives with "lucky stars" to enhance the collective karma of the in-laws.

Meeting Your Bane

The Scandinavian sagas I read as a child often spoke of the hero "meeting his bane." We don't have a similar concept in the modern West, but it was an important notion to many of our ancestors. It meant the hero had met the person, object or circumstances destined to cause his death.

When traditional Hindus go to see an astrologer, they expect him to tell them when they'll die. Here is the West, if an astrologer made such a statement her clients would probably sue her. I remember expressing my astonishment that a professional jyotishi would actually give out such information. The Indian astrologer looked at me incredulously. "How can you plan your life if you don't know when you're going to die?" he demanded. Hindus are very practical.

I have somewhat mixed feelings about recommending that people see an astrologer when they go to India. On the one hand, traditionally trained jyotishis who spend hours a day in worship and meditation and who've been practicing the science since childhood can offer readings with predictive precision hardly a handful of Western-born Vedic

OUR BODIES AND OUR STARS

BODY	DEFINITION	ASTROLOGICAL STATUS	INDICATION
Sthula Upadhi	Physical Body and Vital Force	Mortal. Begins dissolving at death. Subject to planetary influences.	Read from the Ascendant.
Sukshma Upadhi	Subtle Body (Mind)	Mortal. Dissolves at rebirth. Subject to planetary influences, but capable of freedom through self-knowledge and selfless love.	Read from the Moon.
Karana Upadhi	Causal Body (Soul)	Semi-immortal. Dissolves at liberation. This "Higher Self" carries karmas from its previous physical body to a new one at the moment of reincarnation.	Read from the Sun.
Atma	Pure Consciousness (Spirit)	Eternal. Unaffected by karma. On the contrary, planetary energies are subject to Spirit.	Unreadable.

astrologers can match. On the other hand, the Indian tendency to "tell it like it is," expecting that if a client has come for a reading they want to be told the whole truth, can be a very disconcerting experience for an American or European. Very traditional Hindu astrologers are amazingly frank about character flaws they see in a chart, as well as about both positive and negative experiences they foresee. Western-born jyotishis are generally far less technically accomplished, but relate the information in the chart more delicately.

Since that most trepidacious of all questions, "When will I die?" holds a fascination for us all, let me address the issue here. While all of us are destined to die, the date on which we'll pass away is not fixed in most charts. As I stated earlier, most of the karma an astrologer reads in a horoscope is either very flexible or can be altered with some effort. A well-trained jyotishi can glance at a chart and say with a fair degree of certainty whether an incarnation will be short, mid-length, or long. But only a small number of people are firmly fated to die on a particular day. Most of us either have the prarabdha karma to die young, die in middle age, or die in old age, but when we'll die within that broad range is to a large extent up to us.

The 11th century Jyotish master Sri Pati explained, "People are more likely to enjoy the full range of longevity promised by their horoscope if they live disciplined lives, follow the guidance of the wise, and eat wholesome foods. If they choose to eat poorly, engage in an unhealthy lifestyle, or go through life with an attitude of disrespect, they are less likely to live as long as they might have otherwise." (Apparently the importance of a holistic lifestyle has been known for centuries.) Within the critical age range the chart may suggest several periods during which a person might die. Someone who smokes heavily, drives drunk or engages in unsafe sex may die in an earlier period rather than a later one.

According to my horoscope, I will probably die in middle age. For me this is useful information. I'm less concerned with stashing money away for retirement, and more preoccupied with accomplishing as much as I can in the limited amount of time I have left. In the West however, most Vedic astrologers refuse to discuss the time of death except in the most general terms, and then only if the client specifically requests the information.

READING KARMA IN A VEDIC HOROSCOPE

The planetary combinations in your birth chart reveal the karma you created in your previous lives. This forms your destiny in this life.

In India karma is read from the sidereal zodiac, using the backdrop of the stars. This is different from the tropical zodiac used in Western astrology, which begins with the first day of Spring.

Karma is shown by:

1. The placement of planets in the 12 signs *(rashis)* and 12 houses *(bhavas)* of the zodiac.
2. The placement of planets in the 27 lunar constellations *(nakshatras).*
3. Special patterns and combinations *(yogas)* formed by the planets.
4. Major and minor planetary cycles *(dashas* and *bhuktis).*
5. Transits *(gochara)* showing the planets' current position in relation to their placement in the birth chart.
6. Subcharts *(amshas)* that emanate out of the birth chart.
7. Horoscopes for the moment a question is asked *(prashna).*
8. Horoscopes for the moment a new project is launched *(muhurta).*
9. Horoscopes for groups of people *(samhita).*

Acknowledge Your Power

At the risk of sounding like a broken record, let me repeat a vitally important point. According to Vedic astrology, the planets merely signal the time when our karmic debits and credits come due; they don't actually cause us to do anything. Think of a traffic light: it signals when it's time for us to go, but it's our stepping on the accelerator that makes the car move. The choice to act comes from us, not the lights in the sky.

A horoscope is just a symbolic representation of forces at play in our unconscious. Traditional Hindu astrologers will tell you the universe was projected out of a limitless cosmic mind. Therefore thoughts and symbols are as real as physical objects. This is why not only actions, but also thoughts produce karma. Although a horoscope is only a symbol, it can be just as helpful as a road map—another symbolic representation that helps us find our way. And because horoscopes were designed by illumined sages, they can act much like a *yantra,* a device for focusing, clarifying and directing consciousness.

Since the single most common criticism of Vedic astrology you'll hear from people who don't know anything about it is that "it's fatalistic," I want to be absolutely certain you're clear on this fundamental point before you go on to the next section, in which you'll learn how to set up your Hindu horoscope. A Vedic chart is no more fatalistic than the report cards you receive in school. These assess your past, but they don't dictate your future. You live out the promise of your high school grades, for better or worse, only to the extent that you continue to live out your past. The power to change lies with you. Because of its avowal of kriyamana karma—your absolute freedom to choose your own course in the present moment—Vedic astrology provides one of the most radical affirmations of free will in any philosophical system.

The horoscope is a starting point, a platform to work from, not a judge's sentence leaving no opportunity for an appeal. Your destiny isn't written in stone but is a living thing that changes subtly as your level of consciousness expands or contracts. Many deep-rooted problems shown in the chart can vanish completely if sincere and consistent effort is applied.

If your physician tells you, "Your cholesterol is high. This puts you at increased risk for a heart attack," or "Your blood pressure is too high.

This puts you at risk for a stroke," her goal is not to make you spend the rest of your life quaking in fear. Her point is to encourage you to change some facets of your lifestyle that may be contributing to the problem. She may even prescribe medication to help reduce the risk. In Vedic astrology also we are assessing risk factors. If you learn you're about to enter a challenging cycle, there's no need to react fearfully. This information is designed to help spur you to use your intelligence and willpower to manage the upcoming cycle successfully. Imagine if your stockbroker could tell you in advance the market was going to dip precipitously during a certain period. This information shouldn't scare you—it should inspire you to take sensible action.

For example, I recently noted that Mars, which is extremely powerful right now because it's the closest it's been to the Earth in 60,000 years, is passing through the nakshatra (Vedic Moon sign) on my Ascendant. The part of the body this nakshatra governs is the jaw. Mars represents, among other things, surgery. I had a swelling in my mouth which I'd simply been ignoring, assuming it would disappear by itself. Seeing this planetary transit made me think I might wind up needing surgery on my jaw. I scheduled an appointment with my dentist and it's a good thing I did: the swelling turned out to be a tumor that needed to be surgically removed. Knowing about the transit guided me to take the proper action at the proper time.

We are not the victims of fate—we're the creators of it. Through noble thoughts and deeds we can shape a more auspicious destiny. When we read our future, we need to keep in mind that we ourselves are its authors.

We in the West are an independent people who like to believe we're in control of our own destiny. Vedic astrology vividly demonstrates that this belief is absolutely true. My meditation teacher, Swami Rama of the Himalayas, would constantly repeat, "You are the architect of your destiny." Remember that the word karma comes from the Sanskrit root *kri,* which means "to do." Through our thoughts, words and actions—the things we do—we shape our own future, in this life and the next.

Now we're ready to focus on what your Vedic chart says about you.

Part 2
A Vedic Astrology Primer

Astrology uncovers the consequences of good and bad deeds
done in previous lives, just as light reveals objects
concealed in the darkness.
Laghu Jatakam 1.3

Astrology is not just knowing your future.
It is planning your future.
Gayatri Devi Vasudeva

Faith in divine protection, and right use of man's God-given will,
are forces more formidable than are influences
flowing from the heavens....
Seeds of past karma cannot germinate if they are roasted
in the fires of divine wisdom.
Paramahansa Yogananda

5

What's Your Karma? Setting Up Your Vedic Chart

All this information leads up to the most important question of all: What does your Vedic chart say about you? In this chapter you'll learn how to set up your Hindu chart. In the following chapters you'll learn how professional Vedic astrologers integrate and interpret the many components that make up your horoscope.

Well-trained astrologers in India analyze literally thousands of factors when they examine a birth chart. Jyotish is a complex system thousands of years old with numerous different branches. To learn even one of its schools thoroughly you would need to master at least one Indian language and spend a minimum of ten years apprenticed to an experienced jyotishi. Your teacher would require you to memorize, word for word, dozens of classical texts, and to learn the mantras and spiritual practices prescribed in your astrological lineage, so that when you read the charts of people in serious trouble you can offer them techniques that will make a real difference in their lives.

Learning Jyotish well is easily the equivalent of doing a Ph.D. program at an American university. In this book you'll simply be introduced to important astrological basics, primarily those found in Parashari Jyotish, the most widely practiced system of astrology in India. Then you'll learn how Vedic astrologers help clients identify and heal problem areas in their charts.

The Hindu Zodiac

First things first. If you're familiar with your Western horoscope, you're in for a huge surprise the first time you see your Vedic chart. It looks completely different. Even more bewildering, it puts your planets in different signs. It's got extra planets you've probably never heard of (Rahu? Ketu?) while some familiar ones (Uranus, Neptune, Pluto) are missing. It contains signs of the zodiac such as Ashvini and Bharani that don't appear in any map of the heavens you've ever seen. What's going on?

Jyotish places much less emphasis on the three outermost planets (Uranus, Neptune and Pluto) than Western astrology. You need a telescope to track these planets. The ancient Indians preferred to work with the planets you can easily follow across the sky without any special equipment: Mercury, Venus, Mars, Jupiter and Saturn. Curiously, ancient *Nadi* texts in India mention the existence of three additional planets called Prajapati (like Uranus, Prajapati was the celestial father), Varuna (like Neptune, Varuna was the god of the ocean) and Yama (like Pluto, Yama was god of the dead). Instead of the outermost planets Jyotish uses two "shadow planets," Rahu and Ketu (the Moon's north and south nodes respectively), which represent many of the same qualities the outer planets do in Western astrology.

TWELVE SIGNS OF THE HINDU ZODIAC

Western Glyph	English Name	Sanskrit Name	Planetary Ruler	Hindu Symbol
♈	Aries	*Mesha*	Mars	Ram
♉	Taurus	*Vrisha*	Venus	Bull
♊	Gemini	*Mithuna*	Mercury	Two Lovers
♋	Cancer	*Karka*	Moon	Crab
♌	Leo	*Simha*	Sun	Lion
♍	Virgo	*Kanya*	Mercury	Girl
♎	Libra	*Tula*	Venus	Scales
♏	Scorpio	*Vrischika*	Mars	Scorpion
♐	Sagittarius	*Dhanu*	Jupiter	Bow
♑	Capricorn	*Makara*	Saturn	Crocodile
♒	Aquarius	*Kumbha*	Saturn	Pot
♓	Pisces	*Mina*	Jupiter	Two Fish

NINE VEDIC PLANETS

Western Glyph	English Name	Sanskrit Name
☋	South Node	*Ketu*
♀	Venus	*Shukra*
☉	Sun	*Surya, Ravi*
☽	Moon	*Chandra, Soma*
♂	Mars	*Mangala, Kuja*
☊	North Node	*Rahu*
♃	Jupiter	*Guru, Brihaspati*
♄	Saturn	*Shani*
☿	Mercury	*Budha*

Hindu astrology uses both the twelve Sun signs you already know (Aries, Taurus, Gemini, etc.) plus 27 Moon signs (Ashvini, Bharani, Krittika, etc.) called nakshatras. These 27 extra signs are critically important because your Vedic planetary cycles are based on the nakshatra your Moon was in at the moment of your birth. They're a major source of Jyotish's awesome predictive power. There's nothing like them in Western astrology. We'll devote the entire next chapter to these lunar mansions.

Another major difference is that Jyotish is a sidereal (star-based) system, which follows the actual movement of the stars through the sky, rather than a tropical (season-based) system like Western astrology, which is not concerned with the actual placement of the constellations. The Western tropical system was adopted by the Greeks around 285 A.D. when they allied their calendars with the 365 day solar year. The Indians preferred the sidereal system which tracks with the stars, not with the Sun.

This is as extremely important distinction with very dramatic consequences. If your Western horoscope shows that when you were born the Moon was in Leo, there is an excellent chance that had your father been standing outside looking up at the sky, he would not have seen the Moon in the constellation Leo, but in Cancer. In fact, odds are five out of six that every planet in your Western chart was really in the previous constellation when you were born. Your Western horoscope doesn't match with the actual sky at all, which is one of the reasons scientists like to sneer at Western astrology. Your Vedic chart, on the other hand, shows what constellations your planets were really in when you were born.

This surprising discrepancy occurs because the Western tropical zodiac identifies 0° Aries with the exact position of the Sun at the moment Spring begins in the northern hemisphere. Due to a wobbling motion of the Earth, over the centuries this point slips backwards through the sky. Therefore the signs of the zodiac Western astrologers use are now about 24° out of synchronization with the actual constellations after which they are named. In reality, the Western sign Aries actually corresponds more closely with the constellation Pisces. (Incidentally, it's because of the Earth's wobble that astrologers say we'll be entering the Age of Aquarius in a few hundred years.)

In Vedic astrology, however, 0° Aries invariably aligns with the beginning of the constellation Aries in the sky. There's no specially noticeable star there so to find its exact position, Indian astrologers locate the star Spica in the constellation Virgo. Spica is quite bright so it's easy to spot on a clear Spring night. The point exactly opposite it in on the ecliptic is, was, and always will be 0° Aries.

If your Indian horoscope shows that when you were born the Moon was in Leo, odds are 100% that if your dad was standing outside he would have seen the Moon in the 30° portion of the ecliptic that really does correspond to the constellation Leo. In the Hindu zodiac, what you see is what you get.

This does not mean that one system of astrology is "correct"and the other is "false,"merely that their focus is different. The tropical zodiac used in the West may be more helpful in analyzing personality. Vedic astrology is less concerned with personality dynamics and more intent on the life course of the reincarnating soul.

Think of it this way: The West focuses on the personality, which is always changing, so it uses a zodiac which is continually shifting. The East focuses on the spirit, which is unchanging, so it uses a zodiac that doesn't change even as the ages roll past.

Erecting Your Vedic Horoscope

It's easy to get a copy of your Vedic chart these days. Visit the Council of Vedic Astrology at www.VedicAstrology.org for a referral to a Vedic astrologer near you. Also, almost all full feature Western astrology programs now print out Hindu horoscopes too.

Can't log on right now? If you have your Western horoscope in hand, you can convert it into a Vedic one very easily. To make the conversion manually, subtract 23° from the degrees of the planets, Ascendant and lunar nodes in your Western horoscope. When you subtract, keep in mind that astrological signs are exactly 30° 00′ long. If you wind up at 0°, 1°, 29° or 30° of a sign, consult the Degree Conversion Table for a more precise conversion factor. Due to the Earth's wobble, for children born after 2010, you'll have to subtract 24°. If you're mathematically challenged like me, use the Western To Vedic Chart Conversion Table for a short cut method that makes the arithmetic extremely easy.

WESTERN TO VEDIC CHART CONVERSION TABLE

COMPONENT	WESTERN SIGN	WESTERN DEGREE	VEDIC SIGN	VEDIC DEGREE
Ascendant	___	___	___	___
Sun	___	___	___	___
Moon	___	___	___	___
Mars	___	___	___	___
Mercury	___	___	___	___
Jupiter	___	___	___	___
Venus	___	___	___	___
Saturn	___	___	___	___
North Node	___	___	___	___
South Node	___	___	___	___

1. Jot down the Signs and Degrees from your Western chart in the appropriate columns above.
2. In every case where your Western Ascendant or planet degree is23° or less, simply add 7°. Then move the Ascendant or planet back into into the previous sign. Example: If your Western Ascendant is 13° Taurus, add 7°. This comes out to 20°. Since the original degree position of your Ascendant was 23° or less, move your Ascendant backwards one sign from Taurus to Aries. Your Vedic Ascendant is 20° Aries.
3. In every case where your Western Ascendant or planet degree is 23° or more, subtract 23°. The Ascendant or planet stays in the same sign. Example: If your Western Sun is at 27° Aquarius, subtract 23°. This comes to 4°. Since its original degree position was 23° or more, your Sun stays in the same sign, Aquarius. Your Vedic Sun is at 4° Aquarius.
4. Write down your new Sign and Degree positions in the Vedic columns above.

Degree Conversion Table

1. Find the year you were born in the following table.
2. Subtract that number of degrees from the degrees of the Ascendant, planets and nodes in your Western chart. Example: If the Sun in your Western horoscope is placed at 23° 31′ Leo and you were born in 1978, subtract 23° 33′. Your Sun has shifted backward to 29° 58′ Cancer in your Vedic chart. If, however, your Western Venus is placed at 23° 35′ Leo, then subtracting 23° 33′ it would remain in Leo at 0° 02′.

Don't be concerned if your planets change signs. If every Western astrology column you've ever read says that since you were born in late April, you're a Taurus, it can be disorienting to find that your Sun shifts back into Aries in the Vedic zodiac. Relax! Vedic charts are interpreted in a completely different way so, rest assured, everything you've heard about your Western Taurus Sun is still true. Think of it this way. In English the word *soma* means "body." In Sanskrit *soma* is a name for the Moon. But you can't say English is more valid than Sanskrit or vice versa. What you have to do is read the word in the context of the language in which it's written.

DEGREE CONVERSION TABLE

Year	Degrees	Year	Degrees	Year	Degrees	Year	Degrees	Year	Degrees
1930	22° 53′	1950	23° 10′	1970	23° 26′	1990	23° 43′	2010	24° 00′
1931	22° 54′	1951	23° 10′	1971	23° 27′	1991	23° 44′	2011	24° 00′
1932	22° 55′	1952	23° 11′	1972	23° 28′	1992	23° 45′	2012	24° 01′
1933	22° 55′	1953	23° 12′	1973	23° 29′	1993	23° 45′	2013	24° 02′
1934	22° 56′	1954	23° 13′	1974	23° 30′	1994	23° 46′	2014	24° 03′
1935	22° 57′	1955	23° 14′	1975	23° 30′	1995	23° 47′	2015	24° 04′
1936	22° 58′	1956	23° 15′	1976	23° 31′	1996	23° 48′	2016	24° 05′
1937	22° 59′	1957	23° 15′	1977	23° 32′	1997	23° 49′	2017	24° 05′
1938	23° 00′	1958	23° 16′	1978	23° 33′	1998	23° 50′	2018	24° 06′
1939	23° 00′	1959	23° 17′	1979	23° 34′	1999	23° 50′	2019	24° 07′
1940	23° 01′	1960	23° 18′	1980	23° 35′	2000	23° 51′	2020	24° 08′
1941	23° 02′	1961	23° 19′	1981	23° 35′	2001	23° 52′	2021	24° 09′
1942	23° 03′	1962	23° 20′	1982	23° 36′	2002	23° 53′	2022	24° 10′
1943	23° 04′	1963	23° 20′	1983	23° 37′	2003	23° 54′	2023	24° 10′
1944	23° 05′	1964	23° 21′	1984	23° 38′	2004	23° 55′	2024	24° 11′
1945	23° 05′	1965	23° 22′	1985	23° 39′	2005	23° 55′	2025	24° 12′
1946	23° 06′	1966	23° 23′	1986	23° 40′	2006	23° 56′	2026	24° 13′
1947	23° 07′	1967	23° 24′	1987	23° 40′	2007	23° 57′	2027	24° 14′
1948	23° 08′	1968	23° 25′	1988	23° 41′	2008	23° 58′	2028	24° 15′
1949	23° 09′	1969	23° 25′	1989	23° 42′	2009	23° 59′	2029	24° 15′

Your Western horoscope is like a photograph, while your Vedic chart is like an x-ray. The camera and the x-ray equipment both take pictures of you, but they're registering different layers of your being. Your personality may reflect strong Taurean elements just like Western astrology says, but valuable information about the journey your soul is taking can be found by placing your Sun in its correct astronomical position in Aries, just as Indian astrology says. In their proper contexts, both Aries and Taurus placements provide important insights.

Chart Format

Now that you know the position of your Vedic planets, you can place them into a Vedic chart. Over the millennia Vedic astrologers have developed many formats to represent the position of the planets. The two most popular are the South and North Indian styles.

Pisces	Aries	Taurus	Gemini
Aquarius	**South Indian Format**		Cancer
Capricorn			Leo
Sagittarius	Scorpio	Libra	Virgo

In the South Indian chart the upper left hand box is always Pisces, with the rest of the signs placed clockwise. This clockwise arrangement of signs sometimes trips up Western astrologers, who're used to reading horoscopes counterclockwise.

The Ascendant, or *lagna* in Sanskrit, is the sign which was rising over the eastern horizon when you were born. The Ascendant is represented by a diagonal line drawn through the appropriate box. In the sample South Indian chart above, the Ascendant is Leo.

Using the template below, draw a diagonal line through the box containing your Vedic rising sign. If you have Libra rising, for example, draw a diagonal line through the box containing Libra. Then write in the names of your planets and nodes in the appropriate boxes according to their Vedic sign.

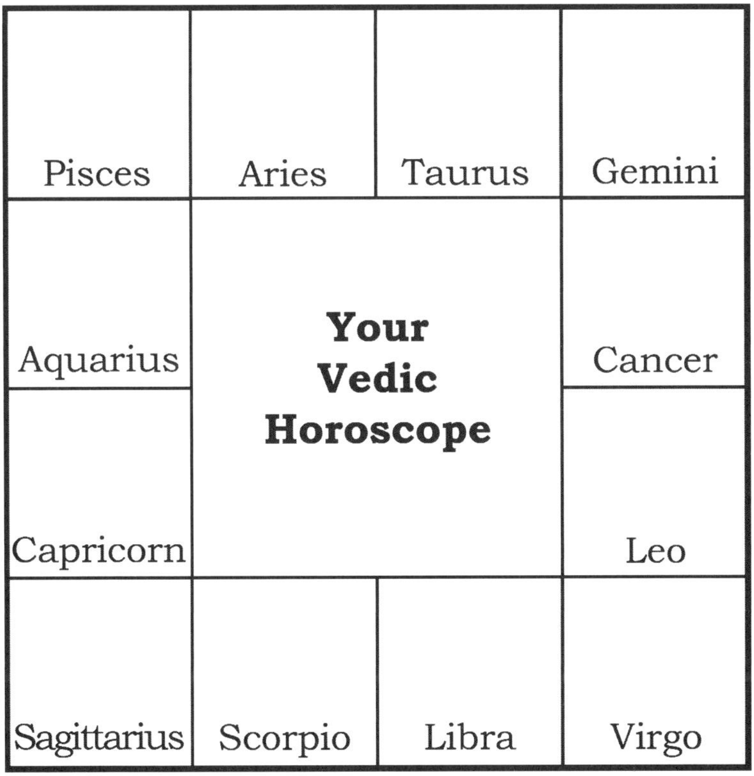

<table>
<tr><td>Pisces</td><td>Aries</td><td>Taurus</td><td>Gemini</td></tr>
<tr><td>Aquarius</td><td colspan="2" rowspan="2">Your Vedic Horoscope</td><td>Cancer</td></tr>
<tr><td>Capricorn</td><td>Leo</td></tr>
<tr><td>Sagittarius</td><td>Scorpio</td><td>Libra</td><td>Virgo</td></tr>
</table>

This is your Vedic chart. We'll be using the South Indian chart format throughout this book because it's the easiest style to read. But you should be aware of the North Indian chart also, since many Vedic astrologers use it.

North Indian Format

The northern format is almost identical to the horoscope style used in Europe till quite recently. (The difference was that Europeans placed the starting point of the chart, or 1st House, where Indians place the 4th house.) As in the West, the chart is read counterclockwise.

This horoscope is designed to highlight the four most powerful areas of the chart: the 1st, 4th, 7th and 10th houses. The 1st house represents the eastern horizon when you were born, while the 7th house was at the western horizon. The 10th house marked the highest part of the ecliptic (the path along which the Sun and planets travel) called the midheaven, while the 4th house represents the lowest point of the ecliptic at that unique moment in time. These are the four corners which mark the parameters of your life. There are twelve houses in all, however, representing twelve important areas in your life.

In the Southern chart the signs of the zodiac stay in the same places while the houses rotate through them. Virgo will always be in the lower right corner, but it may represent the 1st, 2nd, or any other of the twelve houses. In the Northern chart the house positions stay in place while the signs of the zodiac rotate through them, exactly like the Western circular horoscope. The top center portion of the chart always represents the 1st house, whether it contains Aries, Taurus, or any of the other twelve signs of the zodiac.

Twelve Celestial Signs

In the most important book on Vedic astrology ever written, the *Brihat Parashara Hora Shastra,* the sage Parashara briefly describes the twelve signs of the zodiac, called *rashis* (meaning "groups of stars") in Sanskrit. His snapshot pictures of the signs present them in a manner quite different than we Westerners are used to.

PARASHARA'S DESCRIPTION OF THE 12 SIGNS OF THE ZODIAC

ARIES Activating, red, eastern, infertile, fiery, travels in forests and hills, represents rulers, four-legged, rises feet first, more powerful at night.

TAURUS Stable, white, southern, semi-fertile, earthy, found in meadows or farms, represents business people, four-legged, rises feet first, more powerful at night.

GEMINI Flexible, dual, green, western, infertile, airy, found in villages, represents laborers, two-legged, rises head first, more powerful at night.

CANCER Activating, pink, northern, fertile, watery, found in lakes and streams and wells, represents thinkers, many-legged, rises feet first, more powerful at night.

LEO Stable, white, eastern, infertile, fiery, found in castles or mountains or other hard-to-reach places, represents rulers, four-legged, rises head first, more powerful during the day.

VIRGO Flexible, multi-colored, southern, infertile, earthy, dwells in cultivated places and women's areas, represents business people, two-legged, rises head first, more powerful during the day.

LIBRA Activating, dark, western, semi-fertile, airy, found in towns and markets, represents laborers, two-legged, rises head first, more powerful during the day.

SCORPIO Stable, reddish brown, northern, fertile, watery, found in cesspools and swamps and holes, represents thinkers, many-legged, rises head first, more powerful during the day.

SAGITTARIUS Flexible, light brown, eastern, semi-fertile, fiery, found in temples and cities and expensive homes, represents rulers, first half is two-legged, second half is four-legged, rises feet first, more powerful at night.

CAPRICORN Activating, multi-colored, southern, semi-fertile, earthy, found in neglected and run-down areas, represents business people, first half is four-legged, second half is one-footed, rises feet first, more powerful at night.

AQUARIUS Stable, dark brown, western, semi-fertile, airy, found in odd places or sites associated with science and communication, represents laborers, two-legged, rises head first, more powerful during the day.

PISCES Flexible, northern, fertile, watery, found in the oceans or sea or confined places or places of refuge, represents thinkers, footless, rises with both its head and feet first, and is not more powerful during the day or night.

Most of the information here is from the *Brihat Parashara Hora Shastra*. However, a small portion is from the oral tradition which elaborates on Parashara's brief remarks.

You'll notice there's nothing here about Virgos making good secretaries, Librans being indecisive, or Pisceans being dreamy, as you'll so often hear in Western astrology. Keep in mind that this is a completely different system. Indian and Western astrology both use twelve zodiacal signs but they are not interpreted the same way.

In Western astrology, the sign of the zodiac a planet is in is extremely important. It tells you a lot about your personality characteristics. If your Moon is in Cancer, a Western astrologer would say you're probably an emotional person who values family life.

In Vedic astrology, however, the house a planet is placed in is far more important. If your Cancer Moon is in the 1st house, for example, your Vedic astrologer will emphasize that you're likely to be healthy, well-liked, and fortunate. During your Moon cycles, all other factors being equal, you'll probably be quite successful, popular and in good health. This is quite different from the way most Western astrologers will interpret your chart.

Twelve Heavenly Houses

In Vedic astrology, the twelve signs correspond to the actual twelve constellations of the zodiac, beginning with Aries, which spin overhead day and night. The houses, however, are twelve 30° sectors of the ecliptic which don't move. The 1st house is always at the Eastern horizon where the Sun rises. The 7th house is always at the Western horizon where the Sun sets.

Here comes an extremely important point where the Vedic system and modern Western astrology part company. In India, whatever sign was rising on the eastern horizon when you were born becomes your 1st house, no matter whether the beginning, middle or end of that sign was right at the horizon. So if Libra rises in your Vedic chart, your 1st house will contain all 30° of Libra, your 2nd house will contain all 30° of Scorpio, and so on. This system of equating a full sign with a whole house was used in the West in antiquity too, but few Western astrologers use it now.

The twelve houses stand for different departments of your life. Each house reflects distinct qualities and concerns. If a Vedic astrologer wants to learn about your children, he'll look to your 5th house, for example. If he wants to learn about your marriage karma, he'll turn to your 7th house.

THE VEDIC HOUSES

NO.	AREAS THE HOUSE DESCRIBES
1st	Purpose and direction in life, strength of character, the body, appearance, athletics, modeling, self promotion, show business, jobs in which the strength or appearance of the body is paramount, fame, vitality, well being, events of early childhood, head.
2nd	Finances, movable assets, banking, family of origin, clothing and jewelry, food, public speaking, poetic ability, singing, truthfulness, food, face, throat.
3rd	Initiative, courage, adventures, short trips, desires, journalism, the fine arts, TV, film, playing music, the trades, work involving computers, frequent short-distance travel, siblings, arms and hands.
4th	Mother, real estate, fixed assets, vehicles, boats, education, farming, ranching, luxuries, emotional stability, morality, the sea, the last years of life, lungs.
5th	Children, romance, past life credit, intelligence, sports, investments, gambling, creativity, entertainment, stomach area, spiritual techniques, authorship, scholarship, counseling, politics, heart.
6th	Enemies, competitors, subordinates, tenants, the medical field, service-oriented jobs, clerical work, pets and domestic animals, debts, lawsuits, the military, crime, disappointments, minor accidents, brief illness, intestines.
7th	Married life, spouse, sexuality, entrepreneurs, business partnerships, work involving the spouse, residence abroad, open enemies, war, kidneys, lower abdomen.
8th	Longevity, inheritance, loans, insurance, mysticism, psychism, ancient systems of knowledge (e.g. acupuncture, vastu, astrology) archeology, fear, serious accidents, chronic illness, misfortune, reproductive system.
9th	Higher education, law, publishing, philosophy, religion, father, teachers, the guru, long journeys, good fortune, thighs and hips.

10th Vocation, social stature, achievements, earning ability, government, authority figures, corporations, high paying and high status professions, civil service, good deeds, knees.

11th Profits, aspirations, ability to fulfill one's desires, groups, friends, financial windfalls, side jobs, work with or arranged by friends, legs, ankles.

12th Expenses, charitable donations, bed pleasures (sleep and sex), confinement (e.g., in hospitals, prisons, monasteries, convents, ashrams), foreign countries, international commerce, hidden enemies, the state of consciousness after death, enlightenment, feet.

The twelve houses are understood in almost exactly the same way in both India and the West since both developed in part from the same original tradition. There are a few important differences however. Sexual pleasure moves from the Western 8th to the Vedic 7th and 12th houses. The mother is always read from the 4th house, while the father is seen from the 9th and sometimes 10th house. In India speaking abilities are assigned to the 2nd, not the 3rd, house. The Western system reads vehicles in the 3rd house since they relate to travel, but Indians refer vehicles to the 4th house because they're considered fixed assets.

A Wheel with Twelve Spokes

The twin concepts of twelve astrological signs and twelve celestial houses is incredibly ancient. The *Rig Veda* is full of references to a twelve-spoked celestial wheel. Each division of the cosmic wheel stood for the 30 days the Sun spent in its sector, just as our astrological signs do today. But the spokes also represented particular segments of the day, just as our astrological houses do. Particular Vedic deities associated with each spoke were worshiped at different times of the day as the Sun revolved through the twelve houses every 24 hours.

These twelve areas of the sky were called *Adityas* in the *Rig Veda.* Mythologically they were the sons of the primordial Vedic goddess Aditi. Aditi represents limitless space or the unbounded circular expanse of heaven; her name literally means "undivided." Each Aditya was assigned the name of a Vedic deity with his own legends and domain of rulership.

In the myths of the twelve Adityas we find the earliest references to the departments of life associated with the twelve houses.

THE TWELVE ADITYAS

House	Deity	Deity's Role
1st	Savitar	Source of life and light
2nd	Pushan	Lord of food and possessions
3rd	Shakra	Mighty, courageous warrior god
4th	Varuna	God of morality and the cosmic waters
5th	Dhatar	Deity who grants children
6th	Tvashtar	Workman of the gods
7th	Aryaman	God of the marriage contract
8th	Amsha	Lord of debt and repayment
9th	Bhaga	God of happiness and good fortune
10th	Vishnu	Highest god, protector of order
11th	Mitra	The divine friend
12th	Vivasvan	Lord of sacrifice and death

1. Savitar

Orthodox Hindu priests awaken before daybreak. They immediately step outside to invoke the Sun with the holiest mantra in the *Rig Veda:* "With loving reverence we bow to Savitar, the most splendid light in all the worlds. Please illuminate our minds." This sacred prayer calls for the Sun to rise in the sky and simultaneously for divine light to dawn in our awareness. The name Savitar comes from the Sanskrit root *su* which means "to bring forth,"so Savitar is regarded as the source of both light and life. In Vedic mythology he is called the "life giver,"an apt description of the Ascendant.

The *Rig Veda* says Savitar "opens a stall, as it were"so that light can appear. This "stall"represents the 1st house, the place in the horoscope that defines both where the Sun first rises on a given day and the most essential qualities of our personality. The *Rig Veda* actually states, "Savitar tied down the earth, and made the heaven stand still." Ancient astrologers specifically define *Lagna,* the Sanskrit word for Ascendant, as the point which "ties down" the sky, linking a particular moment of time to a specific person or event. The English words ligament (connective tissue), ligate (to bind), and ligature (a band used for tying things down) are related to the Sanskrit word *lagna* and convey a similar idea.

2. *Pushan*

Pushan means "the nourisher." This ancient deity is the guardian of flocks and herds, and the provider of daily sustenance. In Vedic astrology, the 2nd house governs both food and possessions, particularly our "movable assets"and bank balance. In India in 3000 B.C., your cattle constituted your bank account. Fascinatingly, there is a legend that the god Rudra smacked Pushan in the mouth, knocking his teeth down into his throat. In Indian, as in Western astrology, the 2nd house is closely associated with the mouth and throat, as well as with wealth.

3. *Shakra*

Shakra means "powerful."It comes from the root *shak* which means "to be able." In Vedic mythology, *Shakra* is the most powerful of all the gods, a warrior noted both for his strength and courage. In Hindu astrology, the 3rd house is the house of prowess and stamina. It governs both the conscious mind and the arms, which enable you to act.

4.*Varuna*

Varuna is the premier god of the night sky. He governs both the cosmic waters of heaven and the oceans here below. He is pre-eminently the all-seeing god of justice who maintains cosmic order. In the *Rig Veda* he is described as wearing a shining cloak of stars and, as sovereign of the seas, keeping his watchful eye on ships at sail. In Vedic astrology, the 4th house rules boats and bodies of water as well as ethics and morality. As the house corresponding to midnight, it represents the culminating point of night.

5. *Dhatar*

Dhatar is responsible for the production of life, for conception and childbirth. To this day in north India the word *dhatri* means a woman who has given birth. Dhatar is also invoked to bring about marriage. Perhaps this explains why the 5th house is connected both with children and with romance.

6. Tvashtar

The next Aditya is the carpenter of the gods, the divine architect and artisan. When the other deities need a house built, a weapon forged, or a new world constructed, Tvashtar is called in to do the manual labor. His name comes from *tvaks,* which means "to shape or fashion." In Vedic, as in Western astrology, the 6th house governs manual work. Amazingly, Tvashtar is also appealed to in order to grant health and long life — another signification of the 6th house.

7. Aryaman

Aryaman is the Vedic god of marriage, the deity who seals the marriage contract represented by the 7th house in Indian and Western astrology. He also rules over twilight — the very time of day associated with the 7th house. *Aryaman* literally means "one's closest partner,"a fine description of a husband or wife.

8. Amsha

Amsha means "distributor"or "the one who apportions." He regulates what is due you and what you owe others. He especially represents the money you owe the king (taxes) as well as your debt to the gods which can be paid only in the currency of religious practices. Debt and taxes, as well as occult practices, are included under the 8th house in Vedic astrology. This is the most sensitive house of karmic rebalancing.

9. Bhaga

The name Bhaga is derived from *bha,* meaning "to love"or "to support." Bhaga is the most generous of the Vedic gods; his very name is synonymous with "good fortune." He is the divine being who dispenses the results of your good karma, granting prosperity, success, joy and good luck. The 9th house is actually called the *bhagya sthanam,* the "house of Bhaga"or "place of good fortune"in Sanskrit because it is associated with happiness, wisdom, divine favors and devotion to God.

10. Vishnu

Of all Adityas, it is Vishnu who is still most widely worshiped in India today. "The kings gaze up to the highest height where Vishnu gazes back like an eye in heaven. From this most splendid post, he illumines the world,"says the *Rig Veda.* Vishnu maintains order in the universe, even incarnating on Earth ten times to intervene in human history when things here get out of hand. The 10th house represents noon, the height of the day, as well as kingship, the presiding judge, and positions of authority.

11. Mitra

The worship of Mitra (also called Mithras) would eventually spread all the way from India through Persia to ancient Rome. The *Rig Veda* says he's the god who gets people out of their houses in the morning and sends them on their way to work. This would make sense if he's connected with the 11th house, representing the time of morning when people have finished washing up, doing their morning meditation and eating breakfast and are heading to their jobs. The word *mitra* means "friend"or "companion." Interestingly, the 11th house is associated with friendship to this day, both in India and the West.

12. Vivasvan

In the Hindu tradition, Vivasvan is particularly connected with the early morning. He is known as "the sacrificer," because *vivas* means "to worship,"and in Vedic times that meant giving up something valuable as an offering to the gods. Vivasvan is also the father of Yama, the god of death in India. Vedic texts say he "illumines both day and night,"a paradoxical statement that makes sense if he stands for the 12th house in the horoscope, the end portion of which demarcates day from night. In fact, the tradition often associates him with the morning twilight. The 12th house seems to mirror the significance of this deity amazingly well, as it governs death and loss (including voluntary loss such as charitable donations) in Vedic astrology.

These ancient deities play an active part in your life, appearing to you in the form of your twelve houses. Here is what a jyotishi takes into consideration when she examines your houses.

House Rulership

Every house is governed by the planet which rules its sign. If your 1st house is Capricorn, the ruler of the house is Saturn, since Saturn rules Capricorn. Check for planetary rulerships in the table "12 Signs of the Hindu Zodiac"on page 46.

You'll notice that Vedic rulerships are identical to those in contemporary Western astrology with this important exception. The outer planets (Uranus, Neptune, Pluto) do not own signs. Instead, Scorpio is ruled by Mars, Aquarius by Saturn, and Pisces by Jupiter, exactly as in medieval Western astrology.

Planetary rulerships are of primary importance in Vedic astrology. A house cannot be strong if the planet that rules it is weak; a strong lord greatly enhances the affairs denoted by its house. In Chapter 7 you'll discover how jyotishis gauge the strength of a planet.

House Qualities

Most of the houses work in your favor. Others are innately difficult. This is reflected in the qualities associated with each house.

Negative 12th	Very Positive 1st	Neutral 2nd	Mildly Negative 3rd
Neutral 11th	**House Qualities**		Positive 4th
Positive 10th			Positive 5th
Very Positive 9th	Very Negative 8th	Positive 7th	Negative 6th

QUALITIES OF THE VEDIC HOUSES

Houses 1, 4, 7, 10	These four houses form the angles (top, bottom, left, right) of your chart. They are called quadrants or *kendras.* These houses are positive, especially the 1st or rising sign.
Houses 1, 5, 7	These three houses form a triangle in your chart. They're called trines or *trikonas.* They're considered fortunate, especially the 9th, which is the house of good luck. Notice that the 1st house is both a quadrant and a trine, giving it exceptionally positive energy.
Houses 3, 6, 8, 12	These four houses are called *dushthanas,* or sorrow producing places. The 3rd is only mildly negative but the 8th is particularly virulent.
Houses 2, 11	These two houses are neutral in effect.
Houses 3, 6, 10, 11	These four houses can more readily change for the better over time than the other houses. These are called improving or *upachaya* houses because the affairs they govern, if well tended, will do increasingly well.

Because the 6th, 8th and 12th houses have an inherently negative tendency, the planets that rule them tend to cause problems wherever they are located in your chart. If the planet that rules your 6th house of illness and debt is located in your 1st house, which controls your body, you could be prone to health problems or financial upsets. On the other hand, the planets that rule positive houses bring blessings wherever they go. If the planet that rules your 9th house of good fortune is strong in your 1st house, you could be one of those people who seems to get all the lucky breaks.

In some circumstances a planet may rule both a positive and a negative house. For example, if you have Gemini rising, Saturn rules both the very negative 8th and very positive 9th houses. In that case Saturn gives both good and bad fortune at the same time. You might be accepted into a prestigious college (9th house) and get socked with huge debts in the form of bank loans (8th house) in order to pay your tuition during Saturn's cycle.

House Balance

Bhava, the Sanskrit word usually translated "house," literally means "area of action"or "state of mind." It represents a department of your life, whether external in the outer world, or internal in your heart and mind.

The strength and weakness of each of your twelve houses must be weighed against each other in order to generate an accurate reading. For example, the 1st house represents your strength of character while the 12th house signifies serious financial losses. An individual who has a powerful 1st house but a badly afflicted 12th may experience heavy debts when the planet that rules the 12th house is running its cycle. But he'll bounce back when the cycle is over. Another person who has a weak 1st house could go through similar losses while his 12th house karma plays out, but may find it harder to rebuild his life afterwards because the strength and resiliency of the 1st house is compromised.

One individual may have several astrological signatures for a superb singing voice, such as a strong 2nd house. But if her 10th house—which signals her status in her community—is weak, she's unlikely to receive much public recognition for her brilliant vocal accomplishments. Another person may have a mediocre 2nd house, which suggests to the Vedic astrologer that her singing talent is probably not spectacular. But if her 10th house is extremely strong, she could find herself touring with a popular band and singing to packed stadiums. How often have you switched on the television to see singers with minimal talent performing on music videos broadcast to millions, while artists with massive ability spend year after year playing in coffee houses or busking on the street? This might seem incredibly unfair, yet from the Vedic perspective both groups are working out karmic lessons they were born to confront.

A unique feature of Vedic astrology is the way the houses are read in relation to each other in order to produce more detailed information. For instance, the 5th house represents children. The 5th house from the 5th stands for the children of your children. Following this principle, skilled

Vedic astrologers can produce amazingly specific analyses about your parents, cousins or other family members based on planetary placements in your chart. This way of assessing the impact of relatives in one's life is particularly important in India where the extended family system prevails. Because your family's lives are being read from your chart, however, the information reflects your experience of that family member, rather than his experience of himself.

Incidentally, in rare instances astrologers will stumble across a Vedic chart that doesn't fit the person at all. The Parashari system which most jyotishis use fails completely. This is a fascinating phenomenon, reflecting the way exceptions are built into nature. Just as the majority of people are right-handed but a small percentage is left-handed, just as most people are heterosexual but a minority are gay, so most people's charts make sense according to the system outlined by Parashara, but a few individuals' charts need to be read using a different method. Alternate systems were developed by master astrologers like Jaimini and Krishnamurti. Since Parashara's rules work for the vast majority of horoscopes, that's the system you'll be introduced to in this book.

You've just learned a great deal about the twelve Vedic signs and houses. Now let's look at your Vedic planets. We'll start with the most important planet in the Vedic system: your Moon.

6

What's Your Vedic Sign? Finding Your Nakshatra

There's two things you need to know if someone from India asks you what your sign is. First, it's your Moon sign, not your Sun sign, they're asking about. Like the ancient Greeks and Romans, the Hindus consider the Moon more important astrologically than the Sun. Second, they're not asking whether your Moon is in Aries, Taurus or Gemini. They want to know if it's in Ashvini, Bharani, Krittika or any of the other 27 lunar signs they call *nakshatras.*

The Moon, known as Lord Chandra in India, has 27 wives, every one of whom lives in her own mansion along the ecliptic. Each of these lunar mansions or *nakshatras* is 13° 20′ long and is associated with a particular star or group of stars. For example, Krittika is identified with the Pleiades and Rohini with Aldebaran. Lord Chandra spends about a day with each wife as he circles the Earth, lighting the night, shifting the tides and blessing those fortunate men and women who honor him and the energies he represents.

Lord Chandra has two favorite wives: Rohini, who lives in a section of the constellation we call Taurus, and Pushya, whose mansion is in Cancer. His other wives were jealous that he obviously enjoyed himself most in Taurus and Cancer, and complained to their father. He cursed Lord Chandra with tuberculosis, but when the disaffected wives saw their husband wasting away, they begged their father to remove the curse. However, once angry words have been spoken they can't be taken back, so the best dad could do was arrange for the Moon to temporarily recover his health, only to succumb again. Perhaps you've wondered why the Moon waxes and wanes. Now you know.

The phases of the Moon and the nakshatras it passes through have been studied exhaustively in India for more than 6,000 years. It was critical to the Ayurvedic physician, for example, to know that medicines are particularly effective when the Moon is in Ashvini; it was useful for couples to know that Mrigashira or Anuradha are particularly auspicious for weddings; and it was critical for the brahmin priests to know that while the Moon passes through Uttara Phalguni, their rituals will produce especially remarkable results. By setting out on an auspicious nakshatra, one would ensure a safe journey; by first entering a newly-built house during an appropriate nakshatra, life in that house would be filled with blessings.

There's a wonderful story in the *Skanda Purana* which shows that even the gods are mindful of the nakshatras. Lord Shiva, the wildest of the Hindu deities, eloped with Sati, the daughter of a powerful Vedic sage. The marriage soon came to a tragic end when the sage, disgusted by Shiva's hippie lifestyle, insulted his daughter's new husband. Sati was so upset she committed suicide. Shiva was devastated, and retreated into the mountains where he sat in meditation for many ages, guiding and blessing the Himalayan yogis.

Finally, Parvati, a yogini living in the mountains, managed to win Shiva's love, and he agreed to try marriage one more time. But Shiva was determined to get his second attempt started on the right foot. This time rather than eloping, he consulted a famous Vedic astrologer named Garga, and asked him to calculate the most auspicious possible time to begin the wedding. On the great day, Garga sat next to the sundial and at the exact moment the Moon entered Uttara Phalguni, he called out the mantra "Om!" and the wedding vows were exchanged. It worked: as any Hindu will tell you, Shiva and Parvati remain blissfully married to this day, living together at the top of Mount Kailash in Tibet. Knowledge of the nakshatras was considered so important in Vedic society, that traditionally Hindu children were given names that revealed which *nakshatra* they were born under. Years later, illiterate parents might not remember the exact date their children were born, but when he learned the children's names the village astrologer could tell what their Moon sign was,

THE 27 NAKSHATRAS

To find your nakshatra, check the exact degree placement of the Moon in your Western chart. Subtract 23°. Then check the following table. If your Moon is close to the beginning or end of a nakshatra, go back to the Degree Conversion Table in Chapter 5 for a more exact number of degrees to subtract.

No.	Beginning Degree	*Nakshatra*	Marker Star
1.	0° 00′ Aries	Ashvini	Sheratan
2.	13° 20′ Aries	Bharani	41 Arietis
3.	26° 40′ Aries	Krittika	Alcyone (Pleiades)
4.	10° 00′ Taurus	Rohini	Aldebaran
5.	23 °20′ Taurus	Mrigashira	lambda Orionis
6.	6° 40′ Gemini	Ardra	Betelgeuse
7.	20° 00′ Gemini	Punarvasu	Pollux
8.	3° 20′ Cancer	Pushya	delta Cancri
9.	16° 40′ Cancer	Ashlesha	epsilon Hydrae
10.	0° 00′ Leo	Magha	Regulus
11.	13° 20′ Leo	Purva Phalguni	Zosma
12.	26° 40′ Leo	Uttara Phalguni	Denebola
13.	10° 00′ Virgo	Hasta	delta Corvi
14.	23° 20′ Virgo	Chitra	Spica
15.	6° 40′ Libra	Svati	Arcturus
16.	20° 00′ Libra	Vishakha	Zubenelgenubi
17.	3° 20′ Scorpio	Anuradha	delta Scorpii
18.	16° 40′ Scorpio	Jyeshtha	Antares
19.	0° 00′ Sagittarius	Mula	Shaula
20.	13° 20′ Sagittarius	Purva Ashadha	Kaus Media
21.	26° 40′ Sagittarius	Uttara Ashadha	Nunki
22.	10° 00′ Capricorn	Shravana	Altair
23.	23° 20′ Capricorn	Dhanishtha	Rotanev
24.	6° 40′ Aquarius	Shatabhishak	lambda Aquarii
25.	20° 00′ Aquarius	Purva Bhadra	Markab
26.	3° 20′ Pisces	Uttara Bhadra	Algenib
27.	16° 40′ Pisces	Revati	zeta Piscium

Example: Madonna's Moon is located at 11° Virgo in her Western chart. Go backwards through the zodiac 23°. You'll come to 18° Leo. Her nakshatra is Purva Phalguni.

and could then offer some general predictions. Knowing a couple's Moon signs is particularly important in determining marriage compatibility.

Each of the 27 nakshatras is divided into four equal segments called *padas* or feet. The pada the Moon was in at the moment of birth can tell an astrologer a great deal about an individual's personality. In India, rosaries (called *malas*) contain 108 beads, one for each pada or step the Moon takes on his journey across the sky. As they pray their beads, Hindus invoke the blessing energy of all the celestial forces represented by the lunar mansions.

The Hindus also use the twelve zodiacal signs starting with Aries, which were shared by the ancient Greek, Roman and Persian cultures, and form the basis of Western astrology today. The use of the nakshatras is unique to India however, and provides an additional, powerful tool in the amazing collection of techniques skilled Vedic astrologers use to help their clients.

THE 108 CELESTIAL SECTORS

Why did ancient Hindu astronomers divide the zodiac into 108 equal sectors, rather than some more convenient number like 100? Perhaps for these reasons:

- The distance between the Earth and the Sun is approximately 108 times the Sun's diameter.
- The diameter of the Sun is about 108 times the Earth's diameter.
- The distance between the Earth and Moon is 108 times the Moon's diameter.

The Vedic Lunar Mansions

What does your Vedic sign say about you? Here's some information about the qualities associated with each nakshatra. Hindus generally check both the nakshatra of their Moon and the nakshatra that contains their Ascendant degree.

Keep in mind that in India, astrologers read the nakshatras' influence in an extremely sophisticated way, balancing their interpretation on the basis of thousands of other factors in the horoscope. When you read about your Vedic Moon sign here, you're getting a very general picture, as if you were reading your Sun sign description in a Western astrology column. This doesn't take into account the presence of the other planets in your chart, or the relative strength or weakness of your Moon, which will modify how the nakshatra manifests in your personality. Still, this is a good place to begin your exploration of Hindu astrology.

1. 0°00′ - 13°20′ Aries **Ashvini, Horsemen**
Symbol: Horse Head Cycle Lord: Ketu Deity: Ashvins, the celestial healers

Auspicious for starting projects, traveling, buying or selling vehicles, healing. Passionate, impulsive, attractive and intelligent, people whose birth Moons are in Ashvini can also be headstrong, extravagant and sometimes even heroic. They enjoy travel, are often skilled workers, and may have healing abilities. The Ashvins are Vedic gods of light, who joyfully bring health, happiness and inspiration from heaven to earth. People born under their celestial influence have the potential to greatly benefit others by calling on their innate cheerfulness, magnetism and generosity.

2. 13°20′ - 26°40′ Aries **Bharani, Bearer**
Symbol: Vulva Cycle Lord: Venus Deity: Yama, god of righteousness

Auspicious for competitive endeavors, activities requiring bold or aggressive action, agriculture or working with the earth. Bharani folk are usually healthy, happy, skillful and conscientious. They also tend to be somewhat impatient and self indulgent, and find it hard to forgive. They are highly motivated by money. Sometimes Yama, god of justice, sends them suffering and setbacks in order to help them shift their priorities from preoccupation with material gain to spiritual transcendence. They are often long lived and make fine, courageous leaders and successful business people.

3. 26°40′ Aries - 10°00′ Taurus **Krittika, Cutter**
Symbol: Razor Cycle Lord: Sun Deity: Agni, god of fire

Auspicious for competition, debates, assertive action, working with metals. Krittika types are fiery and full of creative energy. They stand out in a crowd and can become quite famous. They may have trouble controlling their appetites though, whether in terms of food or sex. They like to take on big projects and are highly ambitious and self-motivated. Krittika is the constellation Westerners call the Pleiades, which is associated in Hindu mythology with valor and victory.

4. 10°00′ - 23°20′ Taurus **Rohini, Red**
Symbol: Chariot Cycle Lord: Moon Deity: Prajapati, the creator

Auspicious for healing, weddings, spiritual endeavors, putting new jewelry on for the first time. Rohini is one of the best placements for the Moon, giving a loving, truthful disposition, the desire to be of service to others, strength, serenity, and a sense of responsibility. If the Moon is afflicted however, anger, stubbornness and an overly critical nature may appear instead. Rohini is linked with the arts, music, beauty and culture. Rohini people are often well to do, well liked, romantic and appealing. Sometimes there is a serious problem with one or both parents.

5. 23°20′ Taurus - 6°40′ Gemini **Mrigashira, Doe's Head**
Symbol: Deer's Head Cycle Lord: Mars Deity: Soma, god of immortality

Auspicious for beginning construction of new buildings, travel, marriage. Sensitive and highly perceptive, these gentle souls are often drawn to romance, music and the arts. They may be haunted by self-doubt, however, and would rather give in than argue. They prefer a quiet, comfortable life, enjoy children, and can be very hard working. Sometimes their natural timidity, difficulty making up their minds, and attachment to the people and objects they enjoy, can create obstacles to their growth. Nevertheless, they are frequently drawn to spiritual life.

6. 6°40′ - 20°00′ Gemini **Ardra, Moisture**
Symbol: Tear Drop Cycle Lord: Rahu Deity: Rudra, god of storms

Auspicious for combat, working with fire, exorcising demons. People born under Ardra are often full of vitality and make good athletes. They may enjoy physical work more than intellectual pursuits. They live life with enthusiasm and intensity. If the Moon is afflicted they may have a cruel streak, lashing out at others unfairly and failing to appreciate the efforts other people make on their behalf. If the Moon is well disposed, or if the Ardra person has learned the lessons Rudra, the god of violent weather, has sent them, then these can be the most sympathetic and helpful of individuals.

7. 20°00′ Gemini - 3°20′ Cancer — **Punarvasu, Extra Blessings**
Symbol: Quiver of Arrows — Cycle Lord: Jupiter — Deity: Aditi, mother of the gods

Auspicious for healing, construction or repair, starting projects, traveling. Good natured, generous emotionally, and prudent financially, persons born under Punarvasu can be quite content living a relaxed, uncluttered life. They need to guard against complacency however, and watch their health. They make good friends and are usually both self-disciplined and playful. A lot of travel or frequent changes of residence may be indicated.

8. 3°20′ - 16°40′ Cancer — **Pushya, Flower**
Symbol: Udder — Cycle Lord: Saturn — Deity: Brihaspati, priest of the gods

Auspicious for healing, festivals, all positive endeavors—except weddings. Pushya is one of the two best placements for the natal Moon (the other is Rohini). Those who are activating the full potential of their Pushyan nature will not only be intelligent but wise. They have stable, easy going personalities, are prosperous, well educated, popular, virtuous, nice looking and forthright. If they start taking themselves too seriously, however, they can become overly rigid, selfish and arrogant, or may find themselves attracted to friends who're not very good for them. They're often productive and caring people who make good teachers or counselors, but tend to be overly sensitive to criticism.

9. 16°40′ Cancer - 0°00′ Leo — **Ashlesha, Entwiner**
Symbol: Coiled Snake — Cycle Lord: Mercury — Deity: Sarpa, serpent god

Auspicious for competition, business, aggressive action. These self-reliant people can be excellent communicators. They have tremendous concentration, penetrating insight and deep sexual feelings. Because they are so intuitive, they may feel particularly vulnerable, and strike out at others or creatively manipulate the truth to protect themselves. Their candor can cross the border into tactlessness. Because of their innate psychic abilities and powers of concentration, Ashleshans who are attracted to meditation and spiritual life can make amazingly fast progress. Don't humiliate an Ashleshan: they will never forget.

10. 0°00′ - 13°20′ Leo **Magha, Greatness**
Symbol: Throne Cycle Lord: Ketu Deity: Pitris, ancestors

Auspicious for activities requiring courage or relating to water. The children of Magha are regal, ambitious and often physically strong. They can rise to leadership positions easily, and honor tradition. They enjoy being served more than serving, and their grand gestures may impress everyone, or no one. Their desire for respectability sometimes trips over their voracious desire for sex. They are generally well-to-do, pleasure loving, and devote their time to noteworthy projects.

11. 13°20′ - 26°40′ Leo **Purva Phalguni, 1st Fruit**
Symbol: Marriage Bed Cycle Lord: Venus Deity: Bhaga, god of good fortune

Auspicious for construction and conquest. Magnanimous, loyal and delightful conversationalists, those born under Purva Phalguni may find themselves in government service sometime during their lives. Earthy and attractive, these people get their way without intimidating others. Often they are wanderers, drawn to the arts, and enjoy life to the full. The body is usually healthy but the mind is so active and creative, it can sometimes lead to trouble, as they tend to leap without looking first. Fame comes easily to these people, as does money, when the Moon is strong in the chart. If it is weak, conceit, self aggrandizement and a dissolute lifestyle may manifest.

12. 26°40′ Leo - 10°00′ Virgo **Uttara Phalguni, 2ndFruit**
Symbol: Marriage Bed Cycle Lord: Sun Deity: Aryaman, god of marriage

Auspicious for marriage and other ceremonies, entering a new house for the first time, making resolutions. The Hindu god Shiva and the Himalayan yogini Parvati were married under this nakshatra, which often gives happiness in relationships. Phalguni means fruit of the tree, and natives born under both Purva Phalguni and Uttara Phalguni are likely to experience the fruit of good karma earned in previous lifetimes. Uttara Phalguni folks are likeable, generally do well financially, and may earn substantial salaries through their exceptional intelligence. They make wonderful friends, always ready to help their companions. Success, courage and love of adventure may appear, though romantic escapades can lead to trouble.

13. 10°00′ - 23°20′ Virgo **Hasta, Hand**
Symbol: Fist Cycle Lord: Moon Deity: Savitar, god of inspiration

Auspicious for marriage, shopping, travel, starting a course of study. The children of Hasta are hard working, industrious and exceptionally resourceful. They're more likely to be artisans or specialists of some sort rather than leaders. Intelligence and a sharp wit are often seen, and healing ability may be noted. Sometimes there is lack of patience with others, and a determined effort to manipulate others towards their own ends. They are usually pleasant, though a tendency toward depression may occasionally show up. They're fine business people and good teachers. These natives should avoid alcohol and drugs, as their physical constitution is not designed to handle them.

14. 23°20′ Virgo - 6°40′ Libra **Chitra, Brightness**
Symbol: Pearl Cycle Lord: Mars Deity: Tvashtar, the divine architect

Auspicious for healing, rituals, projects related to architecture, clothing or jewelry. Handsome and stylishly dressed, the charming natives of Chitra are drawn to anything that's new or out of the ordinary. They are magnets to the opposite sex, are often artistically gifted, and surround themselves with beautiful things. Chitrans may occasionally be down but they're rarely out of the game for their lively spirit is unconquerable. Intelligence, honesty and efficiency are part of their attractive nature. Less mature Chitrans may waste too much time indulging themselves or may look down at others less fashionable than themselves.

15. 6°40′ Libra - 20°00′ **Svati, Sword**
Symbol: Coral Cycle Lord: Rahu Deity: Vayu, god of the life force

Auspicious for conflict, making weapons or tools, starting benevolent projects. Children of Svati are independent and are rarely overly attached to their material possessions. They're generally quiet, nice people who control their feelings in public. They enjoy helping others, rarely hold grudges for long, and are pleasant to talk with. They like to travel and are strongly attracted to religion or philosophy. They usually have exceptional intelligence (though they may take their time mulling over new information) and have a knack for business. Less mature Svatis may find themselves struggling with chronic discontent, or may become so immersed in their own thoughts and ideas that they lose sight of other people's needs.

16. 20°00′ Libra - 3°20′ Scorpio **Vishakha, Purpose**
Symbol: Potter's Wheel Cycle Lord: Jupiter Deity: Indragni, god of fire and power

Auspicious for healing and activities related to one's home or vehicles. Purposeful and commanding in appearance, these forceful people often meet with success. They're excellent public speakers who enjoy making money. Their courage, ambition and one-pointedness carry them quickly toward their goals, though if they should fail to achieve them they can become quite miserable and impatient. Vishakhas revel in turmoil and enjoy a good argument; some spend their entire lives in a state of revolt. People who want to befriend a Vishakha should be prepared for a fun but turbulent ride, and should not hesitate to remind the Vishakha that they have feelings too.

17. 3°20′ - 16°40′ Scorpio **Anuradha, Devotion**
Symbol: Lotus Cycle Lord: Saturn Deity: Mitra, god of cooperation

Auspicious for marriage, travel, getting in a new car for the first time. Traditionally, the natives born under Anuradha are said to be well-to-do, for they dislike austere lifestyles. They may often be on the move, and not infrequently wind up living a long distance from their birth place. They greatly value their family and friends, though their social skills may need improvement. Anuradhans enjoy organizing projects and managing people. Opportunities seem to naturally roll their way. Anuradhans may also find themselves strongly drawn to mysticism or the occult, and have a deep spiritual nature. Less mature Anuradhans need to watch out for jealousy and depression.

18. 16°40′ Scorpio - 0°00′ Sagittarius **Jyeshtha, Pre-eminence**
Symbol: Earring Cycle Lord: Mercury Deity: Indra, thunder god

Auspicious for courage in the face of enmity, for healing relationships, and for working with metals. Jyeshtha natives are renowned for their adherence to virtue, and testy temperaments. Generally cheerful, they can be quite irascible when provoked. These are the dragon slayers of the zodiac, who gladly fight to defend the helpless. You'll often find them in executive or leadership positions, hoisted there by their own considerable talents and skills. Less emotionally developed Jyeshthans may be arrogant, hypocritical, obstinate or control freaks. Deeply passionate inwardly, Jyeshthans control their feelings in order to gain their ends.

19. 0°00′ - 13°20′ Sagittarius **Mula, Root**
Symbol: Goad Cycle Lord: Ketu Deity: Nirriti, the dark goddess

Auspicious for working outdoors, beautifying the environment, making or breaking pacts. Natives of Mula tend to be set in their ways, to be pleased with themselves, and are generally happy but somewhat suspicious of other people's motivations. Peace-loving and pleasure-seeking, Mulans find their way to money or money finds its way to them. In cases where afflictions to the Moon holds back the prosperity usually associated with this nakshatra, natives still manage to enrich themselves inwardly by finding their way to the root of things intellectually or emotionally. There may be a sense of being somewhat restrained in life. For Mulans drawn to spiritual life, great strides can be taken toward transcendence.

20. 13°20′ - 26°40′ Sagittarius **Purva Ashadha, First Victory**
Symbol: Fan Cycle Lord: Venus Deity: Apas, the cosmic waters

Auspicious for community service, working with the land, healing relationships. Those born under Purva Ashadha are usually lucky in love, and are blessed with warm and lasting partnerships. These proud, outgoing people can make wonderful companions who will stick with their friends through thick and thin. Whether or not they want to be, Purva Ashadhans may often find themselves in conflicts, but odds are they'll come out on top. These people are patient, independent minded, convincing in speech, and tend to be well to do. They value their own opinions significantly more than anyone else's.

21. 26°40′ Sagittarius - 10°00′ Capricorn **Uttara Ashadha, Second Victory**
Symbol: Tusk Cycle Lord: Sun
Deity: Vishvadevas, universal forces

Auspicious for beginning new projects, working in one's home or garden. Natives of Uttara Ashadha are often very popular, idealistic and influential. They're genuinely grateful for the many blessings which fill their lives, and love giving and receiving favors. They make respectable leaders, and are drawn to work which uplifts others. Stable, introspective, and ethical, these people are good both at starting projects and carrying them through to completion. Less mature Uttara Ashadhans may be lazy, easily distracted, or stressed out.

22. 10°00′ - 23°20′ Capricorn **Shravana, Study**
Symbol: Ear Cycle Lord: Moon
Deity: Vishnu, god of cosmic stability

Auspicious for healing, ceremonies, and all other benevolent actions. Shravana people are usually intelligent, well-educated and prosperous. A happy marriage and a certain degree of fame will more than likely come their way. These people love to learn, and make good teachers. They are often drawn to religious life, or a life of service. The danger for them is that they may become rigid or fanatical in their thinking, or may become disillusioned when their efforts to reform the world do not produce positive changes as quickly as they'd like. They enjoy traveling and may be good at picking up foreign languages.

23. 23°20′ Capricorn - 6°40′ Aquarius
Symbol: Drum Cycle Lord: Mars
Dhanishtha, Abundance
Deity: Vasus, the benevolent forces

Auspicious for meeting challenges and for making efforts to grow spiritually. Dhanishtha natives are courageous, generous-hearted and often prosperous. Love of music is shown here. Upbeat and ambitious, these people enjoy taking command. You can't pull the wool over their eyes; they'll carefully analyze any proposition you put to them. Less mature Dhanishthans can be aggressive, avaricious or overly conservative. More mature Dhanishthans can be truly heroic in their efforts to help others. They have a universal outlook, and enjoy bringing people together to promote a worthy cause.

24. 6°40′ - 20°00′ Aquarius
Symbol: 100 Flowers Cycle Lord: Rahu
Shatabhishak, 100 Physicians
Deity: Varuna, god of the cosmic sea

Auspicious for working on vehicles, working on one's house or signing contracts. Those born under Shatabhishak are blunt but honest, refuse to mindlessly conform to other people's standards, and in the end almost always get their way. They are drawn to fields requiring penetrating insight such as science or philosophy. They can be very private people, who keep their real thoughts hidden from view. A less mature Shatabhishakan gives in to depression and may become a mindless workaholic; more mature natives of this nakshatra are sincerely devoted to serving humanity, whether they get credit for their efforts or not.

25. 20°00′ Aquarius - 3°20′ Pisces
Symbol: Death Bed Cycle Lord: Jupiter
Purva Bhadrapada, Front Feet
Deity: Aja Ekapat, the god beyond duality

Auspicious for overcoming danger, farming, manufacturing or selling products. Natives of Purva Bhadrapada are both skilled at making money and hanging on to it. They are usually devoted to their marriage partners, but need to be careful not to be taken advantage of. They have good business skills and often make very fine speakers. Generally, they're fairly serious people, yet they may act impetuously or have a hard time sticking to a decision. Undeveloped Purva Bhadrapadans may be phobic, cynical, or may strike out vindictively at others. These natives may be forced to meet difficult challenges in order to burn through karmic knots which are restraining their spiritual evolution.

26. 3°20′ - 16°40′ Pisces — **Uttara Bhadrapada, Hind Feet**
Symbol: Death Bed — Cycle Lord: Saturn — Deity: Ahir Budhnya, dragon of the deep

Auspicious for weddings, making promises, blessing others. Souls born under the nakshatra Uttara Bhadrapada are generally well balanced and ethical people, who can convince almost anyone of almost anything, and who sincerely enjoy family life. They like to help others, and when conflicts or competition arise, they're likely to hold the winning hand. Kind to the point of self-sacrificing, these people support and protect others. If the finer qualities of Uttara Bhadrapada have not developed yet in the course of the soul's evolution, the less noble side of the nakshatra may manifest, and the person is lazy, irresponsible, and envious. This Moon sign may turn to Tantra as a path of spiritual unfoldment.

27. 16°40′ Pisces - 0°00′ Aries — **Revati, Joy**
Symbol: Fish — Cycle Lord: Mercury — Deity: Pushan, the nourisher

Auspicious for construction, jewelry, weddings, making resolutions. Natives of Revati love people and are warmly loved in return. Healthy, with a sweet disposition and considerable wisdom, these people wish harm to no one. Like the Vedic god Pushan, their instinctive delight is in protecting and nourishing those in need. While they don't seek much for themselves, wealth and joy are often spontaneously bestowed on them. They are sociable and psychic, and find their way into a fulfilling marriage. When a soul fails to reflect the highest potentials of Revati, it may instead display an inferiority complex, a servile nature or fall prey to continual disappointments. Revatis are usually intelligent, good looking and artistically gifted.

The World Tree

Many mythologies from the Old World as well as from the high civilizations of the ancient Americas speak of a cosmic tree from which our universe grows. In the Norse myths I grew up with this tree was called Yggdrasil, but in India it's called the Ashvattha tree. You can easily find it in the sky. The nakshatra Mula is its root (*mula* literally means root). Jyeshtha and the next several nakshatras moving backwards through the zodiac are its trunk and limbs. Purva Phalguni and Uttara Phalguni are the fruit that grow on its branches (*phalguni* literally means "fruit of the tree").

What's so amazingly interesting is that Mula marks the very center of the Milky Way. In fact, the galactic center lies at 6° Sagittarius, which is right in the middle of Mula. Mula is associated with the goddess Nirriti, whom we know today by her modern name Kali. She is the darkness from which light first emerges, the Mother of the World. What an appropriate image for the center of our galaxy.

Many ancient mysteries are encoded in India's lunar mansions. Myths that the ancient Indians shared with the Sumerians and Semites, such as the story of Noah and the Great Flood, the snake in the Garden of Eden, and the seven days of creation, instantly become comprehensible when you understand the world cycles coded in the nakshatras. Very ancient legends associated with these forgotten constellations preserve the inner history of the human race.

7

What the Planets Say: Reading the Sky

When the computer revolution first took off in the last quarter of the 20th century, programmers quickly realized they would have to find a way to condense the vast amount of data they needed to store. Otherwise their data files would become so enormous that saving them on a hard drive would be impossible. So they developed a system of data compression in which each bit of data stood not for one piece of information but for many.

When the file was decompressed numerous dimensions of information would then "unfold" from a surprisingly small file. There was one liability with this ingenious process though: in order to store vast quantities of information, details and precision would sometimes be lost.

These modern programmers had rediscovered a principle used by Vedic astrologers many thousands of years ago. The challenge was to find a way to condense an entire human life—a unique personality and the events it experienced—into a diagram no larger than the palm of your hand. Incredibly, they succeeded! Using a mere 60 bits of data, they were able to describe a full human incarnation.

27	Moon Signs
12	Sun Signs
12	Houses
+ 9	Planets
60	Astrological Factors

The key was to have each astrological factor represent dozens of different things at the same time. You could tell which meaning a factor represented at any given moment in time by checking how it related to the other factors. For example, Venus can represent your spouse if you read it in relation to the 7th house. It can represent your car, however, if you read it in relation to the 4th house. Then again, while the 4th house stands for vehicles in relation to Venus, is stands for your mother in relation to the Moon. But then, if Venus rules the sign in your 9th house (which will happen if you have Virgo or Aquarius rising), it might stand for your father. Think this is confusing? Try programming a computer.

But as experienced astrologers know, this system works beautifully. A Vedic chart looks very simple yet as you "unpack" it, thousands upon thousands of bits of information about you and your life unfold. In fact, a mere 60 factors can combine in so many different ways they can form completely unique portraits of billions of people.

As experienced systems analysts know, elegant systems like this come at a price. Details and precision may be lost; the enormously complex interrelations between so many factors create a certain amount of statistical fuzziness. Your horoscope may show serious problems surrounding your mother, for example. But does this mean your mother has health problems or financial problems, or that she simply doesn't get along with you? Sometimes the jyotishi can tell; other times he has to use auxiliary methods, like the lines on your hands or omens occurring in the room around you in order to guess. Being able to see through the fuzziness in a chart is what distinguishes a master astrologer from a mediocre one.

You've learned about the twelve signs of the Hindu zodiac, the twelve houses and the 27 nakshatras. Once you understand how jyotishis work with the nine planets you'll have all the pieces in place to begin reading your Vedic chart.

THE VEDIC PLANETS

PLANET	SIGNIFICATIONS
Sun	Authority figures, power, the soul, the father, heat, male, Sunday.
Moon	The mind and emotions, mother, the public, cool, changeable, female, Monday.

Mars	Property, sports, technical ability, siblings, conflict, anger, strength, abruptness, male, Tuesday.
Mercury	Intelligence, communications, commerce, humor, quickness, flexibility, pre-pubescent, asexual, Wednesday.
Jupiter	Wealth, children, husband, philosophy, law, benevolence, male, Thursday.
Venus	Beauty, wife, the arts, jewelry, romance, marriage, sensualty, comfort, luxury, female, Friday.
Saturn	Misfortune, delays, restrictions, poverty, longevity, discipline, endurance, maturity, geriatric, asexual, Saturday.
Rahu	Worldly success, physical excess, foreigners, nonconformists, madness, female.
Ketu	Spiritual success, intuition, homelessness, violence, mental derangement, asexual.

PLANET	PROFESSIONS
Sun	Leaders, administrators, CEOs, politicians, doctors.
Moon	Manufacturers, merchants, seamen, food service, public relations, producing or selling women's goods.
Mars	Soldiers, rulers, policemen, athletes, trades people, firemen, surgeons, engineers, technicians, real estate agents and developers, farmers.
Mercury	Business people, salesmen, accountants, computer programmers, stock brokers, writers.
Jupiter	Lawyers, government ministers, counselors, pastors, teachers, scientists, bankers, public speakers.
Venus	Artists, musicians, beauticians, actors, transportation personnel, restaurant workers, fashion designers.
Saturn	The working class, manual laborers, bureaucrats, researchers, medical support personnel, industrialists.
Rahu/Ketu	Revolutionaries, drug dealers, purveyors of alcohol, illicit or illegal jobs, beggars, jesters.

PLANET	QUALITY
Sun	Mildly and unintentionally malefic. Stable effects.
Moon	Benefic if bright, especially if waxing. Malefic if dark (within 72° on either side of the Sun), especially if waning.

	Fluctuating effects.
Mars	Malefic, with abrupt effects.
Mercury	Benefic if predominantly influenced by other benefic planets. Malefic if predominantly influenced by other malefic planets. Gives results quickly.
Jupiter	Very benefic. Stable effects.
Venus	Benefic. Stable effects.
Saturn	Malefic, with slow or delayed and difficult effects.
Rahu	Malefic, much like Saturn, though effects can be sudden.
Ketu	Malefic, much like Mars.

Planets in Houses

Planets bring their personalities into the houses where they're placed. For example, someone with the Sun in the 1st house is likely to have a sunny, powerful personality with a tendency toward hot-temperedness; someone with Venus in the 1st house is likely to be sensual or artistic; someone with Saturn in the 1st house is likely to be serious, perhaps even rigid. A person with Mars in the 1st house is likely to be dynamic or even aggressive, while someone with the Moon in the 1st house may be emotional, vacillating or well-liked by the public.

The innate qualities of the planets also indicate whether your experience in the different areas of activity represented by the houses will be pleasant or unpleasant, smooth or difficult, stable or unstable. Jupiter and Venus bring benefic, supportive energy into any house they enter or affect. Mars, Saturn and the nodes (Rahu and Ketu) bring rougher, less pleasant energy. The Sun radiates his blessings out to everyone, but does this so powerfully it's sometimes hard to deal with his intense energy. For this reason jyotishis say the Sun is mildly and unintentionally cruel. The Moon and Mercury can swing either way. The brighter the Moon is the more benefic he is, but if he's very dark he can be mildly malefic, causing problems wherever he's placed. Mercury is known by the company he keeps. He's easily influenced by the planets affecting him. If he's with Saturn and Mars he can turn malefic; if he's with Jupiter or Venus he uses his energies for the good.

These ground rules regarding the benefic and malefic nature of planets can be modified depending on the planet's placement in a chart. A well placed Saturn, for example, may be far more helpful in a chart overall than a weak Venus. If you're an athlete, a strong Saturn in the 6th house will help you trounce your competitors. A weak Venus there might simply make you nice to them.

But there's still another level of complexity to the planets' effects which you already learned about in the last chapter. The planets also carry with them the energy of the houses they own. A planet that owns the inauspicious 8th house can cause havoc wherever it's placed, while the planet that owns the 9th house will bring the blessing energy of that lucky house with it. Keep in mind that a planet which owns a house is called the house's ruler or lord.

Let's see what this means for your chart. Compare your Vedic horoscope with the Sign Rulers chart. If Pisces is your 1st house, that house is ruled by Jupiter, while your second house (Aries) is ruled by Mars. If you have Cancer rising, the Moon rules your 1st house, while the Sun as ruler

<table>
<tr><td>Jupiter
Pisces</td><td>Mars
Aries</td><td>Venus
Taurus</td><td>Mercury
Gemini</td></tr>
<tr><td>Saturn
Aquarius</td><td colspan="2" rowspan="2">Sign Rulers</td><td>Moon
Cancer</td></tr>
<tr><td>Saturn
Capricorn</td><td>Sun
Leo</td></tr>
<tr><td>Jupiter
Sagittarius</td><td>Mars
Scorpio</td><td>Venus
Libra</td><td>Mercury
Virgo</td></tr>
</table>

of Leo governs your 2nd house. Note down which planets rule each of your twelve houses. Then write down which house those planets are placed in. This information is essential in interpreting your Vedic chart—as critical as knowing what your Sun sign is in Western astrology.

YOUR HOUSE RULERS' PLACEMENT

	Which planet rules the following houses in your chart?	Which house is this planet located in in your chart?
1st	____________	____________
2nd	____________	____________
3rd	____________	____________
4th	____________	____________
5th	____________	____________
6th	____________	____________
7th	____________	____________
8th	____________	____________
9th	____________	____________
10th	____________	____________
11th	____________	____________
12th	____________	____________

Now check the Lord of the House section in the following pages to discover what these planetary placements mean. Remember though, this information applies only to your Vedic chart, not your Western chart. This table gives a very general idea what each placement means, provided other factors in the chart don't offer contraindications. For example, all other factors being equal, if the planet that rules your 1st house is placed in the 2nd house (or "goes to" the 2nd house in Vedic jargon), you're likely to be happy, honorable, good at making money, well-educated, and so on, if that planet is strong and unafflicted. However, if that same planet is extremely weak, you can actually get the opposite effect: difficulties making money could be a central life issue, for example.

THE LORD OF THE HOUSE

Lord of the 1st House goes to the —

1st Healthy, powerful personality, a leader, self-centered, independent, a positive childhood, well-known and well-liked.

2nd Happy, honorable, good at making money, well-educated, loves family, generous, good speaker.

3rd Brave, enthusiastic, intelligent, happy. Drawn to literature, the media, music and the arts.

4th Gains from real estate. Homey, good relations with parents, content, good education, virtuous.

5th Intelligent, gains from investments, possible problems with children, self-centered, yet could be spiritually inclined. Drawn to entertainment, politics or sports.

6th Works hard, overcomes debts and health challenges. Excels in medical field, the military, food-related professions or support positions.

7th Fine business skills, sexually passionate, exceptional spouse but possible marital problems, enjoys travel, good with people.

8th Probing mind, possible interest in yoga or the occult, psychological insights, difficult childhood, health challenges.

9th Fortunate in life, spiritually inclined, kind to others, may travel abroad, benefits from father, well-liked, divinely blessed.

10th Career-oriented, well-known, successful, self confident, ambitious, support from high places.

11th Opportunities spontaneously appear, windfalls, successful in achieving ambitions, successful friends.

12th Excellent for spiritual life, charitable nature, but may lose money or lack confidence.

Lord of the Second House goes to the —

1st Preoccupied with money, inharmonious family relationships, strong sex drive, may be drawn to financial or educational fields. Fine speaker, singer or poet.

2nd Wealthy, career in financial field or education, good speaker, a poet, good looking, loves the family.

3rd Bold, strongly oriented toward material success.

4th Wealthy, well-educated, benefits from mother and real estate.

5th Prosperous, financial investments favored, intelligent, conflicts with family.

6th Much gain after much work, struggles with competitors or employees, could do well in medical field or service professions.

7th Money comes through the spouse, business partners or abroad.

8th Financial difficulties, though may inherit money.

9th Wealthy, spiritual, talented, health improves with the years. Talent in religious or legal fields.

10th Honorable, learned, makes good money, respected. May work in food industry, with jewelry, agriculture or with words or song.

11th Excellent for wealth, money comes easily, good friendships.

12th Needs to be careful with finances.

Lord of the Third House goes to the —

1st Self-made, drawn to the arts or trades, self-assertive, health may suffer.

2nd Needs to learn to work hard, needs to develop motivation.

3rd Animated personality, very good for involvement in the arts or trades or communications fields.

4th Happy and prosperous; some marital problems.

5th Desires are usually fulfilled, drawn to writing and the arts, remarkable children.

6th Good for wealth but only after some exertion. Health and service fields favored.

7th Strong sex drive may cause marital problems, may have run-ins with authority figures, possibly a tough childhood.

8th Needs to cultivate self-confidence and contentment.

9th Lucky breaks, life improves after marriage, conflict with father.

10th Excellent work skills, considerable success through self-effort.

11th Assertive, adventurous, fulfills goals.

12th Conflicts with relatives, insecure, many cravings. Needs to cultivate self respect and abiding tranquility.

Lord of the Fourth House goes to the —

1st Auspicious for real estate, fixed assets, creature comforts, vehicles, and one's mother.

2nd All round beneficial placement for family life, education, real estate and material well-being.

3rd Destined to make lots of money if willing to work hard. Determined and good hearted.

4th Excellent for family happiness, education, real estate and spiritual development.

5th Happy and well-liked, highly intelligent, property investments highly favored, exceptional children.

6th Needs to watch expenses and keep a positive attitude. Conflicts with mother.

7th Excellent for real estate dealings. Good for education and travel.

8th Problems getting one's financial act together. Needs to calm the mind, clarify goals, and work consistently toward achieving them.

9th Favors contentment, material prosperity, spiritual development.

10th Professional success, excellent relations with people in power, surpasses the competition.

11th Good for mother, real estate and material comforts. Friendly and fortunate.

12th Lives modestly for better or worse. Excellent for spiritual life if so inclined.

Lord of the Fifth House goes to the —

1st Good for ministers, counselors, managers, teachers, entertainers and politicians. Intelligent, cheerfully helps others, loves children.

2nd Fame, prosperity, wonderful spouse and children, talent for spiritual practice and astrology.

3rd Artistic talent, things tend to work out for their benefit, good worker.

4th Excellent for all round happiness and creature comforts.

5th Profitable investments, high intelligence, interest in politics, sports or entertainment fields. Powerful indicator of past life credit.

6th Good for work life and health, difficult for romance and relationships with children.

7th Good marriage, good morals, may become well-known. Their children excel.

8th Needs to bring love and awareness into relationships with children, and to cultivate cheerfulness and selfless service.

9th Life is filled with divine grace. Good luck, outstanding character, may be an excellent teacher.

10th Excellent for career. Could be prominent in sports or politics. Favored by those in authority; rises to authority position oneself. May have a famous child.

11th Many gains throughout life. Knowledgeable, skillful, fortunate, successful, intelligent.

12th Excellent for spiritual life.

Lord of the Sixth House goes to the —

1st Competitive, favors military advancement or medical work, could do very well professionally but needs to watch the health.

2nd Fulfilling and potentially profitable for those who enjoy hard work. Needs to watch expenses. Domestic upsets.

3rd Needs to cultivate a tranquil and benevolent spirit.

4th Possible problems with mother, education, cars, houses. Should cultivate a spirit of helpfulness and gratitude.

5th Good for health though children's health may suffer. Possible talent for healing.

6th A healer and a winner. Healthy. Good relations with co-workers.

7th Needs to exercise care in choice of marital and business partners.

8th Need to devote energy and attention to their health, and cultivate good will toward others.

9th Good for health and work-day life, but luck may come and go. Needs to cultivate cheerfulness.

10th May have difficulty clarifying career options. Perhaps work in the medical field or military, or a support position.

11th Consistent, wisely-applied effort more likely to bring results than waiting for lucky breaks.

12th May tend toward self-destructive habits unless they have a clear understanding of their purpose in life.

Lord of the Seventh House goes to the —

1st Powerful personality, happy marriage.

2nd Financial prospects improve after marriage; needs to avoid overindulgence.

3rd Good for the spouse but not necessarily for the marriage. Children's health needs attention.

4th Happy home life. Real estate ventures with spouse or other partners flourish.

5th Wonderful spouse, good business partnerships, happy children.

6th Marriage and partnerships need to be approached with clear-sightedness.

7th Magnetic personality, business skill, possibly a great marriage though with some turbulence.

8th Benefits and losses from marriage and partnerships. Possible significant life lessons in these areas.

9th Favors marriage and long distance travels.

10th Successful spouse and/or spouse helps in one's career. Lots of business travel.

11th Marriage brings significant gains.

12th Empowers sex life but may destabilize marriage.

Lord of the Eighth House goes to the —

1st Excellent for mystical and psychological studies. Possible health challenges, may be accident-prone.

2nd Financial and domestic problems. At all costs, avoid alcohol, tobacco and illegal drugs.

3rd Needs to cultivate courage and confidence. Needs to establish realistic goals.

4th Possible difficulty hanging on to material goods. Intuitive powers could flower into significant spiritual insights.

5th Children, romance and investments need careful attention.

6th Challenging for health but excellent for overcoming competitors. Cultivate patience on the work site.

7th Marriage partner may experience chronic illness. Marital ups and downs. Lasting business success requires extra commitment.

8th Classic indicator of long life, if other factors in the chart support this. Gains through inheritance or insurance.

9th Explores alternatives to their birth religion. Difficulties with the father.

10th It may seem difficult to find one's true vocation or to get one's career off the ground.

11th Favors longevity but creates friction with friends. Patience and commitment are necessary in achieving one's goals.

12th An excellent indicator for those interested in cultivating spiritual life. A challenging indicator for those cultivating material gains.

Lord of the Ninth House goes to the —

1st Blessed life, spiritual, prosperous, respected, full of faith and merit. Helps others, innately wise.

2nd Wealthy, happy, well-read, beloved.

3rd Full of courage and drive, friendly, fortunate, good for communications field and for younger siblings.

4th Excellent for all 4th house affairs: mother, property, vehicles, fixed assets, contentment.

5th Born with much good karma. Blessed life, knows what they were born to do, spiritually inclined, prosperous, intelligent. Exceptional father and/or children.

6th Good prospects for jobs and co-workers, but success still requires hard work. Faith increases as one overcomes difficulties.

7th Success in undertakings, joy in marriage, health, good fortune.

8th Long-lived, unconventional, inherits money, psychic, occasional cycles of hard knocks.

9th Spiritual nature, good fortune, prosperous, idealistic, charitable, inspired and inspiring, father is fortunate.

10th High status, prominent career, fame, prosperity, keeps company with the high and mighty.

11th The passage of years brings increasing wealth, honors and achievements.

12th Money does not come easily though it goes quickly. May be more concerned with benefiting others than oneself.

Lord of the Tenth House goes to the —

1st Excellent career prospects, earns fame and wealth.

2nd Wealthy, charitable, a good speaker or poet, may work with gems, cosmetics, banks or food, peaceful domestic life.

3rd Possible career in the arts, communications or the trades. Courage, self confidence.

4th Happy, successful, good hearted. May be involved in agriculture, real estate, education. Tends to be conservative.

5th Intelligent, successful investments, spiritually-oriented, appreciated by others. May have a remarkably successful child.

6th Skillful, slow but steady financial gains. May work in the military, judicial system, food service, a hospital or prison.

7th Happy marriage and career, relates well to others, fortunate in partnerships.

8th Long-lived, intrigued by the occult, can be a top researcher. Ethics should be a priority.

9th Good luck in career, possibly a career in religion, publishing or higher education. Well to do, dutiful.

10th Powerful career karma, professional success and renown, ample talent.

11th Could become very wealthy. Happy and influential, likes to assist others. May have many different types of jobs.

12th Career instability. Redirecting life to serve others brings fulfilment. Could work abroad or with foreigners.

Lord of the Eleventh House goes to the —

1st Born to financial success, opportunities fall from the sky, desires are fulfilled.

2nd Rich, happiness at home, good speaker, enjoys luxuries, profits through friends.

3rd Bold actions bring success, money from writing or the arts or trades, happy friendships.

4th Acquires real estate and the comforts of life, may be quite learned.

5th Successful investments, happiness from children, prospers through the arts, sports or politics.

6th May prosper through the health field, military, service positions, or through litigation. May have the sense that life is a struggle.

7th Marriage brings fulfillment and affluence, passions are strong, desires are usually fulfilled.

8th Rises and slumps in income, financial gains from spouse or legacies.

9th Fortunate, prosperous, talented, idealistic, charitable.

10th Great for business and career, works for good causes, friends in high places.

11th Gains in undertakings, good friends, desires fulfilled.

12th Either finds making financial contributions to those in need a source of happiness, or finds cycles of financial loss intensely frustrating.

Lord of the Twelfth House goes to the —

1st Needs to focus on staying solvent and staying healthy. Self-esteem may be an issue. Spiritual practices will help a great deal.

2nd Lacks financial or dietary discipline. Kindly, longs for peace. Must stay off alcohol and mind-altering drugs or serious consequences may ensue.

3rd Argumentative, insecure, unmotivated, may be amazingly intuitive.

4th Losses in real estate, car problems, many changes in residence, tends to worry. May have a deeply spiritual nature.

5th Needs to be careful with investments and romances. Needs to cultivate faith and peace of mind. Children need special attention.

6th May have a hard time finding satisfying work, but is a tough competitor. Stay out of litigation if possible!

7th Gains and losses in marriage, may have an ascetic nature.

8th Spiritual nature is very strong, devoted to God and good works.

9th Materially-oriented, does better abroad, conflicts with others.

10th Career may not be the most successful aspect of one's life. Thrives by serving others.

11th Needs to be cautious in investments and to save for a rainy day.

12th An excellent position for serious spiritual seekers. Money spent on good causes, success abroad and possibly an elevated state of consciousness in the after-life.

Planetary Strength

When beginning students compare these meanings in their charts, contradictions almost always appear. Yet when well trained Indian astrologers give readings, they instinctively cut through the maze of confusion. This is because they know how to weigh the strength of planets. The placements of the Ascendant lord in the 10th house is an excellent indication for a strong career focus, yet if the lord is afflicted in the 10th, success may only come only after years of struggle. If the lord is extremely weak in the 10th, the client may never find her career path at all.

GAUGING PLANETARY STRENGTH AND WEAKNESS

PLANET	OWN SIGNS	EXALTATION	FALL	BEST HOUSE
Sun	Leo	Aries	Libra	10th
Moon	Cancer	Taurus	Scorpio	4th
Mars	Aries, Scorpio	Capricorn	Cancer	10th
Mercury	Gemini, Virgo	Virgo	Pisces	1st
Jupiter	Sagittarius, Pisces	Cancer	Capricorn	1st
Venus	Taurus, Libra	Pisces	Virgo	4th
Saturn	Capricorn, Aquarius	Libra	Aries	7th

The Sun and Moon only move in one direction through the sky, but the five true planets (Mercury, Venus, Mars, Jupiter and Saturn) will occasionally appear from the point of view of observers on Earth to stop in their tracks and move in reverse. Planets which are retrograde—that appear to be moving backward in the sky—are extremely strong. Astrologers usually mark a planet "Rx" if it's retrograde. You should be aware that the shadow planets Rahu and Ketu always move backward through the ecliptic, but since that's their natural direction they're not considered extra strong.

All of the interpretations listed above need to be considered in light of the strength of the planetary lord being described. A planet is strong if it is in its exaltation sign or a sign it owns, if it is in its best house, or if it is retrograde. It is weak if it is in the sign of its fall or if it is too close to the Sun. If the planet is neither strong nor weak, it gives average results.

If a planet is within 6° of the Sun it's combust, which means its light is lost in the solar glare. Things in the outer world that planet designates may have trouble manifesting fully. If your combust Jupiter rules the 7th house for example, you could have trouble finding a marriage partner. The inner qualities Jupiter represents however, like a cheerful and generous spirit, are not harmed.

What happens if a planet is strong and weak at the same time? For example, what if the lord of your 1st house is both fallen and retrograde in the 10th house? Astrological effects don't cancel each other out; they both play out. If your 10th lord is both strong and weak, sometimes your career will go great guns, other times it will hit the skids. Or one signification of your 10th house, such as your status in your community, may be excellent, yet your relationship with government officials (another 10th house designation), may be disastrous. A professional jyotishi knows how to tease out these distinctions.

Aspects

There is one last technical matter you need to be aware of to gauge whether your planets are able to deliver their full promise in your chart, for better or worse. The seven classical planets (not Rahu and Ketu) send their energy out to other houses in the form of aspects. Thus the planets not only affect the houses they're in and that they rule, but the house(s) they direct their influence toward in the form of aspects, as well as toward any planets that may be in those houses.

Each planet (including Rahu and Ketu) affects every other planet in the same house with it, no matter how far apart they are within that house. However, the effect is stronger the closer the planets come to each other.

Planets and houses are supported and stabilized by aspects from the positive planets Jupiter, Venus, an unafflicted Mercury, and the bright Moon. They're mildly undermined by aspects from the Sun, an afflicted Mercury, and a dark Moon, which are all weak malefics. However, planets and houses are seriously destabilized by aspects from Mars and Saturn, which are potent malefics.

Is Saturn casting a malefic aspect on your otherwise beautiful 11th house, causing constant frustrations with your friends and the organizations you're involved with? Is Venus casting a benevolent aspect on your 7th house, smoothing out your business partnerships? Here's how to tell what aspects are influencing each of your twelve houses.

PLANETARY ASPECTS

Every planet (including Rahu and Ketu) influences every other planet in the same house with it. In addition, every planet (excluding Rahu and Ketu) also influences the houses and planets it aspects.

PLANET	NO. OF HOUSES FROM ITSELF IT ASPECTS
Sun	7th
Moon	7th
Mercury	7th
Venus	7th
Mars	4th, 7th, 8th
Jupiter	5th, 7th, 9th
Saturn	3rd, 7th, 10th

Extremely Important: Although the mathematical concept zero was invented by the Hindus, Indian astrologers start counting house numbers not with "0" but with "1." Counting the 7th aspect of the Sun in Aries, therefore, you will arrive at Libra, not Scorpio. Libra is seven houses from the Sun if you count Aries as "1," Taurus as "2," Gemini as "3," Cancer as "4," Leo as "5," Virgo as "6," and Libra as "7."

All planets except Rahu and Ketu aspect the 7th house from themselves, as well as all planets in that house. Mars, Jupiter and Saturn each cast two additional aspects. Note that in Vedic astrology planets aspect not only other planets but entire houses, whether there are any planets in those houses or not.

Rahu and Ketu are malefics which usually cause problems for the house they're in and any other planets in the same house with them. However, they do not cast aspects outside the houses they occupy.

You won't understand how to read your Vedic chart till you understand how aspects behave. Let's work through an example in detail to make sure you're clear on Vedic aspects.

Take a look at George W. Bush's Vedic chart. You'll notice the rising sign or Ascendant is Cancer.

Take note that Mercury, Venus and Saturn are all conjunct (together) in the 1st house. All three planets influence each other as well as aspecting the 7th house (Capricorn). In addition, Saturn aspects the 3rd house (Virgo) as well as the Moon and Jupiter, and the 10th house (Aries).

Mars is in the 2nd house (Leo). It aspects the 5th house (Scorpio) as

Pisces	Aries	**Ralm** 27° Taurus	**Sun** 20° Gemini
Aquarius	**George Bush Jr.** **July 6, 1946** **7:26 a.m. EDT** **New Haven, CT** **72W55 41N18** From Hospital Records		**Mercury** 16° **Saturn** 3° **Venus** 28° **Asc** 14° Cancer
Capricorn			**Mars** 16° Leo
Sagittarius	**Ketu** 27° Scorpio	Libra	**Moon** 23° **Jupiter** 25° Virgo

well as Ketu, the 8th house (Aquarius), and the 9th house (Pisces).

The Moon and Jupiter are in the 3rd house (Virgo). They both influence each other and aspect the 9th house (Pisces). In addition, Jupiter aspects the 7th house (Capricorn), and the 11th house (Taurus) as well as Rahu.

Ketu in the 5th house (Scorpio) and Rahu in the 11th house (Taurus) do not cast aspects.

The Sun is in the 12th house (Gemini) from which it aspects only the 6th house (Sagittarius).

We'll discuss what Bush's chart tells us about him in more detail later, but here's a sample of how aspects act. All three benefics or "good" planets (Mercury, Venus and Jupiter) aspect the 7th house of marriage, showing that Bush has a wonderful wife who's been a good influence on him. The malefic Saturn also aspects the 7th house. However, since Saturn owns the house (because Saturn rules Capricorn), it behaves like a good landlord and contributes its better qualities (such as Saturnine stability) rather than its worse ones (such as sorrow and resentment) to the marriage.

In general, aspects from the Moon, Mercury, Venus and Jupiter are helpful. (The Moon's capacity to do good is weakened if it's waning or within about 70° of the Sun, Mercury's if it's influenced by a malefic.) Aspects from the Sun, Mars, and Saturn are usually problematic.

Astrologers in India saw that planets together in the same sign had a dramatic effect on each other, even if they're 20° apart. Two planets 1° apart might not influence each other at all, however, if they're in different signs. Think of your horoscope as a building with twelve rooms. People in the same room, whether they're standing close to each other or not, can still easily carry on a conversation. However, two people only a foot apart won't be able to hear each other if there's a wall between them. Mars at 1° Taurus knows exactly what Venus at 20° Taurus is saying and can influence her easily because they're both in the same room. If Mars is at 1° Taurus and Venus is as 2° Taurus, so much the better: Mars can now hear even Venus' softest whisper. However, Mars at 1° Taurus doesn't know what Venus at 29° Aries is doing even through she's just 2° away because she's in a completely different room.

In Vedic astrology, planets at 30° or 0° of any sign are considered uninfluential because they're in the process of passing through the door from one room into another. Their presence isn't making itself felt strongly yet in either room.

COSMIC QUESTIONS

In Chapter 1, I promised to show you how a very skilled astrologer in India can tell in advance what question you're going to ask, and what the answer is. There are many techniques for doing this. You now have enough knowledge of Jyotish to understand the simplest method.

Here is a case I witnessed myself. A worried-looking woman walked into a Vedic astrologer's office. Before she even spoke, the astrologer mentally visualized the position of the planets at that moment, a technique called *prashna.* The first three planets that flashed through the field of his awareness were Mars, Venus and Saturn. He didn't need to analyze any more planetary positions because he already knew the woman's problem and the solution. "Don't be concerned about your husband. He's still on the boat," he said. "There's been a delay. He'll be home in a few hours."

"But the boat should have docked this morning!" the woman

wailed. Her husband was on a river boat and was late getting in. It turned out he arrived home a couple of hours after the reading, just as the astrologer predicted.

How did the astrologer know all this?

The 1st house of the prashna chart represents the person asking a question. There the astrologer saw Mars in Scorpio (strong in its own sign) aspecting Venus in Taurus (also strong in its own sign). The malefic Mars shows that the woman is worried about some danger. Venus is in the 7th house, which it also rules (Taurus). The 7th house —and Venus, which in this case rules the 7th house —represent the marriage partner. Mars' aspect to Venus shows she is concerned her husband may be in danger. Because Mars is very strong the woman is very worried. But the fact that Venus is strong tells the astrologer the husband is fine. If Venus had been weak, her husband might actually have been in trouble.

So what's happening with the husband? Saturn is in the 7th house with Venus. Saturn represents, among other things, delays. Why is the

<table>
<tr><td>Pisces</td><td>Aries</td><td>Venus 4°
Saturn 7°
Taurus</td><td>Gemini</td></tr>
<tr><td>Aquarius</td><td colspan="2" rowspan="2">Prashna for Worried Woman</td><td>Cancer</td></tr>
<tr><td>Capricorn</td><td>Leo</td></tr>
<tr><td>Sagittarius</td><td>Mars
Scorpio</td><td>Libra</td><td>Virgo</td></tr>
</table>

husband delayed? Saturn owns Aquarius, the 4th house, which represents ships and bodies of water. So the husband is delayed on a boat.

As lord of the 4th house, Saturn also represents the home in this chart. Venus is at 4° Taurus. Saturn is at 7° Taurus. Venus as ruler of the 7th represents the husband. Saturn as ruler of the 4th represents the home. Venus is a fast moving planet; Saturn moves through the ecliptic very slowly. Venus needs to travel only 3° to reach Saturn. In his mind the *jyotishi* equates degrees and hours. So he foresees that in about three hours the husband will arrive home. He was correct.

This is very, very simple astrology. But try doing it yourself. Most of us will be hopelessly confused wondering which of the hundreds of different things Venus, Mars and Saturn represent actually apply in this case. We'll also probably be looking at the other planets trying to figure out how they affect the reading. Because the jyotishi had the blessings of a long lineage of teachers as well as many years of experience, he instantly screened out the irrelevant data and intuited the truth. This process is very much like a talented and deeply knowledgeable physician who knows which of your symptoms to focus on in order to make a correct diagnosis. This phenomenal intuitive ability is what distinguishes truly great astrologers—and great doctors—from the rest of us.

The Fundamental Principle of Vedic Chart Interpretation

The single most important principle of Vedic chart interpretation is this. No element of the horoscope is ever read in isolation. Vedic astrology is 100% holistic, fully respecting the fact that everything in the universe, and certainly every element in a birth chart, is fundamentally interrelated.

If the planet that rules your 12th house is in your 4th house, you may have read that you'll experience losses in real estate. However, if your astrologer double checks and sees that you have excellent financial karma as a whole, and that the planet that rules your 4th house itself is very strong, she'll note that any losses you incur may be minimal. The reason astrologers in India study for years before giving professional readings is to learn how to integrate the many factors that comprise your chart into a comprehensive whole that respects the complexity of your experience in life, as well as your inner resources in handling events both good and bad.

Now let's turn to the two mysterious planets that can't rule a house or cast aspects because they don't really exist: the shadow planets.

8

Shadow Planets: The Karmic Axis

Rahu and Ketu are two of the most powerful and malevolent beings in the sky. That's why at my local Hindu temple, the priest regularly offers rice and barley into the sacred fire to propitiate them. They're the two demons so dangerous they can actually eat the Sun and the Moon. We in the West know Rahu as the Moon's north node and Ketu as its south node, the only points along the ecliptic at which solar and lunar eclipses can occur. But Vedic astrologers know them as the Sun and Moon's bitterest enemies.

These demons almost ate my husband. I was warned by a Hindu yogini that when Rahu transitted my Sun, my husband would experience a serious health crisis. The Sun represents my husband in my Vedic chart because it's the lord of the 7th house of marriage, and it's also in the 7th, so it doubly represents marriage.

The day before Rahu crossed my Sun, Johnathan seemed fine. I sighed in relief. But the night of the transit he collapsed—a nerve in his leg stopped working. Suddenly he couldn't walk.

I came to fully appreciate why Hindus fear the nodes so much when our friend Will died. Will had a wonderful Vedic chart which clearly revealed his generous, spiritual nature. There was only one serious problem in the horoscope: the planet ruling his Ascendant was extremely weak. Since the Ascendant rules the body, a weak Ascendant lord can place the health at risk during malefic transits. Unfortunately, the day

Rahu transited over Will's Ascendant degree, Ketu was simultaneously transitting over his weak Ascendant ruler. He was found dead the next day. Something had gone terribly wrong with the generator in his home and it had filled his house with carbon monoxide.

The Moon's north and south nodes are comparatively minor players in Western astrology. But in the Vedic system Rahu and Ketu are immensely important—we ignore their influence at our risk. However, even though they are first class malefics, depending on how our charts are laid out their powerful energies can often be harnessed to work for our benefit. For this reason it's important to know where the nodes lie in our Vedic charts, and how to make peace with their dynamic and sometimes destructive energies.

Mythology of the Nodes

The gods and demons are constantly at war, according to Hindu scripture. For thousands of years the demons battle the gods, forcing them down from the heavens and stealing their place in the sky. The gods fight back, eventually chasing the demons down into the underworld and resuming their original place in heaven. Yet even as the gods are relaxing on their astral thrones, the demons are plotting a counterattack. Till the universe perishes, absorbed back into the consciousness of Brahma the Creator, this war goes on and on.

This ongoing battle represents the precession of the equinoxes. The gods of heaven are the stars above the celestial equator (*deva,* the Sanskrit word for god, literally means "shining one") while the demons of the netherworld are the stars we residents of the northern hemisphere can't see because they're hidden beneath our horizons. As the Earth's axis pivots due to its precessional wobble, constellations seem to rise and fall in the night sky in an ever repeating cycle of around 26,000 years. Stars that have graced the heavens for thousands of years "lose the battle" and vanish below the celestial horizon for long ages, while formerly invisible stars rise to take their place.

One day the gods and demons discovered they could become immortal if they stopped fighting and instead learned to cooperate with each other. Working together, they could churn the ocean of milk to produce the nectar of immortality. So together they plunged the holy mountain Mandara into the ocean, wrapped a gigantic snake around it, and with the gods holding one end of the snake and the demons the other, they began to churn the mountain. First, a deadly poison bubbled out from the ocean depths. But finally the nectar of eternal life floated to the top of the waves.

Astronomically, the mountain signifies the Earth's axis, the ocean of milk is of course the Milky Way, and the serpent is the celestial equator. (You can get a good view of this serpent, called Vasuki in India, if you live at a low enough latitude. He is the constellation Hydra.) The churning motion once again represents the precessional shift of the Earth's axis. However, since this is a yogic story, it's safe to assume it also has spiritual significance. In the yoga tradition a holy mountain always stands for the spine, which remains firm and immovable as a mountain when a yogi sits for meditation. The snake is the kundalini, the inner spiritual energy swirling around the spine which the yogi has learned to consciously control. The nectar and the poison which come from the ocean represent the positive and negative psychic energies released in deep meditation. The ambrosia especially represents the full awareness of your immortal spirit, the Holy Grail of yoga.

The gods didn't want to share everlasting life with the forces of evil, so they hurried to Vishnu, the Lord of the Universe, for help. Vishnu assumed the form of a voluptuous woman, who began serving the divine nectar to the assembly. Since the gods are full of goodness and purity, they remained focussed on their spiritual goal and immediately drank the nectar. The demons however, who are full of lust and greed, were distracted by the woman's beauty and failed to note that the gods were guzzling every last drop of nectar.

Only one quick-witted demon named Rahuketu saw through the ruse. Slinking across the aisle, he sat down near the gods and opened his mouth to receive the nectar. Two of the gods, the Sun and the Moon, noticed this and attacked, cutting him in half. But it was too late—a drop of nectar had just touched his lip, making him immortal. Though the demon had been sliced in two, neither the upper half of his body (Rahu) nor the lower half (Ketu) could die.

Rahuketu vowed to get revenge. To this day, Rahu lies in wait along the ecliptic, hoping to destroy his two bitter enemies, while 180° away lurks Ketu, with similar mischief in mind. And, indeed, whenever the Sun and Moon both wander too close to either Rahu or Ketu at the same time, the demon swallows them whole. However, since he was sliced in half, the Sun and Moon always manage to escape from his severed body. Watching either of the two great lights of the sky disappear into the demon's gullet has terrified people on Earth since time began. Seeing the luminaries triumphantly re-emerge as the eclipse ends has always been cause for rejoicing.

But, as Indian astrologers know all too well, Rahu and Ketu can eclipse any planet in our birth chart, and spoil any house in the horoscope. Therefore, they very carefully examine how the nodes are acting in our chart, and make recommendations for easing their negative impact.

Illuminating the Shadows

In the West we know that the lunar nodes in one sense don't really exist. They're just mathematical points moving along the zodiac, immaterial abstractions. Shadows don't actually exist either—they're not entities in themselves; they merely reveal the absence of light—yet anyone who's stepped out of the hot Sun into the shade knows that shadows are cool and dark. Hindus acknowledge that Rahu and Ketu don't have a physical body like the other planets do, yet the effects of these two "shadow planets" can be dark and chilling indeed.

Traditionally, Rahu is associated with insatiable craving, intense material desires, profound self-delusion, ignorance and sloth. Ketu is associated with loss, nonattachment, psychic phenomena and fear. Both have unsavory connotations of crime, addiction, neurotic and even psychotic behavior, and incurable disease.

According to Hindu astrologers, Rahu acts like Saturn while Ketu behaves like Mars. Rahu is especially hostile to the Moon and Ketu particularly hates the Sun. If Rahu is tightly conjunct the Moon in a natal chart, the native is often deeply emotional or given to periods of deep depression or self-delusion. One of my close friends has natal Rahu less than 1° from her Moon. During her recent Moon-Rahu planetary cycle, we had to watch her carefully—she was so depressed she was on the verge of suicide. A few days after her cycle shifted into Moon-Jupiter, she received a promotion and raise, and her self esteem soared.

In many charts, however, Rahu and Ketu can actually work very positively. Rahu is said to work well in Aquarius, the sign it co-owns with Saturn, while Ketu shares ownership of Aries with Mars and tends to do well in that sign. While malefics never completely lose their malevolent charge, their aggressive energies tend to support the 3rd, 6th, 10th and 11th houses. The 3rd house rules courage, the 6th rules competition, the 10th rules career success, and the 11th rules the ability to achieve one's goals. In these houses aggressive energies are generally welcome and useful. For example, a well-placed Rahu in the 10th house can give spectacular professional success during its cycle—Vedic astrologers see this again and again. Rahu's ruthless drive and insatiable greed can signal a one-pointed determination to succeed at all costs. In the 6th house well placed nodes signal triumph over one's competitors since this is the house of competition. However, since the 6th is also the house of illness, the nodes' malefic energy here will simultaneously disturb the health.

Rahu magnifies and Ketu contracts. If a client is particularly nervous or sensitive, a transit of Rahu over the Moon will intensify these qualifies. But let me emphasize again that if an individual is ambitious, Rahu transits and planetary cycles can give extraordinary success. I've studied the charts of many thousands of celebrities. It continually astonishes me how often people shoot to the heights of success during their Rahu cycle. A well-placed Rahu often brings worldly achievement and material wealth. I haven't seen it bring contentment or peace of mind, however. Usually it makes the person whose consciousness it dominates want more and more and more.

For aspirants seriously interested in spiritual development, Ketu is an extremely important planet. In fact, in India it's known as *moksha karaka,* meaning "indicator of enlightenment." A well-placed Ketu gives a spiritual orientation in life, detachment from materialistic cravings and success in spiritual endeavors. An afflicted Ketu, however, can lead people to mistakenly believe they're psychic or to other misadventures involving occultism. When Ketu or especially Rahu afflict Jupiter, the planet representing the spiritual preceptor, there can be misadventures involving one's guru.

When a Vedic astrologer sits down to determine how Rahu and Ketu are acting in your chart, he or she will carefully consider a variety of factors. The Moon's nodes tend to be strongly influenced by the planet that owns the house they're in (their dispositor), by other planets in the same house with them, by any planets aspecting them and the planet that rules the nakshatra they're in.

The nodes' house position is also critically important. Here is a general picture of how the nodes behave in the houses of a Vedic chart. Remember that these delineations may be altered by numerous other planetary configurations in the birth chart, and depend in part on how strong or weak the node is natally. A particularly well-placed node will turn the negative significations of a placement around for the better, while a badly afflicted node may undercut the positive promise of a placement.

RAHU IN THE HOUSES

1st This person has a powerful, unique personality and is a strong competitor. An egotistical attitude may conceal inner turmoil or self loathing. The person can get wealthy fairly easily, but needs to be more considerate of others.

2nd Home life may be disturbed by quarrels. This native needs to control his or her diet and must avoid addictive drugs and alcohol. These people need to stabilize their finances and cultivate honesty in relationships.

3rd This position lends courage and dynamism to the personality. The person has strong desires which are often fulfilled, and may become wealthy. There may be artistic aptitude, high motivation and good communication skills.

4th There may be a disturbed relationship with the mother or difficulty acquiring a house or land. This individual needs to cultivate contentment and to be a little extra careful financially.

5th Making money is generally a higher priority for this person than developing spiritually. Intelligence may be high, but strong material desires disturb one's inner peace. There may be problems dealing with children.

6th This person may face many enemies or competitors, but tends to get the better of them. He or she is an excellent worker and is favored with good health and prosperity after some initial difficulties.

7th These natives are often obsessed with relationships, but tend to attract partners who harm them in some way. Resolving relationship karma is a major priority for this incarnation.

8th There may be spiritual inclination, but the possibility of material success sometimes seems blocked. These natives should take care not to be taken advantage of, and should not take advantage of others. There may be exceptional sexual desire or attractiveness.

9th This person has solid leadership skills, but gets in trouble with authority figures. There may be intense interest in philosophy, spirituality and travel. Religious interests could be unorthodox. If Rahu is badly afflicted, the person may be hostile toward religion.

10th The native will experience substantial career success, will be respected by others, and will make good money. He or she may be a humanitarian, and could become quite well-known.

11th This position usually indicates people with the drive to attain their life goals and fulfill their desires. Material success is indicated.

12th These individuals need to cultivate thrift, as money tends to slip through their fingers. Sexual fulfillment could be a problem.

KETU IN THE HOUSES

1st Ketu here may reveal a shy, anxious person who is continually struggling with relationships. Well-placed, however, it shows enormous potential for spiritual growth.

2nd There could be difficulty communicating with others. There may have been more than average conflict in the individual's early family life. Finances may fluctuate; the person should avoid becoming financially dependent on others.

3rd This individual usually has high moral standards, and is quick to fight for what she or he considers right. There is courage, and eventual prosperity and success.

4th There are difficulties with one's mother, with real estate, or in getting an education. However, this person is also a truth seeker with discriminating intelligence. He or she may move frequently.

5th The person may be particularly intelligent, but is also a worrier. She or he is attracted to spiritual practices which are mastered with comparative ease. There are few, if any, children.

6th These people are winners, often rising to prominence in their fields. Generally healthy, when they do get sick their disease may be hard to diagnose. They are usually kind and prosperous.

7th Partners may be spiritually inclined or otherwise unusual in some way. If Ketu is afflicted, relationships may be unstable. The person may be charismatic, well-known and talented. He or she may travel extensively for business purposes.

8th These persons may be psychic, but are drawn to using their intuition for material rather than spiritual benefit. Inheritance may be disappointing. These people need to attend conscientiously to their health.

9th These individuals may have a short fuse and get into problems with the government, with their children and with money. However, they can be genuinely self sacrificing, courageous and humanitarian.

10th This person is successful and well-known, though sometimes treats others harshly. Though career efforts are favored, sudden breaks or unexpected or unusual events related to one's job may occur. Spiritual endeavors are favored.

11th The natives are well educated, prosperous, and readily attain their goals. They are charitable and well-meaning. Their friends may be unusual in some way or there may be frequent conflicts with friends.

12th This is not a great position for material prosperity or romantic fulfillment. For the spiritual aspirant, however, this is one of the best possible positions, favorable for rapid spiritual growth and success in meditation.

The Serpent of Time

Most of these nodal house delineations are not happy depictions of physical and spiritual fulfillment, since most of the time the nodes cause trouble. The Rahu-Ketu axis often shows departments of our personality or arenas of our environment that have plenty of room for improvement. (Astrologers sometimes call Rahu-Ketu the karmic axis. Keep in mind that this is a metaphor. In reality, all the planets reflect our karmic content.)

Incidentally, one of the most notorious planetary configurations in Vedic astrology is *Kala Sarpa Yoga,* meaning "the snake of time." This occurs when all seven planets lie between Rahu and Ketu or between Ketu and Rahu. This is taken as an indication that the person's present lifetime is particularly significant in the course of their numerous incarnations. There is tremendous potential for growth in life, for better or worse. Therefore ethical behavior is particularly important, and spiritual practices will be especially effective. If the nodal axis is strongly activated, and the planets are between Rahu and Ketu, there could be great material gains in life, perhaps followed by a sudden fall. When the planets are between Ketu and Rahu and the karmic axis is active, this lifetime could mark a special spiritual crisis point for the soul. Let's look at an example.

During an eclipse the nodes become supercharged. Astrologically they overpower the Sun and Moon and dominate the entire chart. In all India parents will do special rituals to protect the child and its family when a baby is born during an eclipse, since Rahu and Ketu are likely to hit everyone involved with a wallop.

Pisces	Aries	**Ralm** 27° **Sun** 29° Taurus	**Mercury** 15° Gemini
Aquarius	**Donald Trump** **June 14, 1946** **9:51 a.m. EDT** **Queens, NY** **73W52 40N42** Birth Time From Private Source		**Saturn** 0° **Venus** 3° **Asc** 24° Cancer
Capricorn			**Mars** 3° Leo
Sagittarius	**Moon** 27° **Ketu** 27° Scorpio	Libra	**Jupiter** Rx 24° Virgo

The world famous financier Donald Trump was born on the day of an eclipse. Trump entered his Sun *dasha* (major planetary cycle) in mid-1976. If you have a look at his horoscope you'll see that the Sun, which rules his 2nd house of family finances, is placed in his 11th house of financial windfalls. His well-to-do father gave him several hundred thousand dollars of seed money, and as the Sun cycle progressed Trump invested in real estate. Within a decade he was a self-made billionaire. Rahu, barely 2° from the Sun, amplified his financial luck spectacularly.

However, Trump's Moon is in the same degree as Ketu, and was permanently scarred by the lunar eclipse at his birth. Remember, while Rahu expands, Ketu contracts. And in Trump's Moon dasha the New York real estate market collapsed. Trump, formerly one of the wealthiest men in America, found himself $900,000,000 in debt. The rise and fall associated with a potent *Kala Sarpa Yoga* had taken its due. Trump's Moon is in his 5th house, which governs financial investments, and is severely afflicted by Ketu, so that's the area of life where the karmic axis took its toll.

A Vedic astrologer would note that Trump's Moon is fallen, meaning it's located at its weakest sign position in Scorpio, which is not so good. But the Moon is almost completely full, which is very good. Both the exceptional strength and weakness of the Moon are reflected in Trump's life. He took a big hit, but had the mental resilience (remember the Moon rules the mind) to bounce back. While Trump will never be as rich as he was before, he is no doubt a wiser man for the experience.

Keep in mind that many of the problems signified by the nodes can be alleviated by living truthfully and ethically, not harming others, cultivating compassion, self-discipline and contentment, and devoting a portion of each day to prayer, meditation, selfless service and honest self-examination.

In the next few chapters you'll learn how Vedic astrologers use planetary configurations called *yogas*, planetary cycles called *dashas* and *bhuktis*, and harmonic charts called *amshas*, to further understand the currents and eddies in the stream of your karma.

9

Planetary Patterns: The Knots of Destiny

Yoga. The word probably makes you think of difficult physical postures like standing on your head. But in Sanskrit *yoga* actually means to "yoke" together. That's why Hindus use the term yoga for spiritual practices that help "unite" you with a deeper reality. You already know that health enthusiasts and spiritual aspirants do yoga. But you probably didn't know that planets do too!

When planets "yoke up" with each other they form yogas, unique planetary patterns that mark the contours of your destiny, yoking you to your fate. Think of the planets as a nine-letter alphabet. Yogas are the different sentences they spell out when they combine in very specific ways.

Yogas are perhaps the single most important tool in a Vedic astrologer's repertoire. Well trained jyotishis have memorized thousands of yogas which give them very specific information. For example, I have a planetary configuration which says that my hands will be cut off. Fortunately for me both hands are still in place, but the yoga is still in full effect: a few years ago I developed carpal tunnel syndrome which makes it extremely painful for me to work with my hands.

Yogas can signal a person who's likely to become fabulously wealthy or abruptly poor, who'll plunge into one romantic affair after another, or skyrocket to fame as a scientist, or move constantly, or develop diabetes, or wander in the mountains. One of my acquaintances has a shocking yoga: it says he'll sleep with his mother. Needless to say he's never committed incest, but he lived at home with his mom till his mid-30s, and even now ten years later has never had a girlfriend because of his obsessive preoccupation with his mother. She's the only woman he'll allow into his life.

Interestingly, descriptions of the effects of yogas in Indian astrological texts are often vivid and grossly exaggerated. There's a reason for this. In ancient times astrology students didn't simply invest in a computer program to spit out yogas for them. They memorized thousands of them one-by-one. Powerful images stick in the mind, so instead of saying you'll have problems with your hands, the texts say your hands will be cut off. Instead of saying you devote too much emotional energy to your mother, they say you may sleep with her. Please keep in mind that these colorful expressions are carefully crafted (though rather tasteless) devices to jog the memory. A statement such as "will die before the age of six" really means "will probably experience a serious disease, such as chicken pox or pneumonia, in early childhood." Only when the planets involved in the yoga are very severely afflicted in both the birth chart and the divisional charts you'll learn about in Chapter 11, are these dire predictions likely to play out literally.

Yogas can give a broad spectrum of results depending on how strong and stable they are. For brevity's sake, the texts describe simply the worst—or best—case scenario. So if you discover you've got a yoga that says you'll be "like an emperor, reigning over the three worlds," remember you've got to read that within the context of your chart as a whole. Seen against the backdrop of the rest of your horoscope, it could merely indicate you'll become vice-president of a franchise of fishing equipment outlets. What distinguishes a truly great astrologer is the ability to synthesize the many different yogas and planetary placements in your chart into one unique gestalt that authentically represents your karmas. This is just like a truly skilled homeopathic physician or acupuncturist who's able to synthesize the different physical and mental symptoms you describe into a coherent picture of the condition of your vital force.

Yogas signal whether your life experience will be outside the norm. For example, many people have a strong Ascendant lord in the 2nd house. That's a pretty solid indicator for material prosperity. But does that mean you'll have $50,000 in your bank account or $500,000? If in addition to the 1st lord in the 2nd you have several strong *dhana* yogas (wealth producing combinations), look for big bucks. If you've got the 1st lord in the 2nd but you've got a number of *daridra* yogas (poverty producing combinations), your financial luck will be blocked, forcing the 1st lord's promise to be expressed through some other 2nd house channel. Maybe you'll be a talented singer or public speaker, for example. If you have both powerfully activated dhana and daridra yogas in your chart, hang on for a bumpy ride. Both types of karma will play out in your life depending on the planetary cycle you're running. In one cycle you'll rake in the dough. In the next money will evaporate like a puddle on a hot day—until another planetary cycle reactivates your wealth yoga again.

Yogas are important because they can dramatically modify other components of your chart. If your horoscope doesn't look too good for romance but it turns out you have a fabulous relationship yoga, that yoga will override the other indications. You might have trouble finding your mate, but once you make the connection you're likely to be very happy.

Will I Be Famous?

Are you destined for fame and fortune? Some people rise rapidly to the top of their profession; others remain unknown and unappreciated in spite of their considerable talent. According to the sages of India, our current life is just one of many in a long incarnational cycle, and each rebirth comes with its own set of lessons. For some the lessons involve living in the limelight, enjoying the benefits and pitfalls of public recognition. For others they involve playing one's part on a smaller stage.

Astrologers in India have a variety tools to gauge whether your life is likely to be largely average, or whether you'll soar so far above the baseline that everyone in your profession—perhaps even everyone in the world—will know your name. One of these is Raja Yogas, planetary configurations that promise an exceptional rise in life.

In India the word *raja* means king. So a Raja Yoga is a planetary pattern that makes you "like a king" in terms of prominence in your community. Depending on the strength of the yoga, you could become the head of your church group, the mayor of your town, or the president of the United States. It doesn't just mean political leadership, though. Depending on which house it appears in in your horoscope, a Raja Yoga can indicate above average success in a variety of fields. In the 7th house it could lead to renown in the business world. In the 5th it might bring exceptional success in sports or entertainment.

What makes a Raja Yoga so powerful is that it combines the influence of two types of houses, those governing personal initiative and those that show good fortune. Hindus say that when self-effort "yokes"with luck, it's like God making love to the Goddess. You've got a winning combination.

YOUR RAJA YOGAS

Here's how to tell if there's a Raja Yoga in your chart.

1. Make a note of every house in your Vedic horoscope in which two or more of these planets appear: the Sun, Moon, Mercury, Venus, Mars, Jupiter or Saturn.
2. Check to see which houses these planets rule.
3. Check whether one of the planets rules the 1st, 4th, 7th, or 10th house. Then check to see whether the other planet rules the 1st, 5th or 9th house. If they do you've hit the jackpot. That's your Raja Yoga.

Note: If one planet happens to rule houses from both groups, that's excellent, but it's not as powerful as a Raja Yoga which will always involve two planets or more.

The two most powerful Raja Yogas are:

1. The 9th lord and the 10th lord are in the same house.
2. The 4th lord and the 5th lord are in the same house.

The houses of initiative in a Vedic chart are the 1st, 4th, 7th and 10th, the angles which form the four corners of the horoscope. The houses of luck on the other hand are the 1st, 5th and 9th, the triangle around which the chart is shaped. You'll notice that the 1st house qualifies under both categories. It's the most important house in the horoscope, with a host of special powers including this double ability to produce a Raja Yoga.

You'll often find Raja Yogas at work in the charts of leaders and celebrities. Take Karl Marx's horoscope, for example. Because 1° of Aquarius was rising at the moment of his birth, the sign Aquarius corresponds to his 1st house, Pisces to his second house, and so on. You'll find one Raja Yoga in his chart, in the 4th house, governing education. Venus, which rules both the 4th house itself and the 9th house of law and publishing, appears together there with Mercury, which rules the 5th house of politics. Here the lord of an angular house (the 4th) joins the lord of a trine (the 5th), forming one of the two most powerful Raja Yogas.

Marx studied law and was involved in publishing too as a writer and newspaper editor. He didn't go out and start the Communist Revolution himself; nevertheless he was spectacularly successful in educating the public concerning his ideas about politics and economics. Do you see how the yoga blended together the meanings of all the houses involved? This powerful Raja Yoga in his birth chart greatly amplified his impact on society.

If you're a sharp-eyed student of astrology, you noticed that Marx was born on the day of a solar eclipse. (When Rahu closely joins the Sun and Moon an eclipse occurs.) That and several other spectacular yogas (including two Maha Purusha Yogas you'll learn about later in this chapter) signal that this was a man destined to leave his mark on the world.

Pisces	**Ralm** 17° **Moon** 19° **Sun** 22° Aries	**Venus** 6° **Mercury** 12° Taurus	**Mars** 29° Gemini
Saturn 24° **Asc** 1° Aquarius	**Karl Marx** **May 5, 1818** **2:00 a.m. LMT** **Trier, Germany** **06E06 49N45** From Birth Records		Cancer
Capricorn			Leo
Jupiter Rx 21° Sagittarius	Scorpio	**Ketu** 17° Libra	Virgo

Actually dozens of different kinds of Raja Yogas are recognized in Vedic Astrology. The one you've just learned is the most important, and is technically called a *Dharma Karma Adhipati Yoga.*

Will I Be Rich?

Dhana is the Sanskrit word for "wealth." A Dhana Yoga is a planetary pattern that promises prosperity in the appropriate cycle. Of the numerous types of wealth-promoting yogas, the best known involves any combination of two or more planets ruling the 1st, 2nd, 5th, 9th and 11th houses placed together in the same house. The 1st, 5th, and 9th are the houses of luck, you may remember. These are the Ascendant and its trines, the houses that contribute to ease of life if their planetary lords are strong and well-placed. The 2nd and 11th are financial houses. The 2nd reflects the financial status you were born into, whether your parents were rich or poor. The 11th indicates gains and profits that come to you easily through the course of your life.

Take a look at Christina Onassis' birth chart. Two degrees of Taurus were rising at the moment of her birth, so Taurus is the first house, Gemini the second house, and so on. Onassis has two Dhana Yogas. Venus, lord of the 1st house, is joined in the same sign with Mercury, lord of both the 2nd and 5th houses. This is an excellent combination for wealth, bringing three houses of prosperity together in one amazing combination:

- Lord of the 1st house plus lord of the 2nd
- Lord of the 1st house plus lord of the 5th

Unfortunately, this combination occurs in her 8th house, so most of her money came through her parents' death. (The 8th houses signals money from inheritances.) She became fabulously wealthy when her shipping magnate father, Aristotle Onassis, passed away.

Let me also mention Doris Duke. During her lifetime she was one of the richest women on Earth, wealthier even than the Queen of England. In her 1st house she had a massive Dhana Yoga combining the lords of the 1st, 2nd, 5th and 11th houses — four of the five prosperity-promoting houses. The lord of the 8th is also involved, so once again massive wealth came in part through an inheritance. If the yoga had been in the 7th house the money might have come from a husband. In the 4th it might have come from real estate. In the 12th it might have come from international business deals.

Ralm 0° Pisces	Aries	**Asc** 2° Taurus	Gemini
Jupiter 8° Aquarius	**Christina Onassis** **December 11, 1950** **3:00 p.m. EST** **New York, NY** **73W57 40N45** From Hospital Records		Cancer
Moon 0° **Mars** 4° Capricorn			Leo
Venus 2° **Mercury** 15° Sagittarius	**Sun** 26° Scorpio	Libra	**Ketu** 0° **Saturn** 8° Virgo

Your Dhana Yogas

Do you have a Dhana Yoga in your chart? Here's how to find out.

1. Make a note of every house in your Vedic horoscope in which two or more of these planets appear: the Sun, Moon, Mercury, Venus, Mars, Jupiter or Saturn.
2. Check to see which houses these planets rule.
3. Check whether one of the planets rules the 1st, 2nd, 5th, 9th or 11th house. Then see if the other also rules one of these same houses (the 1st, 2nd, 5th or 9th, or 11th). If so, you've got a Dhana Yoga.

If this planetary combination is strongly activated, it will bring you prosperity during its cycles.

Activated Yogas

Not everyone has a Raja Yoga or Dhana Yoga in their chart. Still, these yogas are not uncommon. Yet very few people are spectacularly wealthy or powerful. In India, astrologers are trained to recognize which yogas are waking, dreaming or asleep. If a yoga is asleep, it gives no effect at all. If it's dreaming, the person only fantasizes about great prosperity or spectacular success in their field; it never actually occurs. If the yoga is awake, however, it can propel a person to fame and fortune.

There are a number of ways to tell if a yoga is wide awake. For example, you want the planets involved to be exceptionally strong. Ideally, at least one of the planets in the combination should be in a sign it rules, the sign of its exaltation or retrograde.

Astrologers in India will always check to see whether your Ascendant is strong before predicting greatness on the basis of a powerful looking yoga. If a person's Ascendant is weak, money or success may roll her way but she may not have the savvy or psychological strength to make good use of them. So instead of rolling into her hands they just roll right past her.

For this reason a weak Ascendant is said to "break"or undermine even the best yogas. This is why Indian jyotishis often recommend special spiritual practices to help strengthen a weak Ascendant. This makes the personality stronger and more positively focused, and therefore better able to take advantage of good yogas. Christina Onassis' Ascendant isn't strong at all. Her massive wealth sent her on an orgy of self-destruction, leading to a tragic premature death.

Another way to check whether a yoga is highly active is to count the house the Moon is in as the 1st house, and see if the yoga reoccurs from this new Ascendant. Then do the same thing using the sign the Sun is in as the 1st house. Indian astrologers use this method, called *sudarshana,* believing that while the rising sign at the moment of your birth is the Ascendant for your physical body, the Moon's sign is the Ascendant for your subtle body, and the Sun's sign is the Ascendant for your causal body. If the same yoga forms from all three Ascendants, that yoga is incredibly powerful and will almost certainly play out dramatically in your life.

Ready to learn some more yogas?

MAHA BHAGYA YOGA

Combination for Exceptional Good Fortune

For a female:

Birth at night when the Sun, Moon and Ascendant all occupy even signs (Taurus, Cancer, Virgo, Scorpio, Capricorn, Pisces).

For a male:

Birth during the day when the Sun, Moon and Ascendant all occupy odd signs (Aries, Gemini, Leo, Libra, Sagittarius, Aquarius).

This is an extremely auspicious influence. The native delights others by his or her mere presence. He or she exhibits sterling virtue and warm hearted generosity. These people become well-known and are fortunate and long-lived.

In the Vedic tradition, night means between sunset and sunrise. Day means between sunrise and sunset. The results of this yoga can be extremely dramatic especially if the Ascendant, Sun and Moon are strong and stable.

PANCHA MAHA PURUSHA YOGAS

Five Combinations Indicating An Exceptional Person

These yogas occur when either Mars, Mercury, Jupiter, Venus or Saturn is in its own sign or its exaltation sign in an angle (houses 1, 4, 7 or 10).

Ruchaka Yoga: Mars is in Aries, Scorpio or Capricorn in houses 1, 4, 7 or 10. This Mars yoga promotes high energy, martial spirit and leadership qualities. The person may own property or have success in competition, athletics, war, technical fields or others of Mars' significations. He or she is victorious over competitors, is courageous and perhaps also arrogant. The face may be long.

Bhadra Yoga: Mercury is in Gemini or Virgo in houses 1, 4, 7 or 10. This Mercury yoga makes the native friendly, well-dressed, talented in communications, helpful to relations and/or skilled in business. He or she is intelligent, well-liked, long-lived, prosperous, and impressive. Honesty and leadership skills are evident.

Hamsa Yoga: Jupiter is in Cancer, Sagittarius or Pisces in houses 1, 4, 7 or 10. This Jupiter yoga is very benefic. The person may be wealthy, healthy, well-educated, have good friends and a good heart. He or she is "good looking, virtuous and praised by the wise."

Malavya Yoga: Venus is in Taurus, Libra or Pisces in houses 1, 4, 7 or 10. This Venus yoga gives wealth, a sensual orientation, determination, fame and mental balance. The native has a wonderful family and owns a number of fine vehicles and may be overweight.

Shasha Yoga: Saturn is in Libra, Capricorn or Aquarius in houses 1, 4, 7 or 10. This Saturn yoga makes the native productive, responsible, influential, and long-lived, but not necessarily considerate of others. He or she acquires wealth and has a strong work ethic. The native rises to eminent positions and benefits from conscientious employees.

Look for these yogas to give their maximum effects during the cycles (dashas and bhuktis, which you'll learn about in the next chapter) of the planet forming the yoga.

PARIVARTANA YOGA
Combinations that Exchange Places

Two planets occupy each other's signs. This is called a "mutual exchange" in Western astrology. Example: Mars, which rules Aries, is in Taurus. Venus, which rules Taurus, is in Aries.

Maha Parivartana Yoga: The exchange occurs between planets in any of the good houses. These are houses 1, 2, 4, 5, 7, 9, 10 and 11. Gives excellent results, tying together the houses involved in a positive way. Good fortune is indicated for these houses. Predict wealth, success and good luck, especially during the cycles of the planets involved.

Viparita Parivartana Yoga: The exchange occurs between planets in difficult houses 3, 6, 8, 12. This yoga gives good results, though it generally delivers its constructive effects after first creating some difficulty. Opposition, losses and problems are eventually decreased or eliminated, especially during the planets' cycles. The mutual exchange of negative influences helps to cancel the inherent negativity, and the problems associated with the houses involved are lessened to some degree. However, if a benefic planet aspects either of the planets, this yoga loses some of its power to help the individual.

Dainya Parivartana Yoga: The exchange is between a planet in a good house (1, 2, 4, 5, 7, 9, 10, 11) and a planet in one of the three most difficult houses (6, 8, 12). Produces rocky effects in the matters involving these houses. Unsuccessful or interrupted undertakings may occur in relation to their affairs. The person meets with difficulties and may not be particularly sensitive to the needs of others, especially when the cycles of those planets are running.

Khala Parivartana Yoga: A planet in the mildly difficult 3rd house exchanges signs with a planet in a good house (1, 2, 4, 5, 7, 9, 10, 11). This gives fluctuating fortunes. It's hard to stabilize matters governed by the two houses involved. The cycles of the two planets forming this yoga are, however, less bumpy than those configured in a *Dainya Parivartana Yoga.*

Here are some general examples of the types of results you might expect to experience when a mutual exchange occurs in a Vedic chart. When looking at a specific chart though, be sure to interpret the exchange in the context of the horoscope as a whole.

1st & 2nd Does well financially. Preoccupied with money. Good speaker or singer.

1st & 3rd Benefits from—and conflicts with—siblings and neighbors.

1st & 4th Gains from mother, real estate, education. Plenty of fixed assets.

1st & 5th Highly creative. Gives and gets good advice. Intelligent. Self-assured.

1st & 6th Possible debts, legal hassles, health challenges.

1st & 7th Successful partnerships. Marriage is a major and generally happy focus.

1st & 8th May have chronic health problems or unhealthy habits. Occult interests.

1st & 9th Fortunate. Divinely protected. Spiritually oriented person.

1st & 10th Fame and fortune. Career may heavily involve the body. Professional success.

1st & 11th Great for achieving goals. Wonderful friends. Sudden financial gains.

1st & 12th Lacks self love. Many expenses. Highly sexed. Feels confined.

2nd & 3rd Fluctuating finances. Earns through arts, trades, or communication fields.
2nd & 4th Great for real estate, agriculture, vehicles and education.
2nd & 5th Good investments. Children prosper. Creative projects succeed.
2nd & 6th Domestic upsets. Legal expenses. Conflicts over money.
2nd & 7th Prosperous spouse. Business deals show a profit.
2nd & 8th Financial problems. In extreme cases, illegal profits.
2nd & 9th Lucky with money. Access to higher education. Prosperous father.
2nd & 10th Career may involve banking, food, singing or public speaking, or luxury items.
2nd & 11th Money gained easily or with help from friends.
2nd & 12th Poor for financial prospects. Needs to work hard and watch expenses.

3rd & 4th Car troubles. Arguments with mother. Aggravations with home ownership.
3rd & 5th Children get on your nerves. Creative juices flow, then lock.
3rd & 6th Ultimately rises over competitors. Mends quickly from injuries and disease.
3rd & 7th Ups and downs in marriage and other partnerships.
3rd & 8th Benefits from insurance, inheritance or litigation.
3rd & 9th Minor conflicts with father, teachers and religious authorities.
3rd & 10th Career highs and lows. May work in arts, trades or communications.
3rd & 11th Wins some, loses some. Friends come and go.
3rd & 12th Good sex. Good experiences with foreigners. Controls expenses.
4th & 5th Gains through real estate investments, shipping, or from the mother.
4th & 6th Debts or lawsuits involving real estate or vehicles.
4th & 7th Strong, prosperous marriage. Good business sense.

4th & 8th Difficulties with mother. Bothersome household expenses.
4th & 9th Fabulous for education. Fortunate and well-to-do.
4th & 10th Could be a fine teacher, real estate agent, or farmer. Stable career.
4th & 11th Plenty of fixed assets. Great for earning wealth. Good friends.
4th & 12th Losses through real estate, vehicles, or schooling.

5th & 6th Care needed in investments. Illness or minor accidents for children, or difficulty conceiving.
5th & 7th Happiness in marriage. Good partnerships.
5th & 8th Difficulty getting creative projects off the ground. May show poor judgment.
5th & 9th Prosperous, lucky, spiritual, intelligent, divinely blessed.
5th & 10th Could be an entertainer, counselor, sports figure, politician or priest.
5th & 11th Lucky with money. Successful and supportive friends.
5th & 12th Possibility of losses through investments. Problems with children.

6th & 7th Difficulty finding or holding on to a mate. Health or legal challenges for spouse.
6th & 8th Gains from court cases, inheritance, medical field, insurance.
6th & 9th Problems with father figures. Conflicts with one's birth religion.
6th & 10th Difficulty finding one's career path. Low-paying or boring work, or work involving the sick.
6th & 11th Has to work hard for any gains. Fights with friends.
6th & 12th Pays off debts. Recovers from health crises.

7th & 8th Hard to find right partner. Health problems for spouse; bumpy marriage.
7th & 9th Fortunate marriage partner. Benefits from business partnerships.
7th & 10th Prominent spouse. Succeeds in business.
7th & 11th Financial gains through spouse. In business with friends.
7th & 12th Business losses. Partners may wind up in jail—or in an ashram. Foreign spouse or business partners.

8th & 9th Not always lucky. Father has major difficulties. Trouble getting higher education.

8th & 10th Career frustration. Checkered reputation. Work involves hidden knowledge or other people's money.

8th & 11th Trouble with friends. Conflicts in organizations. No easy money.

8th & 12th Excels at bed pleasures. Benefits from foreigners. Great for spiritual life, if that's an interest.

9th & 10th Fortunate. High status. Exceptional success.

9th & 11th Very lucky. Achieves goals. Wonderful friends. Prosperous.

9th & 12th Needs to work hard for benefits in life.

10th & 11th Successful, variegated career. Prominent friends. Stature in organizations.

10th & 12th Struggles to get career going. May need to change career field.

11th & 12th Gains spiritually, but may have trouble gaining materially.

Remember that what one of these exchanges signifies in your chart will depend heavily on the context of your horoscope as a whole.

RAJA YOGAS

Royal Combinations

You've already learned the most important Raja Yogas. Here are a few more combinations that can also bring fame and success. Remember: the stronger and more stable the planets involved, the more dramatic the yoga's effects will be.

Raja Yoga #1

The lord of the 5th house is in the same house with the lord of the 9th house. Gives exceptional luck, especially in the areas of life governed by the house in which the yoga occurs.

Raja Yoga #2

The lord of the 9th house is in the same house with the lord of the 11th house. Easily attains goals. Maximum gains with minimum efforts. Prosperous.

Raja Yoga #3

The lord of the 10th house is in the same house with the lord of the 11th house. Tremendous career gains and social prominence result.

BUDHA ADITYA YOGA

Combination for Exceptional Intelligence

1. The Sun and Mercury are in the same house.
2. At least one of the two planets must be strong.
3. The Sun and Mercury must be configured with the 1st and 5th houses. This means they must be placed in one of those houses, or own those houses, or aspect those houses, or some combination of these.
4. The closer Mercury is to the Sun, the better.

The intellect is illuminated. The person is brilliant.

SARASVATI YOGA

Combination for Exceptional Artistic Talent

1. Mercury, Jupiter and Venus are in any of the following houses: 1st, 2nd, 4th, 5th, 7th, 9th or 10th.
2. Jupiter is in Aries, Cancer, Leo, Scorpio, Sagittarius, or Pisces.

The person may be particularly learned and articulate or exceptionally artistically or musically gifted.

VIPARITA RAJA YOGA

Reversal of Fortune Royal Yoga

Two more planets owning difficult houses (houses 3, 6, 8 and 12) occupy another difficult house (3, 6, 8 or 12).

Eventually turns negative conditions associated with these houses for the better. Rough beginnings lead to happy endings.

Well-trained jyotishis have memorized many thousands of yogas, some of which are quite complicated. Being able to quickly identify yogas and correctly interpret their significance in different peoples' charts is the mark of a truly skilled astrologer.

Now let's suppose you've got a terrific yoga in your chart. It's strong because the planets involved are exalted or are in signs they own. Why haven't you seen the results of the yoga yet? Some yogas kick into effect the moment you're born and stay active throughout your life. But many yogas don't become activated till later in life. It's by understanding how your planetary cycles operate that the best Vedic astrologers can make amazingly accurate predictions about dramatic events and surprising changes coming up in your life. Let's take a look at the cycles jyotishis use to read the times and tides of your life.

10

Unfolding Time: Your Planetary Cycles

Until the beginning of the 20th century Western astrology, like Jyotish, was primarily predictive. Clients didn't go to astrologers to be get psychological counselling or to analyze their personality types; they wanted to know what was going to happen next in their lives. With the blossoming of humanistic astrology, the Western system lost its predictive focus, and many Western astrologers today feel that "predicting the future" is an inappropriate and perhaps even unethical thing to do.

In India astrology has retained its original mission: unfolding the possibilities inherent in time. Hindus looked particularly to the Moon, whose rapid movement across the sky and continually changing phases most aptly represented the passage of our lives. On this basis they formulated a number of dasha systems, or ways of looking at planetary cycles. The most widely used is the Vimshottari Dasha.

The Vimshottari system slices the enormous mass of karma you've accumulated over your lifetimes into 120-year chunks (*vimshottari* means "120"). Each of the nine Vedic planets rules a piece, with the Ketu dasha running seven years, Venus running twenty years, and so on in the same order every time. Sub-cycles called *bhuktis* run in the same sequence and similar proportions within each dasha. Where you enter into the sequence depends on the nakshatra your Moon was in when you were born. Remember that the Moon represents your mind in India. The Moon starts the cycle because it's your mind that organizes your sense of time.

VIMSHOTTARI DASHA CYCLES

LORD OF CYCLE	YEARS IN CYCLE
Ketu	7
Venus	20
Sun	6
Moon	10
Mars	7
Rahu	18
Jupiter	16
Saturn	19
Mercury	17
	120

Before you learn about your current dasha, let's examine the way Hindus think about time and how their ideas differ from ours in the West.

Lines of Time

You may not know much about Zoroaster. He lived at the very beginning of recorded history in or near Afghanistan. And he is in a very real sense the founder of the worldview we identify as uniquely Western.

According to ancient Greek sources, Zoroaster flourished around 6300 B.C. Modern Western scholars scoff, but the Indian tradition supports a very early date. He was already a legendary figure by the time of the *Rig Veda,* composed prior to 3100 B.C., in which he is mentioned several times. He spoke a dialect of very ancient Sanskrit almost identical to the language of the *Rig Veda* and was an opponent of the Vedic priest Vasishtha, a fact noted in both the *Rig Veda* and extremely ancient Zoroastrian texts. The Greeks believed his name meant "star (*astra*) worshipper." His followers, priests called Magi, were renowned throughout the ancient world as phenomenally skilled astrologers and wonder workers. Our words "magic" and "magician" are derived from their name.

Zoroaster was one of the single most influential thinkers in human history. What made him stand out so dramatically from the other great men and women of his age was that Zoroaster denied the cyclic nature of time. He insisted that time was linear: that it had begun in the recent past

(9000 years before he was born) and would end in a few more thousand years. Unlike most people of the time who believed that divinity permeates all things, Zoroaster claimed God exists apart from nature. He also believed in a Devil, and taught that at the end of time God would destroy the Devil as well as all human evil-doers. Everyone who believed in Zoroaster's God and followed the moral precepts outlined by Zoroaster himself would be resurrected in a physical body and spend the rest of eternity in happiness and tranquility here on Earth.

If these beliefs sound familiar, it's because some Jews absorbed them into their own faith in the 6th century B.C.E. during their stay in Babylonia, and later passed them on to the Christians and Muslims. Today Zoroaster's idea that time is progressing forward toward Judgment Day is the basis of much of Western thought. Even our scientists' belief that people in ancient times were hopelessly primitive and superstitious while we ourselves represent the most advanced civilization ever to have appeared on Earth can be traced back to Zoroaster's linear thinking.

The sages of India, though, had an entirely different concept of time. They taught that the universe is billions of years old and virtually endless in expanse. They even claimed that before our universe came into being, an infinite number of previous universes had also existed. The Indians were convinced that time is cyclic, beginningless and endless, switching back and forth between periods of manifestation and non-manifestation, life and death. The cosmos, they believed, is a living thing, and it reincarnates.

In Vedic thought, cycles and cycles within cycles are the very basis of existence. And even more startling from the Western point of view, Hindus believe all cycles are interrelated. The cycles of the planets spinning over our heads are related to the cycles of our breath, which in turn are connected to the karmic cycles playing out in our lives. Sages like Jaimini, Bhrigu and Parashara knew how to read the celestial cycles, and this gave them extraordinary insight into the dynamics of human life, the course of civilizations and the beginning and end of world systems.

The Great Hindu Cycles

Many ancient cultures believed that human history moves through four great cycles. The Hindus call these *yugas* or world ages.

THE HINDU WORLD AGES

WORLD AGE	WORLD CYCLE	SUB-CYCLE	GREEK NAME
Satya Yuga	1,728,000 Years	4,800 Years	Golden Age
Treta Yuga	1,296,000 Years	3,600 Years	Silver Age
Dvapara Yuga	864,000 Years	2,400 Years	Bronze Age
Kali Yuga	432,000 Years	1,200 Years	Iron Age
	4,320,000 Years	12,000 Years	

Destined Duration of our Solar System: 8,640,000,000 Years. Note that the Sub-Cycle corresponds to approximately half a precessional cycle, the cycle marked by the Earth's wobble. About 12,000 years ago the North Star was Vega, not Polaris, and Mula—the nakshatra containing the galactic center—was at its highest point in the sky.

Hindu texts trace human history back for millions of years, through several different types of humanity. In fact, we are the seventh human type to appear on the planet, according to the Hindu *Puranas*. In light of the discoveries of Neanderthal, Cro-Magnon, Homo-Erectus and other fossilized human remains, these claims are extremely thought provoking.

Humanity has gone through four world ages and numerous sub-cycles, the *Puranas* say. In the *Satya Yuga,* people lived in harmony with nature and each other, and cultivated wisdom. In the *Treta Yuga,* they began to forget their inherent divine nature and started losing their intimate communion with gods and animals. In the *Dvapara Yugu,* wars began in earnest, people started deceiving each other, and religion degenerated to animal sacrifices. By the *Kali Yuga,* it became hard to find an honest person anywhere, violence and lust dominated human consciousness, and people almost completely forgot that they are one with divine being, and one with each other.

Hindus say the Kali Yuga or cycle of darkness (literally "the Age of Total Loss") began about 5,100 years ago. Just as we Westerners date our years from the birth of Christ, orthodox Hindus date their years from the beginning of the Kali Yuga. Full-feature Vedic Astrology programs will not only print out your Vedic horoscope, they'll tell you how many years have passed between the start of the Kali Yuga and the day you were born.

Ancient Hindu texts made many predictions about events which would occur during the Kali Yuga, such as:

- Grains will lose their nourishing quality. Herbs will no longer have healing power.
- Rulers will become completely corrupt and degenerate.
- Family members will condemn and abandon each other.
- Crime will be so violent and widespread that authorities will be unable to stop it.
- Even the streets of wealthy countries will be filled with beggars.
- Religions will no longer teach people the sacredness of nature.
- Meditation will no longer be taught in the temples.
- The wisdom of ancient astrologers will no longer be honored. Most of their priceless techniques will be lost. People will practice astrology without having first purified themselves through asceticism and spiritual disciplines.

This is a rather gloomy picture, especially considering that there are 426,900 years left to go till the Kali Yuga ends. At that point the *Satya Yuga,* or "Age of Truth," will at long last begin again. However, there are sub-cycles within the greater cycles, mini-yugas during which conditions improve to some extent. Different cultures are running different sub-cycles, so as one civilization crumbles, another arises. For thousands of years, India was one of the strongest, most wealthy and best educated civilizations on the planet. But, by the start of the 20th century, its name had become synonymous with poverty and illiteracy, while northern Europe—a hopelessly primitive backwater in the days of India's greatness—now controlled much of the world.

While humanity as a whole goes through these longer cycles and sub-cycles, each of us as individuals has the power to create our own yuga, a pandit from Allahabad assured me. If we fill our lives with harmony, wisdom and respect, our homes can become centers of light where the Golden Age still flourishes.

Very old Indian and Iranian texts speak of the conflict between Zoroaster's followers and the Hindus. Their opposing views of time and nature continue clashing even today in the antithetical worldviews of the linear Judeo-Christian-Islamic cultures and the cyclically-oriented Hindu-Buddhist-Taoist civilizations.

The Cycles of Our Lives

Just as all of nature goes through predictable cycles, so do each of us individual souls. Many centuries ago, Hindu sages identified the planetary cycles which steer our lives. Therefore, skilled jyotishis are often able to make astonishingly accurate predictions. I've often sat with Vedic astrologers who would randomly ask people in the room for their birth time, and on the basis of their dashas and bhuktis, would correctly give the year the person married, their first child was born, a major promotion occurred, or the period of a critical illness or accident.

While every person goes through these cycles, each of us experiences them very differently. This is because the cycles reflect the unique disposition of its planetary ruler in the individual's natal chart. For example, if a person has exalted Moon in the 10th house (the house governing status and career), she may experience her Moon dasha and bhuktis as periods of tremendous professional success and popularity. Another person who has a weak and afflicted Moon in the 6th house (a house associated with manual labor), may experience his Moon cycles as periods of drudgery and professional frustration.

I was born halfway through my Saturn dasha. Because Saturn is exalted in the 9th house of my Vedic chart (the 9th house governing religion), and Saturn rules my rising sign, an Indian astrologer can glance at my chart and instantly tell that I had a strict religious upbringing emphasizing Saturnine virtues like thrift, hard work and self-discipline.

In February 1964, my Saturn-dominated life completely changed. Overnight I developed a whole new set of interests (triggered by a case of Beatlemania) leading me to reject the rather joyless Saturnine strains of my childhood. Checking my planetary cycles many years later, I discovered that I had entered my Mercury *dasha* the first week of February 1964. At exactly that point, Saturn's constricting energy began phasing out of my life while Mercury quickly took over. Because Mercury rules the powerfully activated 8th house of occult phenomena in my Vedic chart, Indian astrologers are immediately able to see that during my Mercury *dasha* I developed an obsessive interest in the occult, had many psychic experiences, and started studying astrology.

Some years back my friend Kay was complaining bitterly about her inability to find a man she could truly love. Looking at her chart I noticed she was coming to the end of her Venus dasha. In her Vedic chart Venus is in terrible shape, debilitated and seriously afflicted. This is a disastrous combination for romance. Then I noticed that she was about to enter her Sun dasha. Kay's natal Sun is in its own sign Leo in the 7th house (the house governing marriage). The powerful, unafflicted 7th house Sun was finally primed to offer an excellent, fulfilling marriage. I asked Kay to be patient just a few more months, until her Sun dasha began. Kay was skeptical, but several months later she phoned, her voice trembling with excitement, to report that on the day she entered her Sun dasha, a friend at work confessed that he was—and had been for a long time—hopelessly in love with her. He'd been afraid to say anything for fear she'd reject him, but that day he just couldn't restrain his feelings any longer. I'm delighted to report that their marriage has been an enormous success.

Vedic astrologers can help people in two ways when they see extremely challenging planetary cycles playing out. First, by noting when the present difficult cycle ends, they can point to the light at the end of the tunnel, reassuring the client that the present painful time is a small part of a much larger cycle, that it's not going to go on forever. Secondly, they can prescribe astrological remedial measures to help ease the impact of the painful karma arising from the past, just as doctors prescribe medicines to treat illness and infections.

Some planetary cycles, such as those of Mercury, give results very quickly, since Mercury is a fast moving planet. Saturn moves through the ecliptic very slowly; its dashas and bhuktis usually unleash their karmic store more slowly. Transits—the position of the planets at this moment of time in comparison to their place at your time of birth—are used as an important supplementary tool to work out specific timing within a cycle. Dashas are the hour hand, bhuktis are the minute hand, and transits are the second hand in the ticking clock of our destiny.

In India, the strongly predictive nature of Jyotish was not considered fatalistic. Instead, astrology was regarded as an extremely useful tool to help people plan their lives. The natal chart and planetary cycles are like a river pilot's map. Pilots successfully navigate even the most treacherous section of the river because they know what to expect, and arrive at rough waters fully prepared.

Your Vedic astrologer will help you map out your life, showing you which areas of life are most karmically activated at any given time. But remember, the fact that something you really want (business success, a new relationship, a baby) isn't strongly indicated in your present cycle does not necessarily mean you should stop working for it. The famous yogi Paramahansa Yogananda used to ask his astrologer for the least favorable period for completing a particular project. Then he would purposely start the project in that period. Yogananda realized that no one becomes a master by ducking out of life's challenges. It's not by accomplishing something when the going is easy, but by accomplishing it when the going is tough, that we develop stamina and inner strength.

If you see an extremely positive period coming up, promising abundant career success for example, it's a mistake to simply wait for the good cycle to roll around. The extent to which the positive cycle can deliver its full promise depends in part on how well you've prepared. If you're not already up and running when your good dasha or bhukti arrives, you may be wasting an opportunity not scheduled to cycle through again in this lifetime.

<table>
<tr><td>Pisces</td><td>Aries</td><td>Taurus</td><td>Mars 0°
Venus 12°
Jupiter 14°
Sun 22°
Gemini</td></tr>
<tr><td>Moon 7°
Aquarius</td><td colspan="2" rowspan="2">United States of America</td><td>Mercury
3° Rx
Ralm 15°
Cancer</td></tr>
<tr><td>Ketu 15°
Capricorn</td><td>Leo</td></tr>
<tr><td>Asc 8°
Sagittarius</td><td>Scorpio</td><td>Libra</td><td>Saturn 25°
Virgo</td></tr>
</table>

Dashas in the U.S. Chart

Here is a more detailed example of how *dashas* work. This is the chart of the United States of America. The birth time is based on Thomas Jefferson's remarks about when the Declaration of Independence was signed. This delineation is based on the brilliant work of the American-born Vedic astrologer James Kelleher, who thoroughly researched the U.S.A.'s astrological history.

AMERICA'S *DASHAS*

Jupiter Dasha began Mid-October, 1913

Jupiter is the benevolent planet of expansion, cheerfulness and well being. The Jupiter dasha carried the United States into the ebullient "Roaring Twenties."

Saturn Dasha began Mid-October, 1929

Saturn is the planet of poverty, hardship and hard work. It gives mental depression and unhappiness. Yet for those who weather its storms it also gives strength, endurance, self-reliance and lasting success. The Stock Market collapsed in October 1929, plunging the U.S. into a major depression. Through hard work and self-discipline, Americans pulled their country up out of the Dust Bowl. By the end of the Saturn dasha, the U.S. was the strongest country in the world.

Mercury Dasha began Mid-October, 1948

Mercury represents, among other things, communication and trade. In the Mercury dasha the communications era took off, with telephones and televisions entering virtually every American home, tying the country together as it never had been before. American business boomed.

Ketu Dasha began Mid-October 1965

The positive side of the shadow planet Ketu is the illumination of consciousness. The most negative side is horrendous physical violence. The Ketu dasha gave the U.S. hippies, free love, the Civil Rights movement, psychedelic drug use, and explorations in consciousness. It also gave the Vietnam War and devastating riots.

Venus Dasha began Mid-October 1972

Venus is the planet of material luxury. In the Venus dasha hippies gave way to yuppies. The Reagan era substituted money management for consciousness raising. In the Ketu dasha the most popular course of study at most colleges was psychology. In the Venus dasha most students majored in Business Administration.

Sun Dasha began Mid-October 1992

America's powerful Sun (fortified by numerous Raja Yogas—power-promoting planetary patterns) is lord of the 9th house of good luck. In this dasha sunny Bill Clinton took office, the U.S. economy boomed, and the United States relished its role as the single world superpower.

Moon Dasha began Mid-October, 1998

The Moon in the U.S. chart is the lord of the crisis-promoting 8th house. Scandal, political manipulation and financial fluctuations marked the start of this ten-year period. Then on September 11, 2001, the World Trade Center was destroyed and the Pentagon badly damaged by Islamic terrorists. On that day, the two Vedic planets of sudden violence, Mars and Ketu, were transitting directly over the U.S. Ascendant at 8° Sagittarius.

Mars Dasha begins Mid-October 2008

The battered U.S. markets should improve substantially during the Mars dasha. Look for more aggressive and extremely expensive military action on the part of the U.S. against powerful but faceless adversaries. (Mars rules the U.S. 12th house, the house of "secret enemies.")

What's Your Dasha?

In Chapter 6 you discovered which nakshatra your Moon was in when you were born. The following table will tell you the dasha that was running at that time. You would have been born earlier or later in the dasha depending on whether your Moon was in an earlier or later degree of the nakshatra.

YOUR MOON NAKSHATRA	BIRTH DASHA
Ashwini, Magha, Mula	Ketu
Bharani, P. Phalguni, P. Ashadha	Venus
Krittika, U. Phalguni., U. Ashadha	Sun
Rohini, Hasta, Shravana	Moon
Mrigashira, Chitra, Dhanishtha	Mars
Ardra, Swati, Shatabhishak	Rahu
Punarvasu, Vishakha, P. Bhadrapada	Jupiter
Pushya, Anuradha, U. Bhadrapada	Saturn
Ashlesha, Jyestha, Revati	Mercury

To find out what dasha you're running right now, contact the American College of Vedic Astrology at ACVA108@aol.com for a referral to a professional astrologer who can provide you with a print out of your dasha/bhukti cycles. The math you'd need to calculate your cycles on your own is just too complex to teach you here.

You now have enough knowledge about the basic principles of Jyotish to make an educated guess what the qualities of your dashas will be. To make a preliminary judgment, ask yourself the following:

If the planet that rules your current dasha is badly destabilized, you could be in for a rocky ride. If it's well-placed and aspected by benefics, you could be having the time of your life. More often though, dashas give mixed results depending on what's favored and what's disadvantaged in your chart, and what sub-cycle and transits are in progress.

If you're running the dasha of a planet in or owning or aspecting your 7th house, relationships are a primary focus right now. If the 2nd house is activated, finances could be a major preoccupation. If you're about to enter a cycle involving your 4th house, you may soon buy a new home.

A professional Vedic astrologer has vastly more information about what your dasha means, and how the sub-cycle you're running within the dasha may alter the picture. Your jyotishi can also recommend spiritual practices you can do if you'd like to improve the quality of a dasha.

When and Why?

The astrology we practice in the West today is partly based on the Persian model—a system influenced by the Zoroastrian Magi. These brilliant astrologers used horoscopes to delineate what people were like and what might happen to them, but they could not explain why. Things just happened; presumably they were simply God's mysterious will.

The master astrologers of India tackled head-on that vexatious question, "Why?" Unlike Western scientists, Hindus don't believe that events are random and ultimately purposeless. In the ever revolving cycle of our lives which the Hindus call samsara, there is no abrupt beginning or end, and no one responsible for our fate but ourselves. Life is the eternal expression of the universal consciousness which incarnates through us. It is always growing, always changing, always asking, "Why?" The Vimshottari Dasha system helps us answer that other nagging question, "When?"

ASSESSING A PLANETARY CYCLE

NATURE OF THE DASHA

1. Which planet rules the *dasha*?
2. What are the qualities (positive, negative, neutral) of the house that planet is placed in in your natal horoscope?
3. What are the qualities of the house(s) that planet rules?
4. Is the planet strong (in its own sign, exaltation, best house, or retrograde)?
5. Is the planet weak (in its sign of fall, combust)?
6. Are any benefic (stabilizing) or malefic (destabilizing) planets in the same sign with that planet?
7. Are benefic or malefic planets aspecting that planet?
8. Important! What types of yogas is that planet involved in?

AREAS MOST ACTIVATED DURING THE DASHA

1. Which house is the planet that rules the *dasha* placed in?
2. Which houses does that planet own?
3. Which houses does that planet aspect?

11

Vedic Subcharts: Hidden Dimensions of Your Horoscope

You've got just one horoscope, right? The one showing the position of the planets at the moment you were born? If you believe this, you'll be in for a surprise if you have your horoscope read in India. There your astrologer may calculate over a dozen charts for your time of birth.

As I was just saying, Westerners tend to see life in linear terms. Something is either true or false, good or evil, dead or alive—you're either logged on or you're logged off. To the Hindus, however, the world is multi-dimensional. Apparently contradictory statements are recognized as overlapping versions of the same reality, and layer after layer of truth conceals and at the same time reveals the all-pervading essence. Your birth chart also reverberates with numerous dimensions of significance, resonating out into dozens of harmonic frequencies which then coalesce in the astrologer's intuition as she melds all the pieces back together into a meaningful reading.

Parashara, the grandmaster of Vedic astrology, lists 16 *amshas* or zodiacal divisions into which the birth chart expands harmonically. The Nadi and Tajika schools of Indian astrology add even more. These subcharts are like increasingly stronger lenses of a microscope, which help you peer deeper into your birth chart and provide much more information about specific areas in your life. The 10th subchart, for example, offers a wealth of information about your career, while the 7th subchart is scanned for additional details about your children and grandchildren.

Traditionally trained Indian astrologers are so adept at working with these amshas that if you simply hand them your Vedic horoscope they can instantly mentally calculate up to 20 separate subcharts, superimposing all of them on top of each other in their minds.

I've watched jyotishis making interpretations based on all 20 subcharts at once—a feat of integral concentration I could never hope to duplicate in my entire life. Once an American student showed K.N. Rao an anonymous horoscope—actually the chart of Jeffrey Dahmer. (Dahmer, you hopefully don't recall, was the fellow who invited young men over to his apartment where he sexually assaulted, killed and ate them.) To the beginning level astrology students in the room the chart didn't look particularly remarkable. But Rao instantly recoiled and angrily demanded why the horoscope of such a person had been drawn on the board. He'd never heard of Dahmer, but by mentally visualizing the subcharts he was immediately able to tell this was the chart of a dangerous psychopath.

Decompressing Your Horoscope

The amshas (or *vargas* as they're also called) were specially designed to make details in your birth chart easier to see. Your 1st amsha, the birth chart itself, is so condensed that any one house stands for dozens of different things. You'll see your relationship with your father broadly reflected in the 9th house, along with many other matters such as your religion, long distance travel and higher education. But if you turn to the 12th amsha you'll find a subchart devoted more specifically to your parents. The amshas decompress the data in your horoscope. Fascinatingly, planets in the amshas also interact with planets in the birth horoscope to form special multi-dimensional yogas.

Esoterically, while your birth chart refers primarily to events of your present life, the 12th divisional chart reflects your previous incarnation, and the 9th divisional chart offers a glimpse into your next birth. The 2nd amsha, they say, even shows whether your most recent incarnation was on this physical planet or whether you arrived in this body from some other dimension of reality altogether. Throughout history a minority of people have reported that they feel extremely uncomfortable on Earth, that being in a physical body seems completely unnatural, that they feel like aliens here. According to the Vedic system, there really are "drop ins" from other worlds.

THE HINDU SUBCHARTS

Subchart	Name	Information the Subchart Provides
1st	*Janma Kundali/Rashi Chakra*	The birth chart itself. Gives general indications for 12 departments of life.
2nd	*Hora*	Wealth, native's residence (plane of consciousness) before birth.
3rd	*Drekkamsha/Dreshkanna*	Siblings, prosperity, personality tendencies, kundalini experiences, illness, death.
4th	*Chaturthamsha*	Fixed assets, savings, real estate, general fortune.
5th	*Panchamsha*	Spiritual inclination and capacity.
6th	*Shashtamsha*	Disease and accidents.
7th	*Saptamsha*	Children and grandchildren, spouse's wealth.
8th	*Ashtamsha*	Length of life, circumstances of death.
9th	*Navamsha*	Marriage, general life themes, second half of life.
10th	*Dashamsha*	Career, prestige, power.
11th	*Ekadashamsha*	Financial windfalls. Luck with money.
12th	*Dvadashamsha*	Parents and grandparents, past lives.
16th	*Shodashamsha*	Vehicles.
20th	*Vimshamsha*	Religion, ritual practices.
24th	*Siddhamsha*	Intellectual capacity, educational accomplishment.
27th	*Bhamsha*	Strength of the life force.
30th	*Trimshamsha*	One's pleasures and suffering.
40th	*Khavedamsha*	General indications.
45th	*Akshavedamsha*	Fine tuning of general indications.
60th	*Shashtyamsha*	Differentiates destinies of infants born at almost exactly the same time and place.

Note: Most Vedic subcharts, called *amshas* or *vargas*, are calculated differently than the harmonic charts used in Western astrology.

There's another important reason subcharts are so valuable. Many children have similar horoscopes, yet each child—even a twin—has a unique destiny. To fine tune a reading, uncovering what is specific to a soul who takes it first breath in one unique moment at one unique point in space, jyotishis turn to the amshas.

For example, many boys were born on April 20, 1889. Only one of those boys nearly destroyed the world. What made Adolph Hitler one of the most powerful military commanders in history rather than, say, a tyrannical manager at an Austrian dry goods shop? Hitler's Mars is incredibly activated in his 7th house, the house of war. This is not very uncommon, and could simply signal a domineering person who's difficult to live with. What is uncommon is that in almost every subchart, Hitler's Mars appears again and again in positions of phenomenal strength. The fantastic amplification of Mars' energy raised Hitler to the status of a bona fide war lord.

Many boys were born the same day as George Harrison. Yet, he was the only one of them to join the Beatles and become one of the most famous musicians of his time. In his chart, the Moon, lord of his 10th house, goes to the Ascendant. This is a fairly good indicator for success, popularity and renown. This configuration again is not that rare. What is unusual is that Harrison's Moon is configured in the Ascendant of almost every major subchart. This repeating configuration signaled that he was bound for spectacular success.

There's one catch to working with amshas. It is imperative to have an accurate birth time. The 60th divisional chart, for example, is correct only if the birth time is right to within a minute and a half. On the other hand, if you're uncertain about your exact birth time, a jyotishi can match up your divisional charts with major events in your life until he arrives at what most likely is your actual minute of birth.

Your Marriage Chart

By far the most important subchart is the 9th, called the navamsha. While it serves a variety of purposes, it's most famous as the Hindu marriage chart. Read alongside the 7th house in your original birth chart; it indicates if and when you will marry, if and when you may divorce, the personality, values and probable vocation of your mate and the quality of your marriage. The navamsha is queen of the subcharts. Even if your

Indian astrologer doesn't have time to review all your amshas, she will always carefully examine your navamsha. By the way, *nava* is Sanskrit for *nine.* (Think of related English words like "novile" or "enneagram.")

Pisces	Aries	Taurus	Gemini
Aquarius	**Your Navamsha**		Cancer
Capricorn			Leo
Sagittarius	Scorpio	Libra	Virgo

Use the table on page 147 to calculate your navamsha. How does a jyotishi analyze a navamsha as a mirror for the circumstances surrounding marriage? On page 148 you'll find the first few steps she will take. These may look complicated to a beginner, but skilled Vedic astrologers shoot through all these steps in a couple of seconds, before advancing to more complicated navamsha analysis.

There are numerous additional guidelines Indian astrologers use to read your married life. For example, if the rising sign in your *navamsha* is Taurus, Libra or Aquarius, and that sign and the planet which rules it are unafflicted, you will probably be intensely loyal to your partner.

The Second Half of Life

In parts of South India, some very traditional astrologers will scarcely

HOW TO CALCULATE YOUR NAVAMSHA

Degree	Ari	Tau	Gem	Can	Leo	Vir	Lib	Sco	Sag	Cap	Aqu	Pis
3°20′	Ari	Cap	Lib	Can	Ari	Cap	Lib	Can	Ari	Cap	Lib	Can
6°40′	Tau	Aqu	Sco	Leo	Tau	Aqu	Sco	Leo	Tau	Aqu	Sco	Leo
10°00′	Gem	Pis	Sag	Vir	Gem	Pis	Sag	Vir	Gem	Pis	Sag	Vir
13°20′	Can	Ari	Cap	Lib	Can	Ari	Cap	Lib	Can	Ari	Cap	Lib
16°40′	Leo	Tau	Aqu	Sco	Leo	Tau	Aqu	Sco	Leo	Tau	Aqu	Sco
20°00′	Vir	Gem	Pis	Sag	Vir	Gem	Pis	Sag	Vir	Gem	Pis	Sag
23°20′	Lib	Can	Ari	Cap	Lib	Can	Ari	Cap	Lib	Can	Ari	Cap
26°40′	Sco	Leo	Tau	Aqu	Sco	Leo	Tau	Aqu	Sco	Leo	Tau	Aqu
30°00′	Sag	Vir	Gem	Pis	Sag	Vir	Gem	Pis	Sag	Vir	Gem	Pis

1. Check the degrees of your Ascendant and the planets in your Vedic birth chart. Don't use the degrees in your Western horoscope, which are different.
2. Find the signs they appear in in the navamsha table above.
3. Redraw your chart, placing your Ascendant and planets in these new signs.

Example: If your Ascendant is 5° Taurus, check the row headed "6°40′" since your Ascendant falls between 3°20′ and 6°40′. Now look under the column headed "Taurus." Your navamsha Ascendant is Aquarius.
Note: Don't be concerned with what degree your Ascendant or planets fall into in the navamsha. Vedic astrologers look only at sign and house placements in the subcharts, not at degrees.

ANALYZING MARRIAGE IN THE NAVAMSHA

1. Examine the navamsha's 1st house.
2. Examine the navamsha's 7th house.
3. Are these two houses aspected or occupied by planets that support relationships like Venus* and Jupiter, or that prevent or sabootage them, like Mars and Saturn?
4. Examine the planet that rules the navamsha's 1st house.
5. Examine the planet that rules the navamsha's 7th house.
6. Are these two planets placed in auspicious houses themselves, like the angles (houses 1, 4, 7, 10) or trines (houses 1, 5, 9) of the chart? Are they strong and stable?
7. Now turn back to your birth chart. Find the planet that rules its 7th house.
8. Look to see where the 7th house ruler from your birth chart is placed in the navamsha. What condition is it in?

Example: If these factors are strongly influenced by a malefic like Saturn, the jyotishi will check Saturn's condition to see whether it contributes positive Saturnine qualities like emotional maturity and commitment, or shows coldness, cruelty or victimization in relationships.

* Here is an important exception. Traditional jyotishis do not like to see Venus in the 7th house of the birth chart or in the 1st house of the navamsha. They say these positons may reflect a person more geared toward romance than toward stable partnerships.

bother looking at your birth horoscope. They figure that if you're a mature adult, by now you've already dealt with many of the issues reflected in your natal chart and have graduated to the strengths and challenges shown in your navamsha, which they think of as your second horoscope.

There's a saying in India, "The birth chart is a tree; the navamsha is its fruit." The navamsha reveals how the tendencies shown in the original birth chart are likely to actually play out. It's the horoscope of your second half of life, when you've had enough life experience and reached sufficient psychological and social maturity to begin enjoying (or suffering from) the "fruit" of your earlier efforts.

Ever wonder why some people are incredibly famous and successful in the first half of their lives, then seem to vanish into utter obscurity just when you'd assume they'd be reaching their peak? I think particularly of rock stars, actors or athletes who were world-famous as teenagers or young adults, but after they hit their 30s, we never heard of them again. Vedic astrologers would explain this is reflected in part by having a very strong birth chart but a weak navamsha. In the second part of their lives, the momentum of the birth chart peters out if there's no power in the navamsha to keep the momentum going.

Then there are the kids you remember from high school whom you never for a moment thought would amount to anything, who're now multimillionaire entrepreneurs or award-winning artists. One explanation for this phenomenon is that although the birth chart was not especially remarkable, the navamsha burns up the paper it's printed on with success and good fortune. Bill Clinton and George Bush Jr. both have mediocre birth charts, but their navamshas are dynamite. In his mid-40s, Clinton seemed to rocket out of nowhere to win the U.S. presidency. Bush, who seemed unable to speak a single sentence without tripping over his words, was handed the U.S. presidency by the Supreme Court in 2000.

The Work You Will Do

Discovering your navamsha is like finding out there's a sequel to a book you particularly enjoy, which further develops the lead character and extends the plot line of the original book. The navamsha is an invaluable tool for astrologers working to grasp the depths of human nature and the sometimes intriguing, sometimes baffling, twists and turns of destiny. Here's another example of how jyotishis used this amazing subchart.

Confused about your true vocation in life? Curious about the career path your daughter or son may take? In Vedic astrology we look to the 10th house in the natal chart as well as the 10th subchart for important clues to your life work. However, one of the great classics of Hindu astrology, the *Phala Dipika* ("Effects of the Planets"), offers a short cut to assessing a general career path using the navamsha. I've often been stunned at how accurately this simple technique can reveal one's profession.

My friend Bhagavan Das (whose adventures were chronicled in Ram Dass' 1970 cult classic, *Be Here Now*) has Jupiter as his navamsha career indicator. Jupiter indicates (among other professions) spiritual teachers, and Bhagavan Das is indeed a highly-skilled teacher of Nada Yoga, a meditation system involving sound energy. My husband's career indicator is Mars, which besides ruling government administrators, also indicates technical professions. My husband is a computer analyst. My own career indicator is Mercury. I have always held mercurial jobs, such as writer and editor.

READING PROFESSION IN THE NAVAMSHA

1. Check to see which planet rules the 10th house of your Vedic birth chart.
2. Look to see which sign that planet is in in your *navamsha.*
3. What planet rules that sign? That planet sets the tone for your career.
4. Refer to The Vedic Planets table in Chapter 7 for a list of careers associated with each planet.

Examples: The planet ruling Bill Clinton's natal 10th house, Gemini, is Mercury. In Clinton's navamsha Mercury occupies Scorpio, which is ruled by Mars. So Mars becomes his career indicator.

The planet ruling George Bush Jr.'s natal 10th house, Aries, is Mars. In Bush's navamsha Mars occupies Leo, which is ruled by the Sun. So the Sun becomes his career indicator.

In India, Mars and the Sun are the two planets representing the *kshatriya* caste of kings and warriors, which traditionally includes all highly placed government officials.

Putting It All Together

In the last seven chapters I've given you a brief glimpse of how India's astrologers work. In summarizing these principles and techniques at such an introductory level, I've had to oversimplify shamelessly. To apply these methods with consistent accuracy you need to learn many more technical details from an experienced jyotishi who can answer your questions and clarify exceptions. Still, if you've read these chapters carefully, you've just completed a beginning level course in Vedic astrology.

Ready to try applying what you've learned? Let's take a look at the charts of two U.S. presidents.

On November 3, 1992—election day in the U.S.—if you had looked up at the sky you would have found Jupiter at 11° Virgo. Jupiter is the great benefic of the Vedic planetary pantheon, the planet capable of giving the most unalloyed good. If you look at Bill Clinton's horoscope, you'll find that his Ascendant degree is 12° Virgo. George Bush Sr. had recently driven the Iraqi army out of Kuwait, winning him such popularity with the American public that most leading Democratic politicians refused to even try running against him. At the time, Clinton was embroiled in a scandal with a woman named Gennifer Flowers, if I remember correctly. Yet with Jupiter crossing his Ascendant degree, Clinton could have stripped naked and waltzed around the Capital rotunda and he still would have won the election. It's as if the stars were shouting, "Here's your new president!"

What dasha (major planetary cycle) was Clinton running at election time? If you're having trouble guessing, go back and re-read the last paragraph. Clinton was running his Jupiter cycle. His bhukti (subcycle), incidently, was Mercury. Notice that Mercury is in Clinton's 11th house, the house of "sudden gains," forming a Raja Yoga with Saturn. Remember

Pisces	**Moon** 27° Aries	**Ralm** 24° Taurus	Gemini
Aquarius	**Bill Clinton** **August 19, 1946** **8:51 a.m. CST** **Hope, AR** **93W36 33N40** From his mother		**Saturn** 9° **Mercury** 14° Cancer
Capricorn			**Sun** 2° Leo
Sagittarius	**Ketu** 24° Scorpio	**Jupiter** 0° Libra	**Venus** 18° **Mars** 13° **Asc** 12° Virgo

that Raja Yogas give exceptional success and that *raja* means "king" (or in this case "president").

Let's talk about relationships, since Bill Clinton took such a beating for his affair with Monica Lewinsky. Clinton's birth chart shows some difficulties in the loyalty department. Our former president has Venus conjunct Mars in the first house of his Vedic chart, a classical combination for a "roving eye." This tricky combination is exacerbated by an aspect from malefic Saturn (remember Saturn aspects the third house from itself), and the fact that Venus, which in India represents marriage, is in Virgo, the sign of its fall. Venus is also afflicted by Mars, meaning the energy Mars brings into the conjunction threatens the marriage.

In Clinton's chart Mars is conjunct the Ascendant by less than 1°. Mars rules both the 3rd and 8th houses in his chart. In India these are the houses of "minor scandals" and "major scandals" respectively. Here we see Mars carrying the propensity toward scandal to the core of the personality represented by the Ascendent degree, and causing needless grief to Venus, the marriage partner. Nevertheless, Clinton's 7th house ruler is well-positioned in the 2nd house, where it gives a reasonably stable marital life, and indicates an intelligent, prosperous and supportive spouse.

Note that while many other highly placed American politicians may have been involved in far more dramatic sexual escapades than Bill Clinton, because of Mars' placement on his Ascendant degree (where all our strengths and foibles come to light), Clinton always gets caught.

We learn a great deal more about Bill and Hillary's relationship by turning to the ex-president's navamsha, however. First, we look to the navamsha Ascendant, where we find the Sun exalted and Mars in its own sign in Aries. This is an incredibly potent combination, with both planets powerfully activated by exceptionally strong placements. The 1st house ruler Mars is conjunct the 5th house ruler, the Sun, forming another Raja Yoga or power combination contributing toward extraordinary success.

The Sun is considered a mild malefic in India, while Mars can be seriously malevolent. In their own or exaltation signs, however, malefic energies can more readily be harnessed to work constructively for an individual's benefit. In this navamsha, the only aspect these two planets receive is from the great benefic Jupiter in the 7th house, a strongly stabilizing influence. The Sun and Mars signal significant turmoil in Clinton's marriage, but they also indicate a tremendously dynamic

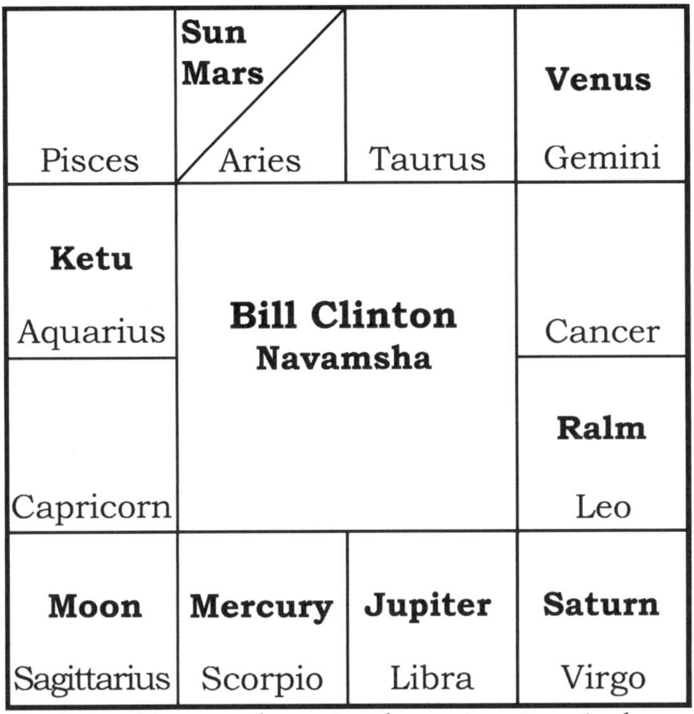

Pisces	**Sun** **Mars** Aries	Taurus	**Venus** Gemini
Ketu Aquarius	**Bill Clinton** **Navamsha**		Cancer
Capricorn			**Ralm** Leo
Moon Sagittarius	**Mercury** Scorpio	**Jupiter** Libra	**Saturn** Virgo

marital relationship supercharged with creative vigor, further enhanced by Jupiter's blessing aspect.

While Jupiter's presence in the 7th house of the navamsha is generally excellent for married life, Venus, ruler of the 7th house (Libra), is in the 3rd house, a house of "desires." In India this is not considered a favorable omen for fidelity due to the native's strong desire nature, all other factors being equal. But Mars, ruler of the all- important 1st house, is in the 1st house itself, suggesting a strong marriage, Clinton's sexual dalliances notwithstanding. The 1st and 7th houses of his navamsha reveals a powerful, self-willed, intelligent and aggressive partner with whom he enjoys an exceptionally animated and empowering relationship.

Vedic astrology students will note that although Jupiter's influence in the navamsha—in the 7th house directly aspecting the 1st—is for the most part positive, Jupiter here also rules the 12th house, the house of loss. This raises the possibility that unless Bill Clinton works with his marriage relationship very consciously, at some point he could lose it. This might occur during a Jupiter planetary cycle or transit.

Let's shift our focus from looking at the navamsha as a marriage chart, and see it as a chart for the second half of Clinton's life. Supercharged Mars and Sun in the 1st house make him an indefatigable fighter and formidable leader. The placement of Saturn, his 10th house lord (signifying career), in the 6th house of obstacles signals to a Vedic astrologer that at every step, enemies attempt to undermine Clinton's professional success. His navamsha Ascendant is so incredibly strong though, that Clinton remains standing after his enemies fall.

In both the birth chart and the navamsha, Clinton has the ruler of the 8th house (Mars in both cases) in his 1st house. This reveals that throughout his lifetime, he undermines his own efforts by courting scandal. Yet the Sun in the navamsha is exalted in the Ascendant, where with Mars it forms the powerful Raja Yoga just mentioned, supporting continuing success.

Vedic astrology, like any science, can be extremely technical, and I don't want to burden you with pedantic details. But very briefly, let me give you a general idea of why any Indian astrologer looking at Clinton's navamsha—even if he or she didn't know this was the chart of a U.S. president—would immediately note this native would rise to exceptional prominence in adulthood. The navamsha contains at least eight rare and/or extremely potent yogas. One is the *Maha Bhagya Yoga* (*maha bhagya* means "exceptionally good fortune") which gives tremendous charisma and popularity, all other factors in the chart being equal. Clinton's navamsha also registers a *Ruchaka Yoga,* lending tremendous force to his personality, and greatly empowering the charm lent by the *Maha Bhagya Yoga.*

Now let's turn to the chart of his successor, George Bush Jr.

In the weeks leading up to the November 2000 U.S. presidential election, along with my fellow Vedic astrology students in the San Francisco Bay Area, I spent many hours poring over the charts of the leading candidates. It was amazing to compare the two horoscopes: for every strength in Bush's chart, there was a commensurate strong point in Al Gore's. For every weakness in Gore's horoscope, there was an equally weak spot in Bush's. Calling the results of the 1992 election had been so easy; this race, however, had us running in circles trying to predict the winner.

Following the November election, the whole country was running around trying to determine who had won. While Gore clearly won the popular vote, the electoral vote was up for grabs. The race was so close it seemed it might be determined by a handful of ballots in Florida.

Pisces	Aries	**Ralm** 27° Taurus	**Sun** 20° Gemini
Aquarius	**George Bush Jr.** **July 6, 1946** **7:26 a.m. EDT** **New Haven, CT** **72W55 41N18** From Hospital Records		**Mercury** 16° **Saturn** 3° **Venus** 28° **Asc** 14° Cancer
Capricorn			**Mars** 16° Leo
Sagittarius	**Ketu** 27° Scorpio	Libra	**Moon** 23° **Jupiter** 25° Virgo

Finally the Supreme Court intervened. Apparently fearing the American public could not be trusted to elect their own president, the Republican dominated court opted to disenfranchise the entire American electorate and placed their own candidate in the White House.

I was stunned by these events for a number of reasons. One was that I had done a prashna and the chart I had cast definitely predicted that Gore would win. Prashna involves erecting a horoscope for the moment a question is asked. It's the most common form of astrology practiced in India—even more common than birth chart analysis. I had had a fair bit of success with the technique and had gotten a bit cocky about it. This bad call was a major failure. My husband consoled me that I had asked the wrong question. Instead of asking, "Who'll win the election?" I should have asked, "Who'll be our next president?" Then perhaps instead of "Gore," who actually got the most votes, the prashna would have answered "Bush."

There are a number of features in Bush's chart that give me pause, particularly because during his term in office a president's chart becomes a sort of de facto chart for the country. (Remember how the scandals indicated by the yogas in Clinton's chart dominated the U.S. media for years?) Bush's chart could reflect significant problems for the U.S. economy. With a malefic in the 2nd house of finances and the 2nd lord gone to the 12th house of losses, you know the man has a problem managing money. Indeed he bankrupted the company he ran before becoming president, and since taking office has plunged the country into astounding levels of debt.

With the Sun in its own sign of Leo in his birth chart, Bill Clinton excelled at foreign policy. (Remember that the 12th house governs international affairs.) Bush also has the Sun in the 12th house but his Sun is very poorly placed. Since becoming president Bush has managed to systematically alienate nearly every other nation in the world, including almost every U.S. ally. On the positive side, Bush's 3rd house is phenomenal, containing a Raja Yoga that reflects the success of his younger brother Jeb Bush who is presently governor of Florida. The 3rd house, you may recall, represents brothers and sisters.

Bush and Clinton are very different personalities but one thing they have in common is spectacular navamshas. As a marriage chart, Bush's navamsha reflects his excellent marriage to a devoted and supportive wife. Note that the lord of its 1st house is well placed in the 10th, and the lord of its 7th house is exalted in the 5th, an excellent placement.

As the chart of the second half of life, Bush's incredible 9th subchart reflects his leap to power. The 5th and 10th are the two houses most closely associated with politics. The 5th in Bush's case contains an exalted planet. The 10th contains an astonishing six Raja Yogas. These involve the 9th ruler, demonstrating the role both his father and pure luck (both 9th house designations) played in getting him into the White House.

On September 11, 2001, the two planets of sudden violence, Mars and Ketu, simultaneously transitted across the U.S. Ascendant. That day America experienced a massive terrorist attack. Bush pulled himself together overnight, transforming from a somewhat bumbling and insecure seeming man into a dynamic, articulate and forceful leader.

One of my friends, a psychiatrist, believes that after September 11, Bush's physicians may have prescribed Ritalin to help him control his

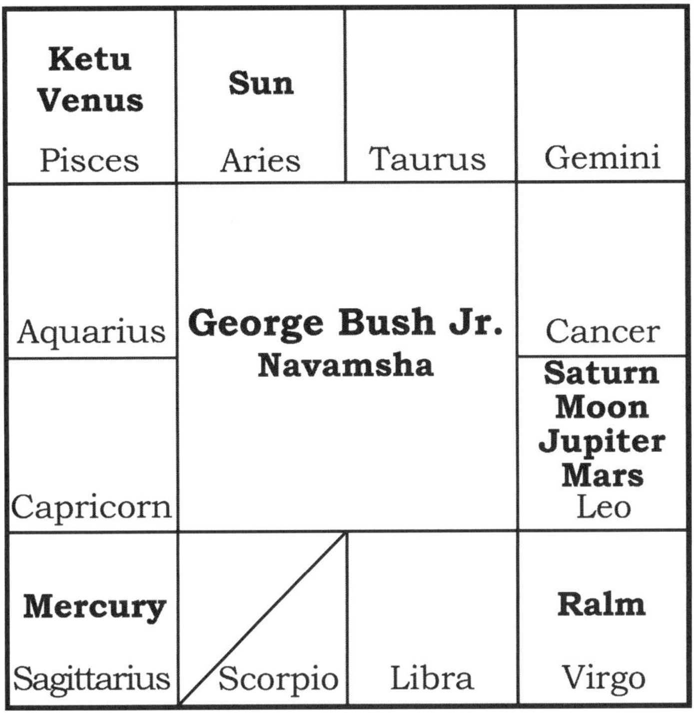

Ketu **Venus** Pisces	**Sun** Aries	Taurus	Gemini
Aquarius	**George Bush Jr.** **Navamsha**		Cancer
Capricorn			**Saturn** **Moon** **Jupiter** **Mars** Leo
Mercury Sagittarius	Scorpio	Libra	**Ralm** Virgo

attention deficit problem. She feels the drug is helping make him much more focused and articulate, but as an amphetamine may also be affecting his judgment and making him act out very aggressively against enemies he perceives everywhere.

I have no idea whether this is true, but I do note that in Vedic astrology we always advise clients with an afflicted 2nd house, like Bush's, to be very cautious with drugs. A weak 2nd house can leave a person susceptible to poisoning. The weakness in this house may also reflect in the excessive drinking of his youth—alcohol and addictive drugs being considered poisons in the Vedic system.

On June 24, 2002, a lunar eclipse occurred exactly on the U.S. Ascendant degree. In India eclipses are believed to "pollute" the degree they occur over for months to come. Following the September 11 attack there was a massive outpouring of sympathy for America from much of the world. But since mid-2002, aggressive White House policies have led to the perception that the U.S. has become an arrogant and malignant superpower. As I write (President's Day, 2003), millions of people around the planet are angrily protesting U.S. policies.

Bush has a *Kala Sarpa Yoga,* a planetary configuration involving the Moon's nodes. This can give a great rise but it can also give a great fall. Remember Donald Trump's *Kala Sarpa Yoga* from Chapter 8? Bush needs to be careful to think clearly and act ethically He's running a dangerous subcycle right now; his Rahu bhukti in fact, which may inflate his sense of himself. He needs to be very cautious in his battle against terrorism to ensure that he doesn't cause more problems than he solves. Nevertheless, with the super-activated and closely interrelated 9th and 10th houses in his navamsha, Bush has experienced spectacular luck in his career.

On June 21, 2001, the Earth experienced one of the rarest astrological portents possible. In fact, it's probably been more than 10,000 years since it happened before. The shadow planet Rahu aligned with the Sun at 6° Gemini exactly opposite the Galactic Center on the day of the Summer Solstice, causing not only a solar eclipse but a galactic eclipse! Soberingly, this occurred less than 2° opposite the United States' Ascendant degree. At the same time, Mars is beginning to make its closest approach to Earth in 60,000 years.

We are entering an extremely critical period for the U.S. and the world as a whole. Rahu is the quintessential planet of materialism and self-delusion. It's imperative that we align ourselves with our inner spiritual resources during this time—or we'll surely suffer the consequences.

So what do you do when you see serious problem areas in a chart? Here is where Vedic astrology really shines. I'll devote the entire next section of this book to the way jyotishis help people correct their karmic imbalances and build a more positive future.

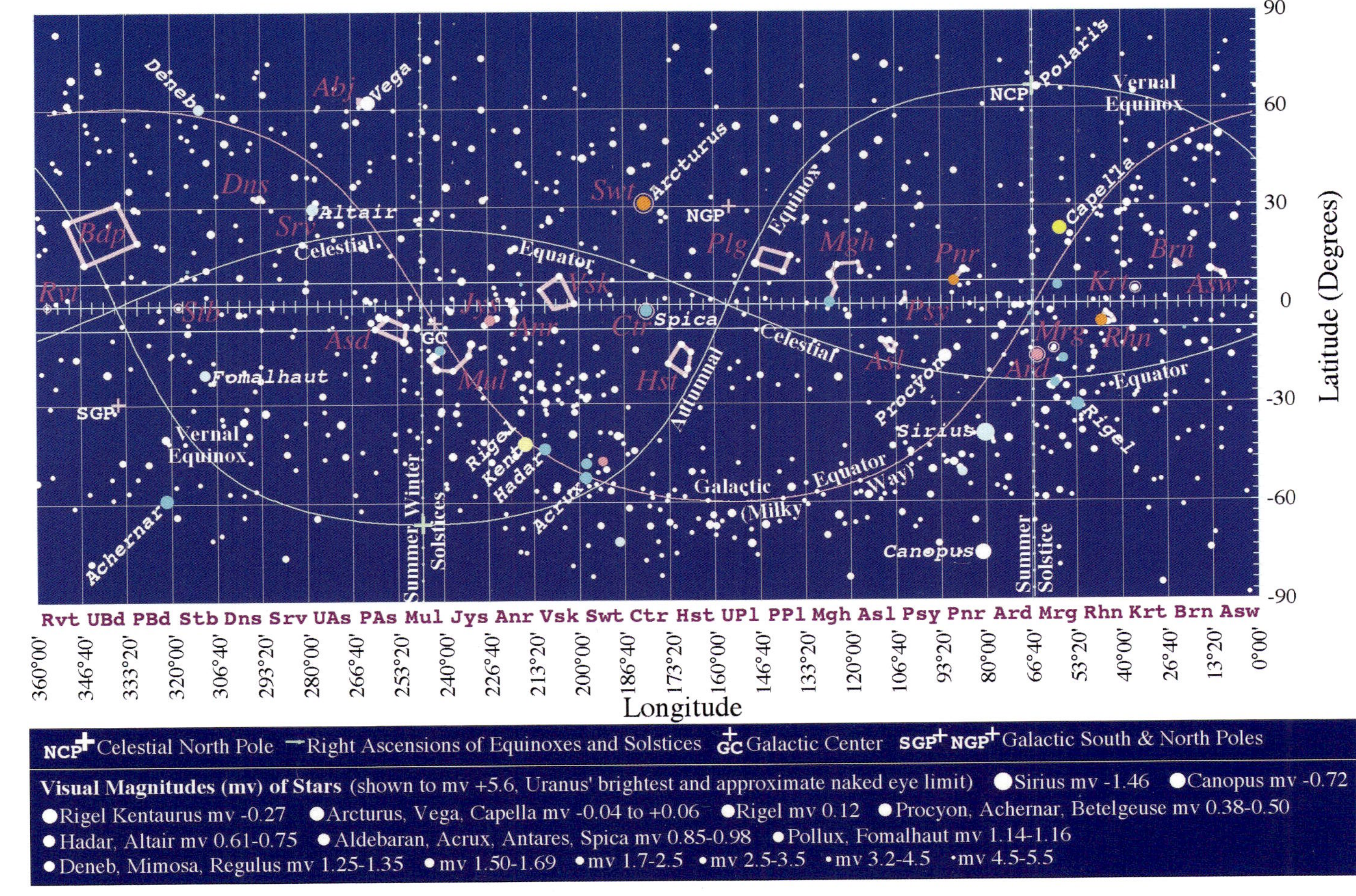
Rvt UBd PBd Stb Dns Srv UAs PAs Mul Jys Anr Vsk Swt Ctr Hst UPl PPl Mgh Asl Psy Pnr Ard Mrg Rhn Krt Brn Asw
360°00' 346°40' 333°20' 320°00' 306°40' 293°20' 280°00' 266°40' 253°20' 240°00' 226°40' 213°20' 200°00' 186°40' 173°20' 160°00' 146°40' 133°20' 120°00' 106°40' 93°20' 80°00' 66°40' 53°20' 40°00' 26°40' 13°20' 0°00'
Longitude
90 60 30 0 -30 -60 -90
Latitude (Degrees)
Deneb
Vega
Altair
Arcturus
Spica
Polaris
Capella
Fomalhaut
Achernar
Rigel Kent
Hadar
Acrux
Procyon
Sirius
Canopus
Rigel
Vernal Equinox
Autumnal Equinox
Summer Winter Solstices
Summer Solstice
Celestial Equator
Galactic Equator (Milky Way)
NCP
NGP
SGP
GC
NCP Celestial North Pole — Right Ascensions of Equinoxes and Solstices GC Galactic Center SGP NGP Galactic South & North Poles
Visual Magnitudes (mv) of Stars (shown to mv +5.6, Uranus' brightest and approximate naked eye limit) Sirius mv -1.46 Canopus mv -0.72
Rigel Kentaurus mv -0.27 Arcturus, Vega, Capella mv -0.04 to +0.06 Rigel mv 0.12 Procyon, Achernar, Betelgeuse mv 0.38-0.50
Hadar, Altair mv 0.61-0.75 Aldebaran, Acrux, Antares, Spica mv 0.85-0.98 Pollux, Fomalhaut mv 1.14-1.16
Deneb, Mimosa, Regulus mv 1.25-1.35 mv 1.50-1.69 mv 1.7-2.5 mv 2.5-3.5 mv 3.2-4.5 mv 4.5-5.5

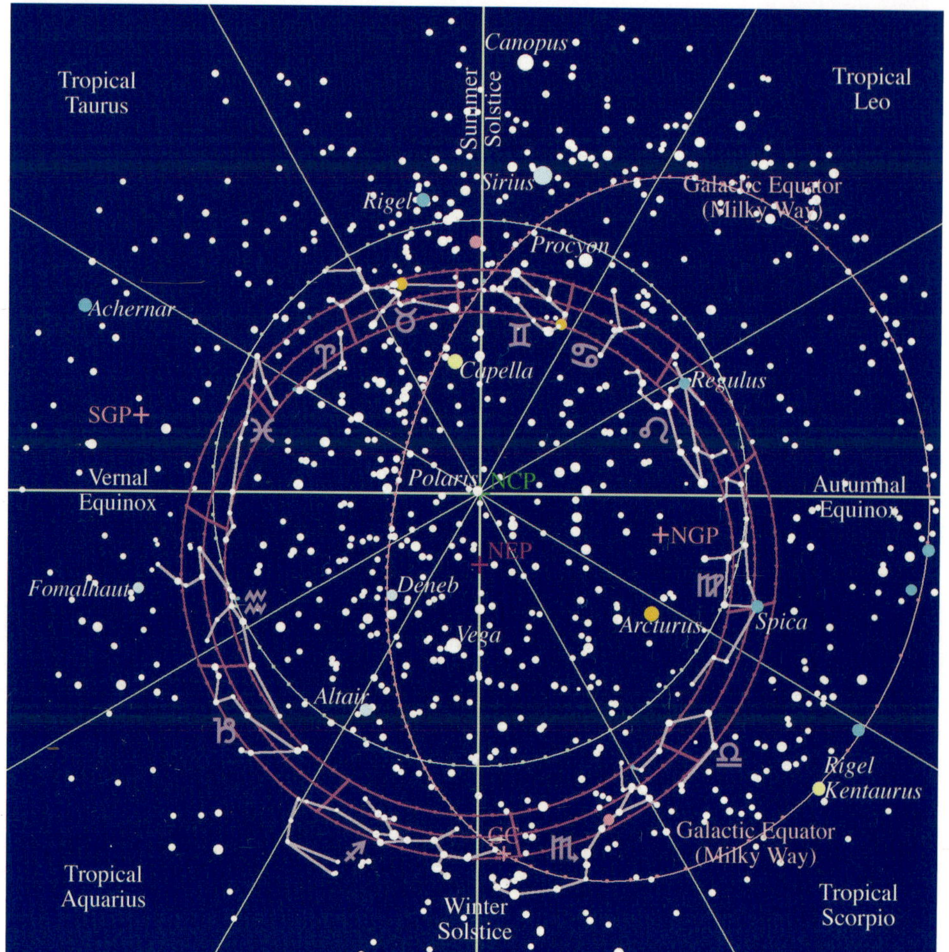

Tropical Taurus
Tropical Leo
Summer Solstice
Canopus
Sirius
Rigel
Galactic Equator (Milky Way)
Procyon
Achernar
Capella
Regulus
SGP
Vernal Equinox
Polaris
NCP
Autumnal Equinox
NGP
NEP
Fomalhaut
Deneb
Arcturus
Spica
Vega
Altair
Rigel Kentaurus
GC
Galactic Equator (Milky Way)
Tropical Aquarius
Winter Solstice
Tropical Scorpio

Part 3
Vedic Astrology in Action

Fate and free will are equally powerful forces.
Yet I consider free will more important,
because it is our conscious choices which create our fate.
Veda Vyasa

Fate can be willed. We are the builders of our fate.
Let us not depend on our fate but on our head and our hands.
We must set about making our own fate.
Swami Rama of the Himalayas

Astrology is not meant to make you a fatalist
but asks you to become intelligently spiritual.
It is the link between ordinary reality and the highest reality.
It reminds you that there is a much greater cosmic force
about which you may have been negligent.
It teaches you to live beautifully.
K. N. Rao

12

Karmic Counselors: Vedic Astrologers at Work

"According to Vedic astrology, the major directions in one's life are determined by the planets at the time of birth. It shows that by making effort, using will power and gaining the grace of God, one can change the direction of one's life, bring happiness and remove unhappiness. It was with this idea that the great sages introduced astrology so that people, by knowing their destiny in advance, could change their lives."

His eyes closed meditatively, Chakrapani Ullal chants the fundamental principles of Vedic astrology to each client who enters his Los Angeles home for a reading. Helping clients understand that Vedic astrology is a spiritual science designed to assist one in working consciously with his or her karma is important to Chakrapani. He had spent seven years with of one of the great yogis of the 20th century, Nityananda of Maharashtra, who advised him to study astrology in order to help guide devotees along their spiritual paths by offering insights into the mechanics of their destiny. Siddha Yoga guru Muktananda brought Chakrapani to the U.S. in the 1970s to help introduce Americans to this incredibly ancient yogic astrological system.

"Mind is the cause of happiness and unhappiness," Chakrapani elaborates. "The ancient sages, being aware of this truth, have been kind enough, in their state of superconsciousness, to say, 'Let us find a way to help future generations. Let us give them tools to help them understand and overcome their problems.' So they found out the influences of the planets, how they are going to affect us, positively and negatively, and they established a formula which is like a gift of God to us."

Chakrapani's skills, and his disarming humility, have won him many thousands of clients, including Hollywood celebrities, and have earned him mention in *People* magazine as one of America's top astrologers. Yet Chakrapani still sits for meditation and *japa* (recitation of sacred mantras) every morning, in order to prepare himself for the demanding task of introducing his clients to their destiny. He sees his work as sacred. "I think astrology is the greatest knowledge a person can have in this world. It allows us to be in control of ourselves, to rise above our situation and to make our life happy. Astrology is the tool which shows us what is our weakness, what is our strength, and why. Once we know that, it is easier for us to correct ourselves if we want to. Once we know the root cause of a problem, there is always a remedy.

"There is no power greater than knowledge of ourselves. It allows us to control our reactions. The chart of the person reveals the influence of the *samskaras*, psychological tendencies brought over from previous births. Once we are able to understand why things are happening, then our intellect can act as an impartial observer and change the course of our action. Gradually, not immediately. Our behavior patterns cannot be changed overnight because samskaras have their own power. You cannot change the course of the river easily, but you can change it little by little, slowly over the years.

"We are all the creatures of habit. That is why the intellect is necessary; it has great influence in shaping our destiny. By observing our own mind impartially, witnessing how we function, we gain the ability to correct ourselves and change the course of our actions."

Hindu astrology, according to Chakrapani, is the ultimate form of self empowerment. It lets us know where we stand. It shows us what we need to change. It puts our future in our hands, and shows us how to mold it. Chakrapani is one of the best known Vedic astrologers in America today. Let me introduce you to a few others.

Astrology and Ayurveda

A few years ago, three leading American-born Vedic astrologers all called me to say, "Dr. Dinesh Sharma is in town. Don't miss him!" With such hearty recommendations, I immediately phoned to make an appointment. Nevertheless, I wasn't sure what to expect as I walked into the small room where Dr. Sharma was conducting consultations. I certainly didn't expect this highly regarded Hindu astrologer to read my pulse. He felt my left wrist, then my right. "You have pressure in the head," he announced. "Also menstrual irregularities." My two chief medical problems were, in fact, migraines and overly frequent periods.

Next he turned to my Vedic chart. "Venus dasha, Rahu bhukti. You should start treatment for the uterine problems immediately, and follow the regime conscientiously." He didn't know it but, without having conducted a single lab test, he was echoing the advice of my gynecologist, who explained that high estrogen levels placed me at increased risk for uterine cancer. But while my gynecologist recommended medication, Dr. Sharma prescribed Ayurvedic herbs, changes in diet, a regular exercise program and meditation.

Ayurveda (the indigenous medical system of India) and astrology have long been allied. But originally Dr. Sharma practiced neither; instead he earned a conventional medical degree. "I practiced Western medicine for years, but finally my conscience would not allow me to go on," he relates. "All I was doing was palliating my patients' symptoms while poisoning them with drugs that had many harmful side effects." Sharma abandoned a lucrative medical career to learn the traditional ways: Ayurveda, Jyotish and Vastu. I asked him how he integrates Vedic astrology into his medical practice.

"Ayurveda gives importance to understanding the constitution of the person before starting treatment. Only then can you prescribe the right type of medicine, the right type of lifestyle. There are three ways to understand a person's constitution. The first is pulse examination. I learned pulse reading from my venerable grandfather. He was unbelievable. He could feel your pulse and tell you you have such-and-such a problem from such-and-such a time in this part of your body.

"Second comes the physical examination. Certain characteristics are typical of certain constitutions. *Vata* persons are lean and thin, anxious and impatient. *Pitta* persons are hot-tempered and cannot tolerate heat. *Kapha* people are generally happy but tend to gain weight. These days we don't find constitutions of one type only because food habits have changed and because of modern luxuries in life. Previously everyone traveled by foot. Now even if you're going to the post office, which is just a half mile away, you go by car. So constitutions are changing and we find more people of mixed types, not just *vata,* but vata/pitta, for example."

PHYSICAL TYPES

TYPE	ELEMENT	QUALITIES	PLANETS
Pitta	Fire	Active, hot, muscular, angry	Sun, Mars, Ketu
Vata	Air	Changeable, spacey, quick, lean, nervous	Saturn, Mercury, Rahu
Kapha	Water Earth	Stable, slow, overweight, calm	Jupiter, Venus, Moon

"In America I have found a maximum number of people with vata or pitta based constitutions. I have rarely found people with kapha predominance, though they're very common in India because of the way we Indians eat.

"A balanced constitution is very rare. Patanjali's *Yoga Sutras* lays out a very strict discipline for yogis. So only yogis have vata, pitta and kapha totally balanced in their bodies. They say in ancient days Indian yogis used to live for hundreds of years. We still have examples in India, such as Devaraha Baba, who finally passed away about ten, twelve years ago. There are people in India over 100 years old, who said they had known Baba for 80 years and he hadn't aged at all. People who were close to Devaraha Baba never saw him eat or sleep. If you can, by strict internal discipline, balance your system, then your body can even start taking nourishment from the atmosphere. Your every organ, your senses, your skin become so active that whatsoever you need, your body will absorb from the atmosphere itself.

"I saw him in Vrindavan. He came down from the raised platform he was sitting on to take a dip in the Yamuna River. He dived in without a diving mask or oxygen. One minute passed, two minutes. After five minutes I said, 'The old man must have drowned! Find him!'

"The people there who knew him said, 'Don't disturb him. Baba is in meditation.' When he came out of the water, I looked at my watch: 25 minutes had passed. I am witness to that, but if I tell this story in your country no one will believe it. They say, 'These Indians, they boast about their yogis and their traditions.' A balanced type of constitution like Baba's is very rare, and comes only when you establish complete harmony between your mind and body, and learn to command your organs.

"I was working at the hospital in Hardwar when a yogi came into my room. He said, 'What you are doing?' I said, 'I am treating patients.' He said, 'Can you see what is wrong with me?' I said, 'You look quite healthy.' He said, 'Yes I am healthy, but please double check.' He gave me his wrist and I checked his pulse. There was no pulse. He was standing there smiling. I asked him to lie down and took out my stethoscope. I couldn't find any heartbeat. I said, 'I should move you to intensive care.' He said, 'I'm just showing you what yoga is. We give suggestions to our organs to stop and take rest.'

"This yogi offered himself to heart specialists who put him on the ECG machine, and his heart was beating normally. He said, 'Okay, now I'm stopping my heart,' and suddenly it stopped. The doctors became frantic. He told them, 'Since you are so worried, I will restart my heart.' And he did. He gave other demonstrations, for example, lying on the ground while a truck drove over his chest. It didn't cause him any problem at all. This is what hatha yogis can do.

"You'll be amazed to know in India there are yogis willing to teach for free but nobody goes to them, because everybody is more concerned with making money. Financial insecurities have taken a big toll on our lives in India. Now these yogis find that everyone is after money and there are no takers for spiritual knowledge.

"But to return to your question. After pulse reading and physical examination, we look at the horoscope. Learning Jyotish used to be a compulsory part of every Ayurvedic physician's education. We find many references that this medicine should be given in this nakshatra, this medicine should be prepared in that nakshatra. Ayurvedic books describe medical problems associated with dashas of different planets.

"What happened was when the Moguls came to India, they would take advice from Ayurvedic physicians, but they never wanted anything to do with astrology because Islam is anti-astrology. They demanded that no Ayurvedic physician should mention Jyotish. The Ayurvedic books related to astrology were singled out and destroyed. Only the books with pure Ayurveda in them were allowed. And so a great treasure is gone.

"When an Ayurvedic physician looks at a patient's horoscope, first he looks at the sign on the Ascendent. The signs have been divided into four categories: fiery, airy, watery and earthy. The fiery signs are pitta, the earth signs are either kapha or mixed. The airy signs are vata, and the water signs are kapha.

"Then we find the lord of the Ascendant. Rahu, Saturn and Mercury are vata planets. Sun, Mars and Ketu are pitta planets, and Jupiter, Moon and Venus are kapha planets.

"Next we see the aspects on the Ascendant. Is the Ascendant being aspected by a vata or pitta or kapha planet or some combination?

"Then we examine the aspects on the lord of the Ascendant, and the sign to which the lord of the Ascendant has gone. We focus on the Ascendant because the 1st house is your body.

"Next it is necessary to check which dasha the person is in. Is it the dasha of a vata or kapha planet? And the dasha lord is sitting in which sign? If the lord of the dasha is a vata planet and it's sitting in a watery sign, it means a vata/kapha disease may disturb the person.

"We might read the pulse wrong, we might make a mistake when we read the person's constitution by physical appearance because appearance can be deceptive. I've seen people who appear very kapha, they're very fat, but when we study their constitution we find they're totally vata because they're so impatient. Only their bodies have become fat, but their constitution is still *vata*. So we look at the horoscope also and synthesize all three factors to come up with a clear picture of the constitution of the person.

"In Ayurveda the definition of a healthy person is: 'The *doshas* (vata, pitta, kapha) in the body should be balanced, the digestive fires should be balanced, the elements of the body (the *dhatus:* bones, blood, etc.) should be evenly balanced, and the excretory system should work perfectly. The consciousness, the mind, the senses of perception and senses of action should be in a happy state.'

"Then we can call a person healthy. It is not that we make a person look very muscular, as it is here in America. Health of mind, health of body, health of soul, that is the total concept of health in Ayurveda."

Astrology and Vastu

In addition to being a physician and astrologer, Dr. Sharma is also a noted expert in Vastu. I had only the haziest notion of what Vastu is, and asked him to explain where this esoteric science fits in with astrology.

"Most people have three types of problems," Sharma began. "First, the person is running into bad planetary cycles. Second, the person is running into some physical problems resulting from dosha imbalance. The third is lack of harmony with the environment. By environment I mean the place where you live and work, where you spend most of your time. If you are physically healthy, if your planets are also good, but there is an imbalance between you and the environment, which means the energy is not flowing in a proper direction where you are working or sleeping or talking or eating for most of the day, this will create a very negative impact. Slowly the energy field which is not conducive to your body and mind works on you without your knowing about it. Despite taking a lot of medicine, you're still unhealthy and unhappy, you still feel a loss of energy in your body.

"You must have been hearing a lot about Feng Shui in this country. Feng shui is in fact Vastu. Indian monks who went to China to propagate Buddhism took the science of Vastu with them. The Chinese experimented and added a few things and came out with this beautiful system called Feng Shui, but the roots of Feng Shui go back to Vastu in India. Vastu teaches us how to align ourselves with the subtle energies around us.

"As you know, if you have a compass or magnet, it always stays north because it aligns with the magnetic lines of the earth's energy field. We cannot see it but there is a constant stream of energy all around us, flowing in a particular direction. When we erect a structure, we trap a space and the energy within it starts moving in a particular direction. If we build the wrong type of structure so the natural currents are obstructed, then the people living in that house suffer. We have seen many examples in India. At a factory designed by a team of modern architects, things went wrong from the first day. The best employees had been hired, the best equipment was purchased, the best raw material was used, but things were going haywire and people were getting sick. Vastu consultation was done and the factory building was modified, the placement of furniture and equipment was rearranged. As soon as this was done, everything started going smoothly. I myself have seen such instances.

"Particularly when we find there is some affliction to the 4th house in the Vedic horoscope, we make sure the person is living in the right type of house. You can certainly move, you can still make changes in your home, but keep in mind the natural flow of the energy field.

"Subtle sciences like Ayurveda, Vastu and astrology complement each other. If you have knowledge of one but not the other, then you are handicapped. If you have a complete understanding of the person, his planets, his body and his environment, you can harmonize the planets, the physical constitution, and the atmosphere in which the person lives. This is a complete approach."

Physicians of the Soul

The Western world abandoned astrology as a medical tool three centuries ago, but its role in the healing arts continues to be honored in South Asia. Dr. K.S. Charak, head of the Department of Surgery at Indira Gandhi Hospital in Delhi, explains, "Diagnosis and treatment of disease are best left to trained medical personnel. However, an astrologer may be able to indicate the time when a person is liable to fall ill and can recommend some preventive steps. Astute astrologers may be able to indicate the severity and outcome of an illness with a fair amount of accuracy, sometimes perhaps better than the medical practitioner. Astrology can also sometimes indicate whether or not surgical intervention is going to help, and when. Modern science can predict how many of a couple's children are likely to inherit a genetic defect, but ancient astrology reveals which of the children will actually develop the malady."

Dr. Charak is the well known author of several excellent books on medical astrology. What a disconnect between Eastern and Western cultures. In India having a surgeon who's famous for his skill in astrology is a real plus. In America a surgeon astrologer might have trouble keeping his license.

While astrology's place in today's medical field may be controversial, its value as a psychotherapeutic technique can hardly be questioned. In India Vedic astrologers are explicitly recognized as "physicians of the soul." Dr. Dennis Harness is a professional psychologist who uses Jyotish in his counseling practice. "My belief is that many psychologists of the future will begin to use astrology as a diagnostic tool," he says. "In particular, Vedic astrology provides both the therapist and the client a bird's eye view of the developmental cycles as they unfold in an individual's life. The planetary periods or dashas reveal the nature and timing of past life karmic patterns as they come to fruition. Health matters, vocational interests, relationship dynamics and even a person's spiritual practice can be accurately reflected through the birth chart.

"Perhaps the transpersonal psychologist of the 21st century who doesn't use astrology will be analogous to an astronomer studying the stars without a telescope. The founder of the transpersonal psychology movement, Carl Jung, often used astrology to reveal the psychological characteristics, patterns and dynamics of his clients. In a letter Jung sent to the prominent Vedic astrologer Dr. B.V. Raman of India, he wrote, 'As I am a psychologist, I am chiefly interested in the particular light the horoscope sheds on certain complications in a person's character. In cases of difficult psychological diagnosis, I usually cast a horoscope in order to have a further point of view from an entirely different angle. I must say that I very often found that the astrological data elucidated certain points which I otherwise would have been unable to understand.'

"Vedic astrology has the same basic goal as psychotherapy, which is to assist the unconscious to become more conscious. The natal chart reflects both the light and dark shadow, our strengths as well as the aspects of ourselves that need to be healed. It can serve the client in developing a 'witness consciousness' or 'observing self' and in cultivating a deeper understanding of the meaning of the life journey, particularly painful or disruptive life experiences. Vedic astrology can help a client in the process of what Jung called 'individuation' and in the discovery of the song the soul intended to sing."

I asked Dr. Harness how he accounts for the phenomenal growth of interest in the Indian system. "Vedic astrology helps people explore the laws of karma and reincarnation in depth, allowing them to see their lives in a much broader perspective. It helps us realize we've spent many incarnations here on earth—our lives today are affected by actions and decisions we made in previous births, as our horoscopes show. It also offers the use of remedial measures which allow a person to take an active role in their healing process rather than just accepting what's happening as one's fate."

One of the most common criticisms of Vedic astrology when it was first introduced here was that it was a "foreign" system, inappropriate for Westerners. Dr. Harness discounts this idea. "The truth is that a number of people who were Vedic astrologers in the past have now incarnated in the West to bring this ancient knowledge to this culture. Many of us have spent many lifetimes in the East. The merging of East and West going on now is laying the groundwork for a global community in which prejudices against other cultures are breaking down. There are challenges in opening the doors to cultural exchange, but we're all enriched when we honor different peoples."

I asked what he considers most valuable about Jyotish. "Vedic astrology helps us to remember our connection with the divine," Dr. Harness answered. "Its remedial measures, like meditation and chanting, help us reconnect with the divine part of ourselves we've split off from. This system helps us extract the nectar from our chart, from both its positive and challenging components, so that we can deal with them consciously. As Carl Jung said, the parts of ourselves we fail to bring to consciousness we're forced to live out as fate."

If medical doctors are the physicians of the body, India's astrologers are the physicians of the soul. As I've mentioned before, nearly every Hindu child has his or her chart read shortly after birth. The insight this provides into the nature of the soul which has just been born into a family can be invaluable. A friend of mine has a chart which strongly emphasizes his passion for music; in fact, from early childhood it was nearly impossible to tear him away from the piano. His parents were unimpressed by his attraction to the arts, however, and insisted he attend dental school rather than following his dream. After ten miserable years filling cavities and capping teeth, he finally walked out of his high-paying job to tutor piano students at the conservatory part time. His parents are furious, but he is finally happy and fulfilled. Perhaps if when he was still an infant, an astrologer had helped his parents understand that he was born to do music, they wouldn't have wasted so much money and effort misdirecting him into a profession that was clearly wrong for him.

Vedic astrologers, with their strong belief in rebirth, diagnose problems which may have begun in previous lives. A man who is having difficulty finding a suitable marriage partner may simply not have reached the appropriate planetary cycle, in which case the astrologer can advise him when meeting the woman he'll marry is more likely to occur. In some cases, however, there may be serious problems in forming partnerships resulting from bitter experiences in past lives. If this is true the astrologer may recommend methods of "propitiating the planets" to help clear away the karmic nexus preventing fulfillment in this lifetime.

Our soul can be sick or lethargic, just as our body can. If we're in the wrong job, living with the wrong people, pursuing the wrong goals, we feel spiritually ill. At this point, a skilled and sensitive astrologer can make a karmic diagnosis based on our birth chart and can recommend a remedy to help us find our way. Instead of fighting with our planets, we learn to work with the energies of time and create the future that our innermost Self intended.

Dr. Harness was so impressed with the clinical results he got applying Jyotish in his work that he co-founded the Council of Vedic Astrology (CVA) and the American College of Vedic Astrology (ACVA), the largest and most active Hindu astrology organization in the U.S. ACVA sponsors in-person and on-line teaching courses and certification programs and publishes a journal. ACVA's delightful annual symposiums give Jyotish enthusiasts by the hundreds a yearly opportunity to get together and compare notes, as well as attend lectures by many leading Vedic astrologers from around the world. Interested? You can learn more at:

The American College of Vedic Astrology
P.O. Box 2149, Sedona, AZ 86339
800-900-6595 ACVA108@aol.com
www.VedicAstrology.org

Destiny Advisors

Canadian Hart deFouw is one of the few Westerners to have undergone a traditional apprenticeship in Jyotish, a formal course of training that lasted, in his case, for over 15 years. His mentor, K.L. Mantri, is one of the greatest Indian astrologers alive today. I asked deFouw what studying in the traditional matter was like.

"In some families and communities Jyotish is still an initiated tradition of formal apprenticeship. The student is initiated into spiritual practices to help build right attitude, understanding and intuition for the subject while concurrently being expected to simply memorize a formidable body of theory and facts," he reported. "First your teacher will test your mettle and your possibilities and your commitment. He or she may start by having you memorize things which they don't teach you how to use until you've demonstrated your allegiance and capacity.

"I wasn't allowed to take notes for the first few years of my studies. The classes, 90% of which were one-on-one with my Jyotish guru, were oral, and I would get as far as I could by just memorizing. I resented this at first because I thought we would end up going too slowly, but it was quite surprising how fast I was able to build up a cumulative momentum. Because of that method of training I internalized many of the principles which other Western students struggle to remember.

"Initially I was introduced to theory, mechanics, methods, Sanskrit terms, and so on. Then we moved on to practical application, which wasn't always a formal thing. Often we would visit other people's houses to enjoy some good quality Indian food while listening to my teacher discourse on their horoscopes. Then afterwards in a private moment he would explain why he said certain things.

"A good Vedic astrologer has one foot very emphatically in the world of spirit and the other foot emphatically in the world of practical reality. They're often very mystical people, devoted to ongoing rituals and spiritual practices. Nevertheless, astrology is used mainly to answer practical questions such as 'Will I get a job?' or 'When will I get married?' or 'How will married life go?' At the same time, astrology texts like the *Mantra Yoga Samhita* explain how to reconnect a person with the mantra or spiritual tradition they were practicing in their last lifetime."

Not long ago an Indian astrologer reconnected deFouw with his own last life. "In India two years ago, I visited a particular Nadi reader," he related. "A Nadi reader is a practitioner of a unique but relatively widespread brand of Jyotish, who has in his possession centuries old preserved leaves upon which have been inscribed many of the main destiny patterns of a consultant, usually in various older Indian regional languages. The information on the leaves is explicitly astrological. An astonishing fact to be emphasized about this Nadi tradition is that the leaves and the information upon them are thought to have been created many centuries before the actual birth of the many people who consult these collections of horoscopes. According to the followers of the Nadi tradition, the Nadi reader simply finds the appropriate leaf and then reads the information found on the pertinent leaf.

"The finding of the leaf, or series of leaves, with the appropriate information is done in a variety of ways. Some Nadi readers take a thumb print of the consultant and based on the patterns of the thumb print are able to locate the corresponding leaf among several thousand. Other traditional practitioners measure the shadow of the consultant and then do a basic calculation to locate the correct leaf. There are several other methods as well.

"My English-speaking Nadi reader measured my shadow on the balcony of his tenth floor Bombay apartment. It took him all of five minutes to locate my leaf and to launch into a matter of fact narration of many past, present and future details of my life. Most of the details of my known past were broadly correct, some exceptionally so. Year of marriage, number of children, along with their age and their sex, my profession (yup, jyotishi!) and other known details were spot on. The reader's narration of the facts of my life to date went on for about a half hour. Then he launched into the future, of which several explicit predictions have already come correct. Not one of this reader's findings involved an interpretation of the psychological nature of any planet in a particular sign of the zodiac as is typical in contemporary Western astrology.

"He then described to me some salient details of my reincarnational past. He read from the leaves that I had been a very successful *jyotishi* in India during the British Raj where I was consulted by many maharajahs and other well-placed people. Then I decided to go and proselytize on behalf of Jyotish in England, only to die there unsuccessful in my mission of having the West recognize the wonders of Jyotish. Before my death in England, I apparently resolved to reincarnate in the West to complete my ambition. Please remember that this is an account of the reading, not me baring my soul.

"My Nadi leaf also stated that I would visit India many times to re-establish my connections with the reincarnated form of my former Indian clients. This particular Nadi reader also informed me that this was my seventh life as a jyotishi, a statement that I have heard independently from other Nadi readers before and since."

After years of shuttling back and forth between North America, India, Europe and Australia giving readings and teaching, Hart deFouw finally agreed to stay in one place long enough each year to begin training us methodically. His Vedic Vidya Institute, based in northern California, offers perhaps the most rigorous training in Jyotish and related Vedic sciences available in the Western world. Those of us fortunate enough to have studied with him count it as one of the truly great experiences of our lives. Because he spent so many years immersed in an authentic Indian *sampradaya* (orally transmitted tradition) under the guidance of an accomplished adept, he is able to transmit not only knowledge, but the living spirit of the science of light. For more information about the Vedic Vidya Institute and *Light on Life,* the classic introduction to Vedic astrology deFouw co-authored with Robert Svoboda, you can log on to www.VedicVidyaInstitute.com.

Qualification Standards

As deFouw intimated, traditional Vedic astrological training is rigorous, and qualification standards are high. K.N. Rao, one of India's leading astrologers, described for me the four qualifications every genuine jyotishi is expected to meet. The first is technical excellence. Those of us who have watched jyotishis take only seconds to mentally calculate horoscopes and complicated planetary periods, can personally attest to the spectacular technical expertise of the Indians.

The second qualification is intellectual excellence. Jyotish is an extremely intellectually demanding discipline. It is not possible to read a few books about Hindu astrology and then hang out your shingle advertising Vedic readings. Mastering the numerous techniques of Jyotish is the intellectual equivalent of completing a medical degree in Western terms. There's a lot to learn: those who don't have the focus to assimilate massive amounts of technical material would be better advised to find another job.

The third qualification is moral excellence. "If you don't have this quality, don't do astrology," Rao emphasized. "The sage Parashara taught that the astrologer must have *jitendriyah,* which means conquest of the organs of action and perception. People are often deeply impressed when you correctly describe events from their lives, and if you don't have self-control you can easily fall into the tendency to exploit people, manipulating them through their subconscious fears."

The fourth qualification is spiritual excellence. "The opening of the *jyotish mati nadis,* subtle inner nerves related to planetary energies, is described in the *Yoga Sutras.* When these nadis are opened, the astrologer no longer requires the crutch of a horoscope to see into your destiny. I have met hundreds of yogis like these. Some of you Western students have met Yogi Karve. Without looking at your birth chart he can tell you the exact degrees in which your planets fall."

Rao grew very serious. "There are three types of astrologers who are cursed by the tradition. Those who are incompetent, those who use their knowledge to manipulate others and those who leave their clients without hope.

"Jyotish must not be practiced with impure motivation. Astrologers concerned only with making money or gaining fame will not succeed. This is because it is not possible to do Vedic astrology properly without *tapas* (spiritual self-disciplines). Real astrology lies beyond the calculations. It is done through the intuition."

Truly great astrologers, like truly great doctors or musicians, are hard to find. Even in India today, standards are rapidly sinking. According to tradition, by the beginning of the Kali Yuga 5000 years ago, three quarters of the world's astrological wisdom had already been lost. The declining standards today are part of an age-long descending arc which will only reach its nadir when the Kali Yuga ends. For this reason, now more than ever, I honor those remarkable adepts who continue to practice the science of light in the old fashioned way: with technical excellence, high intelligence, spiritual integrity and deep compassion.

13

Star Temples: Making Peace with the Planets

It's no secret that orthodox Christianity is intensely hostile toward astrology. In the *Pistis Sophia,* a second century Christian text, Jesus ascends into heaven to combat the planets. After knocking them out of their orbits, he returns to Earth and reports, "I have taken away a third of the power of the planets. I have changed their influences and their squares and their triangles and their octagons." Jesus explains that from this moment on, the predictions of astrologers can never be more than 50% accurate.

Most great thinkers of antiquity had a more accommodating attitude toward the stars. In Plato's *Apology*, the Greek sage Socrates admits that, "just like everyone else," he believes the stars are gods. In the *Timaeus* (a text best known to New Agers for describing the existence of a lost continent called Atlantis), Plato states that the universe is pervaded by a divine intelligence he calls the World Soul, and that this great mind directs the movement of the living planets. In fact, the majority of the ancient Greek philosophers thought the planets were divine beings.

The ancient Romans, though on the whole more cynical than the Greeks, still venerated the planets. One of the few Roman temples to have survived into modern times, the Panthenon in Rome itself, was originally built to honor the stars. The Romans worshipped before statues of planetary deities such as Mercury, Saturn and Jupiter, installed there.

The Sun and Moon, of course, had been worshipped since time

immemorial in the Western world. Diodorus of Sicily, writing in the first century B.C.E., says that the ancient Greeks got along particularly well with the inhabitants of the British Isles since both their cultures were especially devoted to Apollo, the Sun. Modern scholars have speculated that the "magnificent sacred precinct of Apollo...spherical in shape," which Diodorus mentioned, may have been Stonehenge. Diodorus states that the priests at this temple, called the Boreadae, were particularly adept astronomers who worked out the 19-year metonic cycle reconciling the solar and lunar years. Apparently, Sun worship had the fortunate side effect of substantially advancing our knowledge of astronomy.

In the Near East in particular, the planets were actively worshipped. The ancient city of Harran (about 25 miles southeast of Urfa in modern Turkey) was famous for its temples to the planets, where pilgrims came to worship for thousands of years until the city was finally demolished by the Mongols in the thirteenth century. The temple to Venus there, for example, was triangular in shape (the triangle symbolizing femininity) and painted blue (Venus' color). The statue of Venus inside was made of copper, the metal sacred to Venus. The sanctuary was filled with musical instruments since music pleases Venus, and was run by specially-trained priestesses, since Venus is a feminine planet.

In the West, the belief that the planets are living beings persisted well into the Christian era: the famous third century Church father Origen believed the planets have souls. He even thought they could sin! Philo, the famous first century Jewish theologian, wrote that worship of the stars was the next best thing to worshipping God.

Today, the thought of ancient Europeans worshipping the Sun at Stonehenge or of Chaldean hierophants performing rituals to Jupiter and Saturn in Babylonia seems exotic, maybe even foolish. Yet there's one country where the planets are still honored with ritual worship in much the same way as they were thousands of years ago. In India, star worship is still a living practice. *Nava Graha Puja,* the worship of the nine planets, is performed in many temples throughout India. Many Indian astrologers perform the ritual at home as part of their daily spiritual practice. India's astrologers also commonly recommend ritual worship to clients whose charts show serious planetary afflictions.

As an amateur astrologer I was curious to know how these planetary rituals are performed. What are their significance for astrologers and their clients? And what about the Indians' claim that through entering into a ritual relationship with the planets, we can virtually rewrite our horoscopes?

Temples of the Stars

I started my research at a star temple in Trivanderum, a spectacular tropical city near the southern tip of India. It is one of numerous planetary temples founded by Ammachi, the Hindu Mother Teresa. Ammachi is particularly known for her tremendous humanitarian accomplishments: though born in abject poverty, she has managed to build a state of the art hospital in her home state of Kerala, as well as schools, vocational training centers, orphanages, homes for battered and abandoned women, medical clinics, and cultural centers all over the country. Most recently she has set about raising money to build houses for India's homeless at a rate of 10,000 homes per year. She is one of the best known and best loved saints in India today. And, like most traditional Hindus, Ammachi takes astrology seriously.

To the Hindu, all of nature is alive. Thunder and lightning are the sputterings of the god Indra, the heaving of the ocean marks the stirring of the god Varuna, and the Earth itself is the goddess Bhu Devi. The planets also are living beings who deserve our respect. As the lords of time, they delegate the results of our karma to us at the appropriate moment. When she travels, Ammachi often pauses to perform propitiation of Mars, Saturn and Rahu—the three great malefics in Vedic astrology—for the sake of the communities she visits. Negative group karma can be partially offset by making peace with the planetary energies through ritual worship, Hindus believe.

At one of Ammachi's ashrams I spoke with Prasannan, a Vedic astrologer who often travels with her, examining the horoscopes of devotees who come to see her, and recommending spiritual practices such as ritual worship to help them harmonize unbalanced parts of their charts. I asked him why Ammachi considers astrology so important. He explained, "Astrology is something that can help on the path while we're cultivating surrender to God. While we're still in that uncertain zone before we've fully surrendered, astrology can be a road map which shows where the road's washed out ahead and you need to detour. If you want to go to Boston, it's helpful to have a map. Once you're in Boston you can throw the map away.

"The horoscope is a road map to freedom, freedom from the bondage of having to be born again and again in this world. It reveals the obstacles to achieving that freedom, which really means oneness with the universal consciousness.

"The law of karma is expressed in Christianity as 'As you sow, so shall you reap.' The Vedic view is that we're born with a storehouse of karma accumulated during our previous lives, a portion of which is taken into this life. The birth chart reflects the karma that's destined to be experienced in this incarnation.

"Ammachi says that some karmas shown in the horoscope are alterable and others are not. For an astrologer it's important to understand the distinction between these two. If a negative karma was alterable, then the ancient seers prescribed remedial measures to help the person get through the difficult period shown in the chart. They prescribed *pujas* (rituals) or forms of internal worship, gemstones, and mantras; in fact there's a whole science of remedial measures of which puja is an important branch.

"If a karma is completely fixed in the chart, then it may be unalterable. If the person's destined to be childless, for example, then the 5th house will be afflicted, the 5th lord will be afflicted, Jupiter (who represents children in a Vedic chart) will be afflicted, and the affliction will repeat in the harmonic charts. If all of those are seriously afflicted and the person comes for advice on having kids, you've got to gauge their attachment to children and see if they're ready to hear the news that only a miracle would bring them a child. On the other hand, if you see only minor blockages in the 5th house, then resorting to pujas or other forms of worship would bring about the birth of a child. Remedial measures are for that gray area where we have some say.

"It's rare that you find something that's completely unalterable. Most karmas are at least to some degree malleable. For instance, when we're doing regular spiritual practice we gain in some measure the grace of God. In the Christian tradition this might be through regular prayer. In India it might be repeating a mantra. These things build light around the aura of the person and act as a protective shield so even if some difficult event is destined to happen, its impact will be minimized. Instead of breaking their leg, they only break their toe.

"People have pujas done for family members who don't even know it's going on and still they feel the effects. When the birth chart has been examined and the person's name is invoked and at the same time the person's birth star (Moon nakshatra) is invoked, some sort of connection between the star and the person is established, which the puja influences for the better. How is a mystery, but you can't argue with results—and the results are often phenomenal. In India though, people believe that when enlightened masters create a ritual practice to help others, the universe must obey."

The Patron Deity of Astrologers

The star temple I visited in Trivanderum was built according to the principles of Vastu (Hindu Feng Shui), with four doors facing in each of the cardinal directions. Inside is a large black stone into which have been carved images not of the planetary deities themselves but of the divine beings who rule the planets. The Mother of the Universe faces east, representing the divine creative energy which gave birth to the planets. The Father of the Universe faces west, representing the force which will destroy the planets when the cycle of cosmic manifestation comes to an end. Facing north is the ancient snake deity who represents the energy which sustains the world process (in our bodies, this energy takes the form of kundalini). And facing south is Lord Ganesh, the famous Indian elephant-headed god.

Just as an elephant can clear a path through the thickest jungle, so Lord Ganesh can remove any obstacles created for us by the planets. "If you're lost in a jungle, who would you most want to help you?" a Hindu devotee asked me. "An elephant can clear a path for you merely by walking forward. Even if a tree or a large stone blocks your path, he can easily remove it with his trunk." Ganesh is revered as the "Remover of Obstacles" in India.

Before undertaking any new activity—starting a business, beginning a trip—one always asks Ganesh to make the way smooth. Even before propitiating the other Hindu deities, one first invokes Ganesh because he will remove any obstacles that might prevent you from establishing a good "psychic connection" with the goddess or god you want to worship.

Ganesh, Lord of the Constellations
Courtesy of *Hinduism Today.*

Because he is so intelligent and has a powerful retentive memory (elephants never forget), Ganesh is patron of mathematicians, scientists and astrologers. Just as Catholics believe St. Jude looks out for travelers, beggars and thieves, and traditional Chinese appealed to Kwan Yin for safety and healing, Indian astrologers turn to Ganesh for guidance in giving readings. Many classical Vedic astrology texts open with hymns invoking his blessings. "I bow before the lotus feet of Lord Ganesh, son of the Goddess, destroyer of sorrow, who is served by the five elements and has the face of an elephant" begins the *Brihat Parasara Hora Sastra.* Ganapati, as he is also often called, means "lord of the constellations." This elephant-headed deity is as real to Hindus as Jesus is to Christians and Buddha to Buddhists. In fact, on September 21, 1995, Ganesh playfully reminded the entire world that the point of human life isn't to serve oneself but to serve God. Throughout the planet statues of Ganesh began "drinking" milk offered to them during worship. Camera crews in many nations filmed the milk placed before the deity actually dematerializing. This inexplicable phenomenon was personally witnessed by thousands and extensively reported in the world media.

There's a story about the elephant god astrologers tell. One day Ganesh's parents, the Mother and Father of the Universe, challenged him and his brother Skanda to see which of the two could run around the universe fastest. The quickest one would win a piece of candy. It seemed like an unfair trial: Ganesh was strong but somewhat slow, at least compared to Skanda, who was quick as a whip. Skanda leapt up instantly and with lightning speed raced around the world.

When he returned, Skanda was astonished to see Ganesha sitting at his parents' feet eating the candy. "How could Ganesh possibly have gotten back first?" he demanded.

"While you were circling the cosmos," his mother smiled, "your brother got up and walked around your father Shiva and me. He understood that the entire universe is contained in us—Shiva the Supreme Consciousness and me, Shiva's creative power."

This was an important lesson for fiery-minded Skanda, who at last understood that willful action, when it's not grounded in enlightened understanding, may be just so much wasted energy. Would it surprise you to learn that some Indians associate Ganesh with Jupiter and Skanda with Mars? Jupiter is the planet of wisdom and devotion; Mars is the planet of action. In India people hoping to win Jupiter's grace will sometimes keep an image of Ganesh nearby, while people working through Mars imbalances in their horoscopes will often recite mantras to Skanda.

In Hindu homes you'll find images of a small mouse sitting next to Ganesh. The mouse represents your mind, which is always nibbling at the crumbs that fall from the pastries and candies Ganesh—the immense inner wisdom hidden within you—holds in his hands.

In India, many saints and meditators have had visions of Lord Ganesh, who acts in their lives as a living force. Whether or not we Westerners accept the literal existence of Ganesh, we might nonetheless appreciate the yogic conception of the elephant-headed deity. To the Vedic seers he represented the ineffably vast field of intelligence which contains within its awareness unlimited numbers of galaxies. It perfectly comprehends the meaning of the movement of every planet and star, indeed, of every atom in the universe. When they acknowledge Lord Ganesh, it is to this limitless expanse of divine awareness that the astrologers of India reverently bow.

Worshipping the Planets

The technical name for the type of star temple I visited in Trivanderum is *brahma sthanam*, which means "abode of divine energy." The temple was potentized by millions upon millions of repetitions of holy mantras and by special installation rituals performed by great saints like Ammachi. The temples are periodically recharged during festivals when thousands of devotees gather to chant the names of God and Goddess, and when enlightened yogis and yoginis come to visit and give their blessings. In addition, daily rituals are performed in the temple by Hindu priests and priestesses.

Pilgrims come every day to circumambulate the temple in order to offer their respects to the gods and to make peace with the planets whose influences may be disrupting their lives. Sometimes they pay the local priests a small fee to perform propitiatory rituals for them.

On auspicious days, special ceremonies are performed at the star temple to pacify negative planetary forces. Prasannan explains that during *Shani* puja, worship of Saturn, hundreds of people gather to reverently repeat the mantra for Saturn. As each mantra is spoken, the worshipper takes a little bit of a liquid (in which spices and other items sacred to Saturn have been dissolved) and offers it into a special pot. Each drop represents a part of ourselves, whether it is the loving respect we feel for Lord Saturn or the negative qualities in ourselves we want him to help us renounce. At the end of the ceremony all the pots are collected and the fluid, containing our psychic offerings, is poured over the image of the deities in the temple. Saturn accepts and purifies our negativities along with our devotion. "It's a phenomenal, powerful experience," Prasannan relates.

The *Brihat Parasara Hora Shastra*, the bible of Vedic astrologers, recommends that anyone who desires peace, prosperity, good health and long life should worship the planets. Many pages of techniques for establishing a reverent relationship with the planets follow. For example, a statue of the planet representing an affliction can be built from the metal or other material sacred to him, or a drawing of the planet can be made. Then with loving reverence one should offer flowers, appropriately colored pieces of cloth, incense and the types of food the planet prefers. The planet's mantra is then chanted thousands of times, and finally, with a generous spirit, gifts are donated to the needy.

Because of the subtle interlinking of everything in the universe, items with a similar quality to the planet (e.g., milk or pearls with the Moon) are used to establish a connection with the planet itself. Star temples like the *brahma sthanam* I visited in Trivanderum are, in a sense, trans-dimensional portals connecting us directly to the planet which governs those things (poverty, disease, loneliness, etc.) we are having problems with, and allows us to petition for grace.

The *Brihat Parasara Hora Shastra* concludes that the planet which is related to the adverse effects one is experiencing can be appeased through rituals because God requested the planets to do good to those who worship them. "The development, progress and downfall of the people, and the creation and destruction of the universe itself, are all under the administration and authority of the planets. Therefore, they are certainly worthy of our deepest respect."

Worshipping the planets seems silly to us today, either because we believe that rather than divine beings, the planets are just huge balls of dirt and gas, or because we're convinced there's only one God and to worship anything less than the Big Guy himself is sacrilegious. The Hindus also believe there is only one God, whom they call Brahman, the Supreme Being. But everything that exists has been projected from God and therefore partakes in God's divine nature. Trees, rivers, clouds, even planets and stars, are all alive and deserve our respect because they are God's expression of himself. In Hindu scriptures even the Earth is a living being who prays to God when she's in trouble, just as we do. Since the consciousness of the planets, including our Earth, is much vaster than our own, for all practical purposes they're considered gods and goddesses, and it's believed they can be particularly helpful to us if we establish a conscious relationship with them. "They're the ministers in the cabinet and God is the prime minister," explains Prasannan. They have important roles to play in the governance of the cosmos.

When Hindus worship the planets they are expressing their loving reverence to those great beings God placed in the sky to signal the passage of time as well as to indicate when our karmic credits and debits come due. Because the planets are the outer significators of our inner qualities, by propitiating the anger in Mars, the depression in Saturn, the self-delusion in Rahu, the sensuality in Venus, we are making peace with those very qualities in ourselves. Planetary rituals are an age-old technique through which our conscious mind can make contact with the deepest aspects of our personality, and with those same qualities in the living universe around us. That may be why these rituals played a role in the spiritual lives of many ancient civilizations, and why they are still valued in India today.

Time to Worship

There are 19 encyclopedic texts in India called *Puranas,* "Ancient Chronicles," which preserve the sacred lore of the ancient Hindus. One of these, the *Markandeya Purana,* contains an interesting story about a king who fell afoul of the planets.

King Uttama was desperately in love with his gorgeous wife, but his feelings were not reciprocated. For years Uttama tried to win his queen's affection, but she could barely conceal her indifference. One day having tasted a particularly delicious beverage, he offered a sip to his wife. She turned her face from the cup in disgust. It was the last straw. Filled with hurt and rage, he ordered a servant to take the queen out to the middle of the forest and abandon her there. For her part, the queen was relieved to finally be rid of a husband she didn't love.

The king quickly found himself the object of severe criticism. In India, then as now, for a Hindu man to leave his wife was considered deeply disgraceful. He felt bad about his behavior and also seriously missed his queen. Finally he went to a brahmin priest well versed in astrology. "Is my wife still alive? If so, where is she? Is she with another man?"

The astrologer cast a horoscope for the moment of the question and replied, "Your wife is fine. She was rescued from the forest by a Naga chieftain who took her to his home. There she became close friends with the chieftain's daughter, who has been protecting her. She hasn't fallen in love with anyone else."

Uttama was relieved to hear his wife was fine, but the fundamental problem remained. "What can I do?" he wailed. "Even if I go bring her back, she still doesn't love me. We'll both still be as miserable as before!"

NAKSHATRAS FOR PUJA

No.	Nakshatra	Purpose for Puja
1.	Ashvini	For vehicles and for good health.
2.	Bharani	For longevity.
3.	Krittika	For a happy after-life.
4.	Rohini	To conceive children.
5.	Mrigashira	For robust health.
6.	Ardra	For courage.
7.	Punarvasu	To acquire land or other valuable objects.
8.	Pushya	For ample food and material well being.
9.	Ashlesha	For successful children.
10.	Magha	For pre-eminence in one's community.
11.	Purva Phalguni	For good fortune.
12.	Uttara Phalguni	For blessings surrounding one's children.
13.	Hasta	For intelligence and success.
14.	Chitra	For happiness regarding children.
15.	Svati	For success in business.
16.	Vishakha	For love within the family.
17.	Anuradha	To achieve high rank or a promotion.
18.	Jyeshtha	To achieve positions of authority.
19.	Mula	For excellent health.
20.	Purva Ashadha	To become famous.
21.	Uttara Ashadha	To prevent or release grief.
22.	Shravana	For inner illumination.
23.	Dhanishtha	For financial gain.
24.	Shatabhishak	For healing ability.
25.	Purva Bhadra	For abundance (and blessings for and from animals).
26.	Uttara Bhadra	For happiness in love.
27.	Revati	For money.

Looking at the king's horoscope, the astrologer explained that Uttama's prospects of marital happiness were severely marred by aspects from the malefic planets Mars and Saturn. But this didn't mean the situation was hopeless. "You should do the puja to Lord Mitra, god of friendship. This may improve the harmony and affection between the two of you." The king eagerly engaged priests to perform the ritual. Because the karma in his chart was deep set, the priests repeated the rite seven times in full before the king set off to retrieve his queen.

In the Naga household, the queen found her feelings subtly beginning to change. The Naga men there were rude and unfaithful—in comparison to them her own devoted husband seemed like a real prize. In fact, the more she thought about him, the more she found herself actually missing him. When Uttama suddenly rode up outside, she found herself running out to joyfully embrace him. In some mysterious way, the subtle energies released by the puja had healed their marriage.

The *Markandeya Purana* recommends doing pujas for special purposes while the Moon is traveling through specific sections of the zodiac.

The pujas suggested by the *Markandeya Purana* involve honoring the gods and ancestors with rituals and prayer, and offering food and donations to spiritual teachers (who in ancient India did not receive salaries, but lived off donations made by the community they served) and to the poor.

14

Dealing with Disaster: Realigning the Stars

Learning that my husband had bone cancer was a horrible shock. Dr. Connell called with the bad news the very week Johnathan entered his Mercury dasha. In my husband's Vedic chart, Mercury rules the 8th house, making it lord of chronic disease. It is placed in his first house, representing his body, where it's afflicted by aspects from several malefic planets. This is ominous from a Hindu perspective, especially since several other factors in the chart also show serious threats to Johnathan's health.

Even more soberingly, some of the most difficult transits I'd ever undergo in my life started exactly the last week in December, on virtually the same day Johnathan entered his Mercury cycle. I was just beginning to study Vedic astrology at the time, but even as a beginner I had been able to see a challenging period ahead for both of us. Between our two charts, financial setbacks, serious problems for close relatives and friends, and a dramatic health crisis were evident. As long ago as the previous June, Johnathan and I had gone on spiritual retreat to prepare ourselves, chanting the Maha Mrityunjaya mantra (the premier mantra for mitigating the effects of portended disaster), as well as setting our financial affairs in order and making multiple trips to Johnathan's physician in an effort to head off potential disease.

Then as the year drew to a close, one of my employers went bankrupt, and I wasn't paid for a project I had worked on for six months. Two of my aunts died within several hours of each other, and a good friend of my husband's asphyxiated from carbon monoxide poisoning. But Johnathan's life-threatening disease was especially bitter news. The day Johnathan entered the dasha of his malefic 8th house lord we were being forced to face some of the most difficult fixed karma of our lives.

Fixed karma is a karmic potentiality which is definitely destined to manifest in your current lifetime. In some cases so many factors in the birth chart and subcharts converge to predict a specific event at a specific time, that Vedic astrologers throw up their hands and say there is nothing you can do to prevent it from occurring. At that point the only recourse is to appeal for divine grace, because only God has the power to alter fixed karma.

From the Vedic perspective, fixed karma reflects events the soul has chosen to undergo in this incarnation, or if it is a less evolved soul, events it is compelled to undergo, because of past life karma. These are the lessons we can't shirk. Passing these tests is central to our soul's purpose here on Earth.

Unfortunately, the experience of cancer was "fixed"in my husband's chart. Fortunately for us, the outcome of this deadly disease was not fixed. Johnathan's incredibly strong 1st house revealed both luck and physical resiliency. We could beat this disease or the disease could beat us. It was up to us.

The Fire Ritual

Two days after learning how seriously ill he was, Johnathan and I were reminiscing about our tour through India several years previously. I was trying to remember a mantra to Divine Mother Kali (the terrible Mother Goddess who brings devastation to our lives in order to purify and enlighten us) which Shree Maa, one of North India's most beloved saints, used to repeat as we travelled with her through Bengal. Johnathan remembered it instantly and spoke it out loud. Before he reached the final syllable, our phone started ringing. It was Shree Maa.

By coincidence, Shree Maa had arrived in the United States the day before. When she learned how critical our situation was she changed her itinerary. The very next day we were honored to have one of India's greatest saints visit our home in northern California. She sat with Johnathan for several hours, singing devotional songs to the Divine Mother and rubbing his body with sacred ash.

Like many saints and yogis in India, Shree Maa is a firm believer in Vedic astrology. One of her first questions to me on entering our house, was what was happening in our horoscopes. Learning of the grim picture in both our charts, Shree Maa immediately prescribed a remedial measure for both of us to perform in order to work with the difficult planetary energies wreaking havoc in our lives.

Shree Maa taught us a litany of protective mantras we would be required to recite every day till Johnathan's full recovery. She also recommended that on every New Moon and Full Moon day, without fail, I perform the *Nava Graha Puja,* a special ritual propitiating the nine planets.

It's always best to perform a ritual yourself, with full faith and devotion. If a person is too sick to conduct their own ritual, a relative or friend—someone who is psychically close to the person—may perform it for them. Otherwise, a specially trained priest one knows and respects can be engaged to conduct the ritual.

Since Johnathan was too sick to do the ritual, as his wife the duty fell to me to perform the Nava Graha Puja twice each month during the astrologically auspicious hours immediately preceding the Full Moon and immediately following the New Moon. This was why I found myself driving the twisting mountain roads of Napa County to the nearest Kali temple during one of the worst storms in local memory. The road was literally washing out from beneath my tires while rain pelted my car windows so fiercely the rubber on my windshield wiper actually began to pull loose. The time may have been astrologically auspicious but Divine Mother Kali was clearly not going to make the fulfillment of this remedial measure easy.

However, the temple was warm and dry as I sat down on the mat next to the fire pit to perform a fire ritual nearly as old as time itself, a ceremony appealing to the nine Lords of Karma (the Sun and Moon, the planets Mercury, Venus, Mars, Jupiter and Saturn, and the Moon's two nodes Rahu and Ketu) to bless and protect my husband.

Shree Maa sat to my right, guiding me through the procedure. First she "opened" the fire, igniting the firewood and inviting the blessing forces of the universe to be present for our ritual. Subjectively, it was a remarkable experience. As the timber began to blaze, Shree Maa chanted in Sanskrit and suddenly the flames transformed into Lord Agni, the Vedic god of fire who carries our prayers to heaven. From a Hindu point of view, it's completely mistaken to think of earth, air, water or fire as inert. In reality, they're suffused with divinity. When we place ourselves in a sacred frame of mind, veils drop from our eyes and we recognize the divinity that was present in the fire all along.

Swami Satyananda announced Johnathan's name and address, and we all fixed his image clearly in our minds. Next we invoked the presence of Lord Ganesh, the elephant-headed god of Hinduism who removes all obstacles to the fulfillment of our goal. Then we began propitiating the planetary intelligences themselves. In Hinduism, as in many ancient cultures, the planets are experienced as cosmic beings, who have a much vaster degree of awareness than we do ourselves. Shree Maa chanted in Sanskrit,

> With loving reverence we bow to the Sun
> whose exhalation brought this world into being
> and whose inhalation withdraws it from existence.
> With your rising, all beings awaken from the slumber of ignorance.
> When you are at the zenith, all beings find the fulfillment of wisdom.
> When you set, all beings withdraw into their undying nature.
> Your glory is all pervading!

The purpose of praising the planetary intelligences is not to flatter them into granting our requests. As Ammachi, the great saint from South India, told me, "The gods need our praise as much as the Sun needs us to hold up a candle to light its way." We praise the planets not for their sake but for our own, for as we honor the cosmic beings our limited human consciousness begins to attune itself to their greater awareness and majesty, and to the sublime qualities they represent.

Invoking the presence of each planetary lord in turn, we then chanted each of the planets' sacred mantra 108 times. With every mantra we tossed a handful of rice and barley into the fire in token of our self-dedication. In Hindu sacrifices like this one, grains, butter oil and flower petals are offered.

The subjective effect of this ritual is quite profound. We are aligning ourselves with and opening our hearts to Jupiter, Saturn and the other planets as living beings who have tremendous powers to protect and bless. When we enter into a correct, reverent relationship with them, the imbalances in our karma, reflected in planetary imbalances in our natal charts, are corrected, and the impact of our negative karmas is lessened. Orthodox Hindus have great faith in the power of these rituals. It is not faith alone which makes the rituals effective, but faith (revealing a positive movement of will and an openness to blessing power) can greatly amplify the ritual's effect.

We concluded the Nava Graha Puja with the chanting of several healing prayers. Then we circumambulated Lord Agni, the sacred fire, and rang the temple bell loudly to celebrate our communion with the gods.

Shortly after we began our remedial measures, we received a call from the specialist in charge of Johnathan's case. "Uh—there's been a mistake in Johnathan's diagnosis," he explained. "The initial results of the biopsy showed we were dealing with a bone sarcoma. But I just got the final test back and it turns out we're looking at a lymphoma instead. This type of cancer is much easier to treat. John's prognosis just got much brighter."

I actually felt dizzy. It was as if some sort of quantum shift had just occurred and the course of the future had just slipped into a new channel. Of course, there is absolutely no way I can prove the remedial measures are responsible for the remarkable speed with which Johnathan has recovered, though our oncologist calls it nothing short of miraculous. He told us that having a tumor that initially presents as a sarcoma turn out to be a lymphoma is so rare that he was considering writing up the case for a medical journal.

I can't promise that if you apply the same remedial measures your cancer will disappear too. Each person must work through their destiny in their own way. Yet this experience, and many more to follow, opened my mind to whole new ways of working with karma.

Lines of Destiny

One of the major practices Johnathan and I worked with was chanting the Maha Mrityunjaya mantra. Peter Keogh is a personal consultant at the Palmistry Center in Westmount, Canada. Palmistry is a sister science of astrology in India; few professional Indian astrologers are not also thoroughly trained in omenology and palmistry. Recently he participated with several other musicians in the production of a tape in which the Maha Mrityunjaya mantra is repeatedly chanted. Preparing for the taping session, he spent several months chanting the mantra over and over in his mind. "I began to notice significant changes taking place in my hands. A large island on the headline of my left hand was beginning to disappear. As a palmist, I know the challenge and work required to make changes on a major line, yet here I was inadvertently being positively affected by the vibrations of the mantra." According to Vedic astrologers, the lines in our hands, as well as the positions of the stars, reflect the lines of our destiny. Can applying remedial measures like protective mantras and sacred rituals actually alter our fate? Over the years I've seen enough to believe in the possibility that "magic"techniques like mantras and rituals (i.e., focussed attention) can have extraordinary effects.

If the prospect of being able to see difficult times ahead in your futures scares you, you should probably leave Vedic astrology alone. The Vedic chart and its planetary cycles can reveal upcoming events, good and not so good. Working with our Vedic charts gave my husband and me some understanding of why a traumatic event was happening, about how long this cycle would last, and what we could do to help alleviate our misfortune as far as realistically possible. For those who want to work with the energies creating the future, Vedic astrology is an incredible tool. It shows us that as long as we are willing to do the hard work of coming to terms with the problems our planets represent, we can heal our present and reshape our future.

15

Reshaping the Future: Tools for Altering Destiny

Many centuries ago, a worried Hindu mother brought her young son to the local astrologer. The boy did not seem very motivated, and she was concerned about his prospects. Like astrologers in India even today, the jyotishi carefully examined the lines in the boy's palms. "I regret to tell you this," he sighed, "but it doesn't look like your son will ever amount to anything."

Hearing his dismal fate, the boy ran out of the hut sobbing. Outside he found a sharp piece of stone. With painstaking precision, he carved new lines into his palm. Hurrying back to the astrologer's hut, he held up his bleeding hand and demanded, "Now what does it say?"

As anyone familiar with Indian history knows, that young boy, whose name was Panini, grew up to be one of the greatest geniuses of all time. His analysis of language structures was so brilliant that modern Western linguists admit they couldn't duplicate his work even with a super computer. Astrologers in India like to tell this story as an example of a determined soul who literally took his destiny into his own hands.

We don't need to carve up our palms, but we do need to think seriously about what we want from life, where we want to go, and what we want to achieve. If we're not happy with the direction we're going in, we need to begin working consciously with the force of our karma. Then we can redirect the flow of our destiny, rather than passively allowing it to carry us along.

Fixing the Future

There are two tacks in dealing with the karma you see in your birth chart. The first is to sail with the wind. Embrace the future, and live out your destiny with cheerfulness, acceptance and faith. Be your chart. Maximize its positive potentials. Make peace with its weaknesses.

The second is to sail against the wind, applying the rudder of your will. Paramahansa Yogananda's chart showed he would marry three times. Three times his parents selected a bride for him. Each time he refused to go through with the marriage; a shocking act of rebellion in traditional Hindu society. Yogananda's unswerving commitment to spiritual life (also revealed by several dramatic planetary combinations in his horoscope) led him to reject the comfortable domestic life his parents envisioned for him. Instead he consciously chose the life of a monk, and in the process became one of the greatest spiritual teachers of the 20th century, bringing the tradition of yoga and meditation to the Western world.

Sometimes a Vedic chart shows seriously difficult times ahead. As I've mentioned time and again, according to the Indian seers most calamities headed our way may be prevented, or their impact significantly lessened, by consciously preparing for them. Ironically, Westerners sometimes say they're afraid to consult a Vedic astrologer because they don't want to know what disasters lurk in the future. Having lived through the 1989 Loma Prieta earthquake here in northern California, I assure you I wouldn't mind having a little advance notice before the next big earthquake hits. A disaster can knock you off your feet and bring the roof crashing down on your head. Or, thanks to some advance warning, you can be sitting ready with a flashlight, blankets and bottled water, and perhaps even have time to reinforce the walls. The predictions of Vedic astrology are not meant to frighten us, but to prepare us for the future.

Jyotishis in India frequently prescribe karmic remedies, called *upayas*, to help their clients take charge of their fate. Once while scrutinizing a friend's chart, K.N. Rao saw the strong possibility of imminent death. He prescribed the repetition of the Maha Mrityunjaya mantra, the traditional formula for staving off death. A month later while the man was conducting a warehouse inspection, a girder gave way burying him beneath 200 bags of cement. His coworkers were certain he had been killed. When they uncovered him, however, they were amazed to discover that except for a hairline fracture to his hip, the man was unharmed. From the point of view of Vedic astrology, this man's prarabdha karma dictated that he must undergo a potentially fatal accident on the critical date. Repeating the mantra helped this man align himself with the flow of divine grace, and although he still had to suffer the accident, the full impact of the bad karma was blunted. It's like falling out of a tree: the arms of the protective angel invoked in the mantra reach out to break your fall. You still hit the ground, but you don't hit as hard. Hindus believe remedies prescribed by saints, gurus and jyotishis can really help them reconstruct their future, averting accidents, inviting more positive relationships into their lives, improving their financial status, even extending longevity.

The universe of yoga is a universe of justice, but it is also a universe of grace. "What's so beautiful about Hindu astrology is that when we see a bad period coming, there's something we can actually do about it,"says James Braha, a leading Western-born Vedic astrologer. "If there's a seriously difficult period ahead like the periods John Lennon or Marilyn Monroe were going through—in their charts you can see their death being imminent—there are *upayas* or remedial methods you can use to ameliorate these bad periods. What's the good of having predictive astrology if you can't alter what you see?"

Holistic doctors recommend preventive medicine. If diabetes runs in your family, there are lifestyle changes you can make to delay its onset in your life, minimize its destructive effect or perhaps even prevent it from manifesting altogether. Likewise, India's holistic astrologers prescribe preventive measures. In the very last episode of the popular sci-fi TV series *Star Trek: Voyager,* Captain Janeway travels back from the future to warn Seven-of-Nine, a member of her crew, that she's going to die soon. "Now that I know about those consequences, they're no longer a certainty," Seven-of-Nine matter-of-factly replies. For Vedic astrologers, these concepts aren't just science fiction. Many people who've consulted India's famous *Nadi Granthas* reported that their readings were uncannily accurate for their lives up to the moment of the reading itself. After getting the reading, however, the events predicted for the future were less likely to come true. Once people become conscious of a pattern of destiny that's been set in motion in previous lives, they're able to take action to change the outcome. That's the reason knowing your Vedic chart can be so valuable. It brings to your attention the many themes brought over from previous incarnations that may continue to dominate your present life. Once you consciously recognize the karmic vectors working in your life, you have the option to go off automatic pilot and begin living your life manually. Now you're in the driver's seat with your hand on the stick shift.

Once you're clear about what you want to change, it's time to select an appropriate and effective upaya to clean out the karmic debris in your unconscious and help you set a new course. This means making a *vrata*, a sacred vow to complete an upaya or spiritual practice. You'll see people fulfilling vratas any time you visit India. There are the young men who rise before dawn to prostrate, stand up and walk three steps forward, then prostrate again, all the way from their homes to the banks of the Ganges River to greet the rising sun. There are grandparents reciting their mantras millions of times, the beads of their malas slipping endlessly through their bone-thin fingers. There are mothers offering fruit and fried dough balls into a ritual fire on behalf of family members. You'll also hear pandits reciting voluminous holy texts over and over again. All this is part of a special resolve they've made in order to adjust their karmic balance. Hindus are very aware of the mechanics of karma and are working with that process consciously.

There are five reasons a Vedic astrologer may recommend an upaya for you.

1. Paying Your Karmic Debts

The first reason is to burn away bad karma. A Vedic chart may show a knot of grief in relation to romance which may be due to having treated someone cruelly in a past life or having reneged on a commitment, for example. In some cases chronic financial problems may be due to greed or miserliness in a previous incarnation. Hindu codes of conduct, like the *Lawbook of Manu*, describe difficult ascetic practices such as vowing to fast on barley juice and live in a cowshed for a set period to atone for past mistakes. "Repent genuinely, make amends, and never repeat your error again," Manu advises. The Catholic Church has a similar system for expiating misdeeds: you confess, undertake a discipline such as repeating a thousand Hail Marys, and sincerely attempt to mend your ways.

A skilled astrologer can sometimes see that difficulty succeeding in one's career or in building a stable marriage, creating prosperity, or finding a guru may be due to unresolved karma still pending from past lives. Traditional yogis believe that old karmic debts can be paid off through acts of self-discipline or self-sacrifice. This is because unconscious memories of past deeds are stored in a part of our subtle body called the *karmashaya* or "karma container" which we carry with us from life to life. Bad karma can be scrubbed away through the cleansing power of purifying practices undertaken with sincere intent.

While few of us have cowsheds these days, we can commit to austerities more appropriate to our culture, such as promising not to spend any money on ourselves for the next three months. The money saved in this way is then donated to charity. Or for a certain period of time we can fast on weekends, and sit meditating or reading inspiring books instead of watching television or going to the movies.

An upaya to correct a deep karmic imbalance in a chart should not be easy. To be effective, it should be *tapas*, which loosely translated means it should make you sweat. If it's a stretch for you to recite your mantra for fifteen minutes every day, then commit to do thirty minutes. If you normally donate 10% of your income to charity, then for the duration of your upaya donate 20%.

2. Adding to Your Karmic Savings Account

The second reason for prescribing an upaya is to help you create extra good karma so you build enough *punya* or merit to qualify for special blessings. It's like adding to your bank account so that later there's more cash to spend on things you really want like a baby, a house or improving your health. A middle-aged Indian couple I know made a vow to pay their respects to God at the Tirumala Temple in Andhra Pradesh, in hopes of finally conceiving a child. Both their charts showed serious obstructions to their 5th houses, the house of children. Making the pilgrimage to the temple site in Tirupathi involved considerable time and expense, not to mention the hardship of traveling through central India. Once they were there, both of them shaved their heads to demonstrate their devotion in a traditional Hindu fashion, climbed the 10,000 steps up to the main temple and left a substantial donation. Whether by coincidence or not, their son was born eleven months later.

In India, people sometimes think of this as bargaining with God. "If I promise to endure this hardship, I will earn God's compassion and he will grant me a boon." There's something deep in the human psyche that recognizes the legitimacy of this karmic principle. If you think back, you'll probably remember times when you found yourself spontaneously praying that if God helped you pass an exam, or get a job, or recover from an illness, then you would attend church or synagogue regularly, or pray more often or do volunteer work at a local shelter.

You need to run an extra mile each day to start pulling ahead in terms of the karmic merit you're depositing in your karmashaya. Yogic texts describe ambitious individuals who do tapas for years with full determination in order to achieve a particular goal. Many Tibetans—ordinary people, not just monks—recite the mantra "*Om Mani Padme Hum*" 100,000 times every day. The inner "heat" generated by their tapas produces a focused mind, and that power of concentration begins to reshape the future in accord with their desires. In yoga, the focused mind is called *chintamani*, "the wish fulfilling gem." Performing upayas is one time-honored way to acquire this inner jewel.

3. Helping Others

The third kind of *vrata* entails garnering karmic merit not for yourself, but for others. This type of practice is very common in India. You'll most often see it among Hindu housewives, many of whom perform special practices in order to add to the *bhagya* or good fortune of their family as a whole. You will find mothers reciting mantras or fasting to benefit not just their children but their grandchildren and great grandchildren. The Bible says that punishment for a father's sins is meted out to his descendants to the third and fourth generation. The yoga tradition claims that blessings have similar force. Each of us partakes not only of our own individual karma, but of group karma as well. By adding to the karmic balance sheet of the collective, everyone in our family or society benefits, now and in the future. Spiritual masters often spend hours a day in meditation or performing special rites for others.

As I related earlier, when my husband was diagnosed with cancer the great Assamese saint Shree Maa advised me to begin an intense course of spiritual practice on Johnathan's behalf. Many religious traditions teach that by dedicating the fruit of our spiritual practices to others we really can help them. This is what saints do when they bless us, although they have a lot more good karma to spare.

4. Becoming a Better Person

A fourth reason an upaya may be prescribed is to help you develop a desirable quality in your personality, such as generosity, equanimity, endurance or self-control. If your chart suggests that important positive qualities may be lacking in your makeup, developing those traits could be one of the major reasons you were placed on this planet.

In India, people will sometimes vow to give a cow (an expensive item in rural India) or a set of clothes and blankets to the needy at regular intervals. Or they'll promise not to eat each day till they've fed a stranger. This not only generates karmic merit, it helps develop generosity of spirit. Others may make a solemn promise not to respond in anger no matter how seriously they're provoked.

One devotee I know who owned a foundry in Calcutta had made a vow that every two years he would walk from the Himalayas to the southern tip of India carrying two heavy buckets of Ganges water. The strength of will this vow created in him was extraordinary and helped make him a leader in his community.

Will power is one of the most valuable assets any person can have. In India it's called *sankalpa shakti,* "the power to makes one's intentions manifest." It takes a lot of inner determination to persist in completing your *upaya* despite the numberless responsibilities and distractions of your day-to-day life.

5. Spiritual Growth

The fifth reason for doing an upaya is to accelerate your spiritual growth. The renunciate swamis and sadhus of India are continually working with upayas in order to deepen and strengthen their spiritual lives. One of the most common ones they perform is called a *purascharana*. In this practice they a promise to recite a specific number of mantras in a certain amount of time for a particular purpose. The number of mantra repetitions often runs into hundreds of millions. Occasionally yogis commit to an upaya so demanding, it will take them several lifetimes to complete.

Most of us are not that ambitious, yet all of us can benefit from developing a deeper connection with our Higher Self. It's the most valuable source of guidance, healing and creativity in existence. And access to it is free. We need only focus our mind and open our hearts with regular spiritual practice.

An upaya is not a casual undertaking. It's a solemn commitment made to our Higher Self, the living presence of God within us. Yogis in India take upayas extremely seriously because breaking a promise to the divine consciousness within ourselves is like breaking faith with God. Therefore yogis are careful only to begin a practice they're sure they can and will keep. If for some reason a yogi can't fulfill his commitment, he may request another yogi to fulfill it for him. I myself have seen instances where when a disciple loses interest in a long upaya, such as the decision to chant a mantra several hundred thousand times, their guru will complete it for the student rather than allow himto incur the bad karma of breaking faith with God within.

There are four steps to doing an upaya.

1. Clarify Your Goal

You must be very clear about your purpose in beginning this sacred practice. When your intention is firmly fixed in your mind, the physical act of performing the upaya will energize this image. Whether it's better health, more cash flow, or improved relationships, approach the upaya with as much attention and intention as possible.

2. Design the Upaya

Your upaya should be demanding, but not unrealistic. You may want to begin with easier ones such as avoiding solid food from sunrise to sunset one day a week, or adding a half hour of hatha yoga postures to your daily exercise routine. Challenge yourself without harming yourself.

The ideal is for your guru or spiritual mentor to assign the practice for you. An enlightened master has a better sense of which particular upaya is most appropriate for a disciple, and how long the disciple will need to continue the practice till the correct karmic balance is reached and the goal is achieved. An experienced jyotishi is the next best choice for assigning an upaya. If you don't have a guru or an astrologer, tune in to your inner guidance and experiment with creating your own upaya. It is always better to do some spiritual practice than none at all.

3. Energize the Upaya

One person I know memorized some Sanskrit syllables he read in a book and sat down and mumbled the mantra 200,000 times. He had no idea what the mantra meant and no conception of the inner force the mantra was supposed to attune him to. He performed the practice diligently, but completely mechanically, and didn't feel like he got much out of it. Let me promise you right now that if you also practice the remedial measures mechanically, the amount of benefit you experience will be negligible.

Upayas are magic. Magic only happens when there is focussed awareness. If you do the practices in a perfunctory, lifeless manner, there's not likely to be any transformation in your consciousness. Blessings will not be invoked, nor will your destiny be changed.

Your full attention must be engaged or magic simply can't happen. Your car won't go anywhere till you switch on the ignition and step on the gas. An upaya is a vehicle for grace, but it can't move forward without your full conscious participation.

In the Vedic tradition, remedial techniques are said to have "pins" which must be released before the practice can be truly effective. You can toss 200,000 grenades at an adversary, but if you haven't pulled the lynch pin activating the device, there will be no release of energy, no effect, no victory. In India, releasing the pins involves establishing conscious contact with the divine force the practice invokes. How is this done?

Energizing a remedial measure such as a mantra requires three essential components: mental focus, faith and perseverance. In some cases you may be working to counterbalance comparatively superficial "bad karma." In other cases you are trying to put an end to many lifetimes of frustration and karmic mismanagement. By examining your birth chart and its various subcharts, an experienced Vedic astrologer can usually tell how "deep" the karma is, and how much energy you'll have to exert to turn this karma around. If the karma is deeply set, millions of focussed repetitions of the mantra may be required. Persevere.

Vedic remedial measures are not penances. Performing an upaya is a living, joyous experience that puts you in touch with that part of yourself which is most alive, most aware, most self-directed. When you perform an upaya you are becoming more conscious, and consciously taking control of your life. It's an exhilarating experience to undertake these remedial methods, and it's wonderful to experience their healing effects. In twenty years of working with these methods, I have never seen one case where the upaya was correctly, sincerely and consistently practiced in which it did not have a clear and dramatic effect.

4. Follow Through

I have found that unlike the short-lived New Year's resolutions I used to make, I've always been able to complete my upayas. That's because I appreciate their sacred nature and incorporate a renewed commitment to complete the practice into the prayers I say before my morning meditation. My upayas have become such a deep part of my spiritual practice that failing to complete them is no longer a possibility in my mind.

If you are performing a vrata to overcome a limitation in your life such as poor health or poverty, remember that our worst problems often have deep karmic roots. I've seen cases where a saint assigned a particular vrata and a longstanding problem like infertility or, in another case, the inability to afford a home, vanished almost immediately after a fairly short remedial measure was completed. But if the bad karma was built up over lifetimes, it may take years to root it all out. However, no spiritual work is ever wasted. Quickly or slowly, depending on the intensity of your effort, your upaya is cleansing and freeing your soul.

An upaya is a promise you make to your Self, a commitment to free yourself from the bondage of your past negative habits, to generate more positive thoughts and actions in the present, and to create a better, more spiritually enlivened future for yourself and those around you.

In the next four chapters I'll outline some of the upayas I was taught by my spiritual mentors. Please note that the prescriptions recommended here are beginning level. If the karmic complex you're working with is exceptionally deep, you'll need to work with an upaya far more intensely, or work with several upayas at once. For example, instead of chanting a mantra for a few months, you may need to cultivate the blessing power of your mantra over the course of several years. In general, the more tightly a karmic knot is tied, the more effort you need to apply to release it. A serious problem reflected in your horoscope may have developed over a number of lifetimes; it's possible but unlikely it will disappear overnight. Remember that the tighter the knot is tied, the more it restricts the freedom of your soul. Therefore it's all the more important to make a sincere and sustained effort to loosen it.

Please be clear, when you are doing an *upaya* to improve your health, that the techniques I've described here are adjuncts to, and not substitutes for, your doctor's advice.

Have faith in your upaya. Faith doesn't mean deluding yourself or naively believing in magic. Faith means focusing your will with full expectation that you'll see positive results from your spiritual practice. Faith acts as an amplifier, magnifying the effects of your efforts, and invokes the grace of your inner guidance.

16

Vedic Astrological Prescriptions I: Mantric Upayas

Vedic astrology is less about reading your future than writing it. Your Vedic astrologer can help you identify problem areas in your horoscope that you would like to correct, or supportive configurations in your chart that you would like to strengthen. Then he or she can recommend upayas—remedial measures that correct the karmic difficulties you experience in your life.

For example, suppose you have a lot of frustration, maybe even despair, about relationships. This is almost certainly reflected in your Vedic chart where you'll find the 7th house (the house governing partnerships of all types, including marriage) badly afflicted, and perhaps Venus (the planet governing relationships) weak as well. Your astrologer may assign an upaya to bolster Venus and the 7th house or help you make peace with the planetary energies representing the problem.

Suppose you've just entered a period in which every single thing suddenly seems to be going wrong. This is almost certainly reflected in a new planetary cycle you've just entered or a transit you're now running. The jyotishi will determine which planet is ruling this difficult cycle and assign an upaya to help smooth its effects.

Let's take a look at some of the most popular and effective prescriptions well-trained Vedic astrologers typically recommend. There are four basic types of upayas.

• *Vachaka* Upaya	Upayas involving speech
• *Manasika* Upaya	Upayas involving the mind
• *Kayaka* Upaya	Upayas involving the body
• *Tantrika* Upaya	Upayas involving external objects

Words and Will

Indian astrologers all agree that chanting the resonant sounds of mantras purifies the field of your consciousness and neutralizes the effect of bad karmas. Prayers also align you with a higher power—a particularly effective way to invoke the flow of grace into your life. How does this work? The answer lies in *mantra vidya*—the Hindu science of consciousness and energy.

All energy conveys information. Vibrations of a certain wavelength communicate the color red, others the sensation of heat, others the scent of pine, still others the sound of birds jabbering — provided you have the organs necessary to sense them. Vibrations are information, the energy that gives reality its shape. They're the way the universe communicates with and regulates itself.

The Bible says that "In the beginning was the Word, and the Word was with God, and the Word was God." This means that God's will expresses itself through the medium of energy infused with the creative potency of intelligence. ("And God said, 'Let there be light,' and there was light.") Will is the link between consciousness and energy. The material reality we experience around us is the most physical level of divine consciousness, the physical expression of God's will, according to the Hindu sages. This is the core principle of occult traditions worldwide, and lies at the root of mantra science.

There are six sacred sciences, called *Vedangas*, in India. Vedic astrology is one. The second is Vedic ritual magic. All four others, however, have to do with the science of mantras. They entail mastering will and the power inherent in words, using the force of one's intelligence to help others and oneself. In this way we, like God and the angels, consciously shape a new reality.

When we apply this principle in our own spiritual practice we begin to experience the extraordinary power of consciously directed words, thoughts, images and concepts. This is the key to working successfully with mantras, chants and prayers.

LEVELS OF SELF-CONSCIOUSNESS

Vaikari	The ordinary physical sounds you hear with your ears, such as spoken words.
Madhyama	Mental sound, which you hear only in your mind, like your thoughts.
Pashyanti	Visual imagery you see only with your mind's eye. Example: Albert Einstein was able to develop the theory of relativity because he used mental imagery (fantasy) to visualize light speeding through the universe, rather than thinking about it with words. Other physicists of his time had been unable to make this mental leap because they thought only in words, and there were no words for relativity yet.
Para Vak	Intuitive understanding, grasping the very essence of a concept, pure meaning uncloaked in words or images. Sometimes you simply know. You have no evidence, no concrete thoughts, no clear images, but there's a distinct feeling that something is true.
Vag Devi	Beyond these four is the transcendent, undisturbed, living intelligence itself, the source of all insight, which you experience as the silence of tranquil, lucid awareness.

Verbal remedial measures employ five levels of Self-consciousness. The deeper the level you reach while performing your upaya, the more rapid and far-reaching your results will be.

Indications: Mantric prescriptions (upayas involving sound energy, whether sounded with the mouth or in the mind) are very highly recommended in the Vedic tradition. They are superb all-round remedial measures used for burning away "bad" karma and raising the level of an individual's awareness (creating "good" karma). Planetary mantras and divine mantras are ideal for specifically strengthening weak or heavily afflicted planets and the attitudes and experiences they represent in your life.

Contraindications: Upayas involving mantric energy should never be done by people who are fearful, unethical, disinclined to turn their minds inward or mentally unstable. These individuals should be assigned *kayaka* upayas—physical remedial measures. *Kirtan* (devotional music) is the exception—it's the one upaya approved for everyone.

MANTRAS

The most commonly recommended Vedic prescription is mantra. A mantra is a sonic tool which uses vibrations, whether spoken out loud or sounded in the mind, to create a link between your usual state of awareness and the higher awareness and intuitive power that lies dormant within you. It opens a vibratory gateway through which guidance and healing energy can flow. Yogis use mantras with surgical precision to move with full awareness through their unconscious mind. In this way they can operate on unhealthy aspects of themselves, the complexes and neuroses which have been carried over from previous births. In Jyotish, mantras are used to strengthen those aspects of your personality which may be weak or unbalanced. Once inner wounds are healed, the flow of external events often changes dramatically and obstacles begin to melt away.

Incidently, the use of mantras was central to the ancient Egyptian, Chaldean and Greek astrological systems as well. The famous 4th century Neoplatonist Iamblicus wrote that he preferred Egyptian mantras over Greek ones because they'd been empowered by thousands of years of constant repetition. It's extremely unfortunate this tradition has been lost in the West, since mantras are such a superb form of spiritual therapy. They're easy to do, they're extremely effective, they're free, and (practiced correctly) they don't have negative side effects. The mantric tradition has been most carefully preserved in India, so I'll emphasize Sanskrit mantras here.

A Word of Caution: Though you're about to learn some very potent mantras, I do not recommend that you start a mantra practice on your own. In India, mantras are considered extremely sacred and are always transmitted in person by a teacher who has practiced the mantra, experienced its effects, and knows its energies inside and out. Hindus believe that when you give a person a mantra, you are not just giving a sound, you're transmitting a living energy. The *devata* or divine intelligence of the mantra comes not from the sound itself (which is just a vehicle for the *devata*) but from the consciousness of the teacher who is transmitting it. If you feel inspired to begin working with mantras, I urge you to contact a qualified teacher for initiation.

Here's a note for those of you who simply can't wait to try sounding out the mantras. Sanskrit speakers pronounce vowels like Italians do, not like Americans. *Ram* is pronounced "rahm," not "ram" like a male sheep, for example. So you'll have to try speaking the mantras with a European accent. Also, there's no "th" sound in Sanskrit (as is our word "that"); the letters "th" are pronounced more like foo*th*ill. There's no "f" sound in Sanskrit either, so "ph" is pronounced more like u*ph*ill. Please don't play with the mantras. I strongly suggest you to contact a qualified instructor who can teach you how the mantra is pronounced and make sure that mantra is right for you.

Important: If you have been initiated in a spiritual tradition, the mantra your guru gave you takes precedence over all astrological mantras. Stick with the mantra given by a realized master.

Planetary Mantras

There are three reasons to use a planetary mantra.

1. To propitiate a planet that's acting in a malevolent manner in your horoscope, causing problems or blocking the flow of good karma.
2. To strengthen a benevolent planet which has the potential to do great good but is presently too weak to be helpful.
3. To enliven the planet which rules your Ascendant. Energizing this planet greatly empowers your chart as a whole.

In Vedic astrology, the planets are personified as deities such as Surya, god of the Sun, or Chandra, the Moon god. Like traditional people the world over, Hindus experience the entire universe as full of life, permeated by consciousness, and animated throughout by gods and demigods. To them the stars and planets are living intelligences doing the work assigned them by the Creator. The Bible also describes the heavenly hosts as continually singing the praise of their maker, while at the same time serving as "signs" for those of us here below.

When you use a planetary mantra you attune yourself with planetary energies that are "out of focus" in your birth chart. For instance, signal serious problems in a person's life. By chanting tras a person links himself to positive saturnine qualities like stability, loyalty, ethics and hard work, which may be exactly what he needs to cultivate in order to overcome the difficulties inherent in his horoscope.

Here's another example. A client is chronically depressed. The astrologer sees this clearly in her horoscope: her powerfully activated Saturn closely aspects her weak Moon and she's running a Moon cycle. (Saturn can represent depression while the Moon stands for the mind.) In a case like this a jyotishi may prescribe a mantra such as *Om Cham Chandraya Namaha,* "I honor the lunar forces within me and throughout the universe." By offering respect to her inner Moon, the woman is saying in effect, "I honor the strength and joy within me."

If a person lacks self-confidence as shown perhaps by a weak Sun, the jyotishi might prescribe a mantra like *Om Sum Suryaya Namaha* which means, "With loving respect I bow to the Sun and to the radiant solar energy within me and around me."

MANTRAS OF THE PLANETS

Sun	*Om Sum Suryaya Namaha!*
Moon	*Om Som Somaya Namaha!*
Mars	*Om Kum Kujaya Namaha!*
Mercury	*Om Bum Budhaya Namaha!*
Jupiter	*Om Brim Brihaspataye Namaha!*
Venus	*Om Shum Shukraya Namaha!*
Saturn	*Om Sham Shanaishcharaya Namaha!*
Rahu	*Om Ram Rahave Namaha!*
Ketu	*Om Kem Ketave Namaha!*

Each planetary mantra given here begins with the sacred syllable "Om," followed by a *bija* mantra, or activating sound, for a particular planet. The third Sanskrit word is the name of the planet. *Namah* (pronounced *namaha* at the end of a sentence) means "I bow to" or "I offer my deepest respect to."

Divine Mantras

Some Indian jyotishis prefer to have clients chant the mantra of the form of God or the Goddess associated with a planet, rather than the planetary intelligence itself. The logic is, why go to the head of the village when you can go to the duke or duchess?

In India various aspects of the Supreme Being and divine incarnations (*avatars*) are connected with each planet.

PLANETS AND DIVINITIES

HINDU DEITIES	
Sun	Savitar, Agni, Mitra, Shiva, Rama
Moon	Apas, Varuna, Krishna, Uma, Parvati
Mars	Bhumi, Skanda, Hanuman, Narasimha
Mercury	Vishnu, Narayana, Buddha, Sarasvati
Jupiter	Indra, Brahma, Ganesh, Vamana
Venus	Sachi, Lakshmi, Lalita, Parashurama
Saturn	Brahma, Yama, Shiva, Kali, Kurma
Rahu	Sarpa, Durga, Varaha
Ketu	Ganesh, Chhinamasta, Mina

Don't be confused because some gods are mentioned more than once. Traditions vary. According to the *Rig Veda,* all these names are ultimately just different words for the same Supreme Being anyway. Divine names from other traditions (e.g., God, Jesus, Allah, Jehovah, Thoth, Isis, Quetzalcoatl) do just as well. Hindus believe the Supreme Being isn't particular about which name you use, only that your heart be open and your prayers sincere.

You could just as well propitiate the planetary intelligences by the names such as the following if they speak more forcefully to your imagination.

ROMAN	GREEK	SUMERIAN	NORSE
Sol	Apollo	Shamash	Sola
Diana	Artemis	Sin	Skadi
Mars	Ares	Nergal	Tyr
Mercury	Hermes	Nabu	Odin
Jupiter	Zeus	Marduk	Thor
Venus	Aphrodite	Ishtar	Freya
Saturn	Kronos	Ninurte	Loki

Other people feel why should you go to the duke if you can go directly to the king or queen? These people direct their thoughts to the Supreme Being alone, from which all other divine and angelic intelligences are projected.

MANTRAS TO THE SUPREME BEING

Some of the most popular and powerful Sanskrit mantras to the Supreme Divinity are:

Om Namah Shivaya!
With loving reverence I bow to the Supreme Being.

Om Namo Bhagavate Vasudevaya!
With deepest devotion I bow to all pervading Divine Awareness.

Ma Om!
Homage to the Mother of the Universe.

Because they've been chanted will full sincerity by so many millions of devotees for so many centuries, these mantras transmit tremendous blessing force. If your Mercury is weak or afflicted, your jyotishi may recommend that you chant *"Om Vasudevaya namaha!"* which is a mantra connected with Vishnu, the aspect of the Supreme Being most closely associated with Mercury. If feminine planets in your chart, such as the Moon, Venus or Rahu, are playing "out of tune" in your horoscope, the jyotishi may suggest a mantra to the Divine Mother like *"Ma Om!"*

Sometimes a jyotishi will recommend a mantra that directly energizes a facet of your life, rather than a planet that governs it. Here are some highly charged mantras of this type. Please don't try these without first learning how to pronounce them properly. Pronouncing them as closely as possible to the way they've been spoken traditionally helps to release their mantric power.

MANTRAS FOR A SPECIAL PURPOSE

Om Gam Ganeshaya Namaha!
For an auspicious beginning to a new project or to remove obstacles in the way of fulfillment of a cherished goal.

Om Shrim Lakshmyai Namaha!
For prosperity, family harmony and well being.

Om Aim Sarasvatyai Namaha!
For enhanced artistic talent and success, literary skill, intellectual brilliance and eloquence.

Om Hrim Kali Durgaye Namaha!
For courage, will power, and victory in life's battles, as well as to attone for past thoughts and actions you sincerely regret.

It goes without saying that these mantras can be used for ethical purposes only. Every deity—even the most benign ones like Lakshmi—has a wrathful form. Trying to use a mantra to directly or indirectly harm others releases this wrathful energy on the person pronouncing it.

The Maha Mantras

There are three legendary mantras called maha mantras, *maha* meaning "great" in Sanskrit. The first two are the Gayatri and the Maha Mrityunjaya. Both are found in the *Rig Veda,* meaning they're at the very least 5000 years old. The third is the famous Hare Krishna mantra. All three of these mantras have been repeated trillions of times throughout history by saints, yogis, priests and spiritual aspirants, making them fantastically potent.

There are three ways these mantras are used in Jyotish.

1. If a horoscope shows numerous difficulties, these maha mantras may be used like broad spectrum antibiotics, as all-purpose prescriptions to cure many ills at once.
2. For spiritual aspirants, these important mantras quickly enliven one's spiritual life. The Gayatri mantra purifies the mind. The Hare Krishna mantra intensifies devotion. The Maha Mrityunjaya mantra forms a protective shield around the soul. These mantras are related to Brahma, Vishnu and Shiva respectively, who together form the Hindu divine trinity.
3. Each mantra also has a specific function. The Gayatri helps put people in touch with their inner guidance, honing the intuition and illuminating the mind. It is said to "remove curses," meaning both hostile psychic energy directed at you by other people, and self-created mental complexes that tie the soul in knots. In cases of disease, impending disaster or imminent death, the Maha Mrityunjaya mantra (literally "the great mantra for conquering death") is often prescribed. It protects against all threats and, when death finally does arrive, it eases the process of release. The Hare Krishna mantra "washes away sin," and increases love and faith.

THE GREAT MANTRAS

Gayatri Mantra

Om bhur bhuvaha svaha	Om. With loving reverence we bow
Tat savitur varenyam	To the divine inner Sun,
Bhargo devasya dhimahi	The most splendid light in all worlds.
Dhiyoyo naha prachodayat.	Please illuminate our consciousness!

Hare Krishna Mantra

Hare Krishna Hare Krishna	Divine Lord! Divine Lord!
Krishna Krishna Hare Hare	Lord God! Lord God!
Hare Rama Hare Rama	
Rama Rama Hare Hare	

Maha Mrityunjaya Mantra	
Om trayambakam yajamahe *Sugandhim pushti vardhanam* *Urvarukamiva bandhanan* *Mrityor mukshiya mamritat.*	Om. O, All-Seeing One, You who attend to the welfare of all beings, please free us from the grip of death as easily as ripe fruit is released from a vine. May our minds attend always to our immortal Spirit!

In no case is any mantra or other upaya, including the Maha Mrityunjaya, a substitute for consulting a doctor. The mantra invokes divine grace; that grace may come to you in the form of a particularly skilled physician.

Awakening a Mantra

Suppose you're ready to begin mantra practice. The first thing you need to do is activate your mantra.

To bring a mantra to life in your awareness, making it a conduit to higher conscious, you must perform *prana pratishtha* which means infusing it with life energy. When someone gives you a present like a new electronic gadget you have to put in batteries. In a similar way, you want to energize the mantra to make it work for you. Here is the process.

Activating Your Mantra

1. If you are working with a Vedic astrologer, ask him or her for an auspicious date and time to potentize your mantra.

2. Find a quiet spot where no one can hear you. Sit up straight in a comfortable position. Bring your full attention into the present moment by focusing on your breath.

3. Begin chanting your mantra out loud with devotion, keeping in mind the mantra's inner meaning. In this way, you breathe your soul force into the mantra. Do not chant just with your mouth but with your entire body. By this I mean you should be able to feel the physical vibrations reverberating in your skull and in your gut. The air around your body should be charged with the sound of the mantra. If you are sitting in a small room, chant so that the vibrations of your mantra permeate the walls around you. Chant for a minimum of five minutes, although 10 to 15 minutes is better if you can keep your mind focused that long.

4. In the next phase chant more softly. Eventually, whisper the mantra more and more quietly until finally your lips are moving but no sound is emerging. If you do this with full awareness you will still feel the force of the mantra as strongly as you did when you were chanting it loudly.

5. Finally chant the mantra mentally only. From this moment on, you will not speak the mantra out loud again. Don't share your mantra with anyone else. It is now a sacred energy force operating in the field of your awareness.

By the way, the process of potentizing upayas was known and practiced by Western astrologers until a few centuries ago. In William Lilly's classic 17th century textbook, *Christian Astrology,* this process is called "vivification."

When you first start working with your mantra on a regular basis you'll need to make a continual mental effort to keep repeating it. Eventually, the mantra will begin flashing spontaneously in your mind without any effort on your part. At this point, your subconscious mind has received the mantra and is repeating it for you, creating a field of protective and blessing energy around you.

Some people see almost instant effects when they begin working with a mantra. According to the tradition, this is because they've worked with that mantra in a previous life so the mantra "owes" them results. However, if the karma they're working to erase is deep-rooted, most people will need to use the mantra for a some time before extremely dramatic effects appear since this may be the first life in which they've recited it. Very rarely, a person gets only modest results from mantra practice. According to tradition this may be because they treated the mantra disrespectfully in a past life, or have been repeating it without reverence or with impatience or doubt. Therefore the mantra—which is considered a living intelligence in Jyotish—is reluctant to offer its blessing.

How to Use a Mantra

There are two ways to work with mantras:

1. Japa. This is continual mental repetition of your mantra for prescribed periods every day.
2. Meditation. This entails following your mantra to its source in the deepest levels of consciousness.

Mantra japa is similar to the Catholic practice of reciting the rosary. To do japa of a mantra you need a mala, a Hindu rosary with 108 beads. Malas are available through most yoga centers, from companies advertising in yoga magazines, or log on to www.yespublishers.com or www.HimalayanInstitute.org for a mail order source. The 108 beads stand for the 108 steps the Moon takes on its journey around the zodiac. You'll notice there's a 109th bead much larger than the rest called the guru bead. This is where you start. Here is how to perform japa.

Mantra Japa

1. Choose a time each day when you can sit uninterruptedly to do your practice. Fix firmly in your mind your goal for doing this upaya.

2. Sit comfortably with your head, neck and trunk straight. Avoid slumping forward, since slackness in the spinal column breaks the flow of concentration. Hold the mala in your right hand. Close your eyes.

3. For a few moments quietly observe your breath, keeping your attention fixed on the bottom of your nasal septum (the bridge between your nostrils). This is a valuable short cut used by yogis and martial artists to quickly relax the body and focus the mind.

4. Beginning with the bead immediately after the guru bead, run the mala bead by bead through your fingers, repeating your mantra once with every bead. Traditionally, practitioners don't use their index finger to move the beads because it represents the ego.

5. When you reach the guru bead after reciting your mantra 108 times, flip the mala around in your hand and begin your next round. Start with the bead you finished with on your last round.

6. Don't let your attention wander. Focus on the sound and meaning of your mantra. If you suddenly realize you drifted off mentally during the last few beads, go back and do them again.

7. Continue chanting your mantra till you've completed the number of rounds you planned to do. Give yourself credit only for 100 recitations in each round even though you've done 108. The other eight recitations are offered to the universe for the benefit of others.

8. When you're finished, pause for a moment to focus on your breath. Relish the state of focused tranquility you're experiencing.

Rx BEGINNING LEVEL MANTRA JAPA
10,000 repetitions of your mantra. This is 100 malas.
One mala per day will take just over 3 months to complete (100 days).
Two malas per day will take 1 1/2 months to complete (50 days).
Four malas per day can be completed in just over 3 weeks (25 days).

Rx INTERMEDIATE LEVEL MANTRA JAPA
100,000 repetitions of your mantra. This is 1000 malas.
Five malas per day will take 6 1/2 months to complete (200 days)
Ten malas per day will take little more than 3 months to complete (100 days).
Twenty malas per day can be completed in less than 2 weeks (50 days).

Rx ADVANCED LEVEL MANTRA JAPA
1,000,000 repetitions of your mantra. This is 10,000 malas.
Five malas per day will take 5 1/2 years to complete (2000 days).
Ten malas per day will take about than 2 3/4 years to complete (1000 days).
Twenty malas per day can be completed in less than 1 1/2 years (500 days).

Mantra meditation is similar to japa but is a more internalized process. Please be aware that the majority of saints and yogis in India recommend meditation most highly of all upayas. The ancient sage Patanjali states that when your mastery of deep meditative states becomes so complete that you remain in a meditative state 24 hours a day, even while going about your daily affairs, you transcend the karmic process all together. The latent karmas stored in your causal body are destroyed, like roasted seeds which no longer can germinate.

Think of it this way. You may be wildly infatuated with a certain person. You would literally give anything to be with him or her. Then one day you see that person do something that strikes you as stupid or repulsive and instantly your infatuation vanishes as quickly as it appeared. Now you wouldn't want them even if they begged you to go out with them. The "seed" of your desire has been "fried" in the fire of knowledge. It no longer controls your behavior or dominates your fantasy life. In deep states of yogic meditation, you let go of all your illusions and achieve *mukti*, the state of freedom from all the karmic compulsions that had been dictating your feelings and circumstances. You are now a *jivanmukta*, a "free soul." This means your true Self, the divinity within you, not your complexes, habits and neuroses, is in charge of your life.

That's a pretty ambitious goal. Yet almost everyone is able to benefit from at least a beginning level mantra meditation practice. There are two caveats, however:

1. For mantra meditation, you should use a divine mantra or maha mantra, not a planetary mantra.
2. Meditation is not appropriate for people who have difficulty drawing their attention inward, or for the mentally ill.

Mantra Meditation

1. Choose a time every day when you can sit for meditation. Twice a day is even better. You should sit for at least 15 minutes in every session. You may wish to gradually increase the amount of time as you get more used to sitting completely still and keeping your mind focused. Serious yoga students meditate a minimum of 30-45 minutes twice a day. Yogis spend hours a day in meditation.

2. Seat yourself on a meditation cushion or hard chair so that you can sit up straight comfortably. You'll be sitting without moving for some time so make sure you're in a stable position that keeps your head, neck and trunk aligned without strain. Posture is important. It's much easier to stay focused when the nerves in your spinal column aren't cramped by a slumped posture.

3. Bring your full attention to your nasal septum. That's the bridge of flesh at the bottom of your nose which divides your two nostrils. Sense the air flowing in and out of your nostrils here. Spend at least one full minute feeling the cool air enter your nostrils and warm air flow out. This is the single most important centering exercise in the entire yoga tradition. It calms your nervous system and focuses your mind. Bring your full awareness to your third eye (*ajna* chakra). This is the spot inside your brain that's about three inches behind the point on your forehead where your eyebrows meet. You will know you've reached that spot when your mental focus suddenly becomes intensely lucid. If it's difficult for you to hold your attention this high in your body for any length of time, focus instead on your heart area (*anahata* chakra). This is the spot directly between your nipples.

4. Begin to mentally repeat your mantra. (When you're more experienced, the mantra will repeat itself for you.) Focus intently on the inner sound and the feeling of the mantra. Each mantra carries with it a feeling of tranquility, quiet joy and faith.

5. Stay with the mantra. Thoughts, images and desires may enter your awareness. Don't pay attention to them or waste energy trying to force them out of your mind. Instead simply return to your mantra. There will be plenty of time to deal with your thoughts later. For these few minutes of your *upaya,* you're devoting the force of your attention exclusively to the sound and feeling of your mantra.

6. Eventually, you'll begin to feel very, very still. At this point release the mantra and glide into silence. You are fully awake, fully aware and completely at peace. Abide in this space as long as it lasts without your having to make any effort to sustain it. When it slips away, return to your mantra. That still, lucid state is the living presence of your immortal spirit.

7. When you finish your meditation, sit quietly for a moment longer, relishing the sense of physical relaxation and mental refreshment. Be regular in your meditation practice. Do it every day. The effects are amazing.

Traditionally, meditation is done after bathing (at least wash your hands and rinse out your mouth), on an empty stomach, with a clear and concentrated mind. Sunrise and sunset are considered ideal times for meditation. Always meditate during a solar or lunar eclipse. During an eclipse all of nature is supporting your spiritual practice.

Rx BEGINNING LEVEL MANTRA MEDITATION
15 minutes of mantra meditation every day for six months.

Rx INTERMEDIATE LEVEL MANTRA MEDITATION
30 minutes of mantra meditation twice daily for a year.

Rx ADVANCED LEVEL MANTRA MEDITATION
3 hours of mantra meditation daily for the rest of your life.

Schedule your day so that you can realistically complete this upaya. Yogis in India often meditate up to 18 hours a day. However, very long sessions of meditation are better left for retirees and serious aspirants.

PRAYER

Chanting of *stotras* is one of the most valuable and effective upayas according to Parashara, the father of Vedic astrology himself. Stotras are hymns and prayers. Some of the stotras Indians use are hundreds of verses long. A New York lawyer I know chanted all 700 verses of the *Chandi,* a hymn to the Goddess Kali, three times a day without fail for three years.

This took hours to do every day. His goal was purely spiritual: to express his burning love for the Divine Mother and to burn away all his karmas. The results were very dramatic. Today, he is widely acknowledged as a saint and authentic guru; his many books on spiritual devotion are cherished throughout the world.

Most Westerners can't manage that much Sanskrit, so jyotishis working with non-Indian clients must find appropriate stotras for them in their own languages. Clients who are uncomfortable with Hindu prayers are encouraged to pray according to the canon of their own religion.

There are three ways a Westerner can work with stotras.

Prayers and Praise

1. Identify a passage several pages long in a holy text or other inspiring work that speaks to you deeply. For instance:

- "The Sermon on the Mount" from the Bible (Matthew 5 - 7)
- "The Discourse on Creation" from the *Corpus Hermetica* (Hymn III)
- "The Vision of God" from the *Bhagavad Gita* (Chapter 21)

Choose a passage that extols the divine, nature or the spirit. Avoid any passages that are a litany of demands for material things you need or want or that condemn other people. Set aside a regular time every day to read the passage. Don't rush through it, no matter how rushed you are. Read it carefully, out loud if necessary, so that you can savor every word. In this way no matter how many times you read it, each time it will transport you into an exalted state of consciousness. You enter a sacred space within yourself where you make contact with a reality higher than your ordinary awareness. It is attaining that state, not just mindlessly reading the passage, that clears away bad karma and invokes positive new possibilities.

2. Select a prayer you especially love. (I've listed a number of sample prayers in the next few pages.) The words of a favorite hymn will also do. Select a time every day (preferably twice a day) when you can sit for 5, 10 or 15 minutes and repeat the prayer over and over. The point is not to mindlessly repeat the words. If the prayer doesn't come from your heart, it doesn't count. Sit down in a quiet place, relax, focus your mind and open your heart to the living presence of divine grace. Then repeat the prayer with concentration, in a spirit of love and thankfulness. This feels like giving your soul a bath. When you finish, you'll feel spiritually cleansed and filled with joy and hope.

3. Set aside a few minutes each morning before you begin work and each evening before you go to bed. Take a moment to calm your mind by focusing briefly on your inhalations and exhalations. When your thought processes begin to quiet down, open your heart to the living presence of divine love that fills and surrounds you, in fact that permeates the entire cosmos. Mentally speak to God, the Divine Mother or your Higher Self. You don't need a prepared statement or formal prayer. Simply speak as a child would to its parent or a friend to a friend or a lover to the beloved. Don't focus so much on telling the divinity what you want or need. Instead focus on the divine, expressing your love, gratitude and amazement at its grace and majesty. Try to speak not just from your mind but from your heart. If tears come, let them come. They are washing away your bad karma and anointing a special seat for God in your heart. When your prayer is finished, don't get up right away. Sit for at least another half minute in stillness.

Ammachi, the great saint from Kerala in southwestern India, says that five minutes of sincerely crying to God is far more valuable than hours of unfocused meditation. If meditating is difficult for you, try working with stotras and prayer instead. You don't need to spend a lot of time but you do need to make a living connection with the source of healing and grace in order for this upaya to be effective. Don't get up till you genuinely feel you've connected with divine grace, even if only for a moment.

Here are a number of formal prayers you can consider using as an upaya. We begin with the greatest prayer of the Christian tradition, the Lord's Prayer. The last phrase of that prayer is "For Thine is the power and the glory forever and ever." You may be interested to learn that in the original version the words "forever and ever" are actually "throughout all the cycles of time." Blessings for all our planetary cycles are exactly what we're praying for.

Rx PRAISE
Select a special passage, several pages long, describing or praising God or Goddess, nature or the spirit. Read it every day for three months, allowing it to transport you into a state of grace.

Christian Prayers

The Lord's Prayer
Our Father Who art in heaven,
Hallowed be Thy name.
Thy kingdom come.
Thy will be done on Earth as it is in heaven.
Give us this day our daily bread,
And forgive our sins as we forgive those who sin against us.
Lead us not into temptation
But deliver us from evil.
For Thine is the kingdom and the power and the glory
Forever and ever. Amen.

Glory Be
Glory be to the Father, to the Son, and to the Holy Spirit.
As it was in the beginning, is now, and ever shall be,
world without end. Amen.

Hail Mary
Hail Mary, full of grace, the Lord is with thee.
Blessed art thou among women,
and blessed is the fruit of thy womb, Jesus.
Holy Mary, mother of God, pray for us sinners
Now and at the hour of our death. Amen.

Jewish Prayers

Prayer from the Siddur
I gratefully thank You, O living and eternal King,
Because You have returned my soul within me with compassion.
Abundant is Your faithfulness!

Prayer from the Sh'ma Yisroel
Hear O Israel,
The Lord is our God.
The Lord is One!

Islamic Prayer

Everything is perishing but Your face.
There is no God but You.
Do not hold back from me
Your everlasting beauty.

Buddhist Prayer

With deepest reverence I submit my body, speech and mind,
To You who protect all living beings without exception,
To You who conquered everything there is to conquer,
To You who perfectly understand everything that exists.
I offer everything I am and everything I can imagine,
And pray for the welfare of all beings from beginningless time.

Pagan Prayer

To the Sun and the Moon, the planets and stars,
To the wind and the rain, the earth and the rivers,
To the trees and the mountains, the deserts and oceans,
Blessings! Blessings! Blessings!
To the men and the angels, the snakes and the spirits,
To women and whales, the wolves in the forest,
To children and lovers, the dead and the living,
Blessings! Blessings! Blessings!

Hindu Prayers

Vedic astrologers are often inclined to prescribe prayers from Hinduism, the mystical tradition from which their system of astrology arose. People who grew up in monotheistic religions sometimes feel uncomfortable with praying to "false gods." If you prefer a prayer or mantra associated with your own religious tradition, be sure to clarify your feelings with your jyotishi.

Just so you know though, the Hindu perspective is that no matter what god or goddess you pray to, your prayer winds up in the same mailbox with everyone else's, because there aren't any false gods—there really is only one God. The *Rig Veda* uses hundreds of different names for God yet repeatedly reaffirms that they're only different words for the same divine reality. Incidently, the Judeo-Christian name for God, Yahveh, occurs 21 times in *Rig Veda.* Perhaps Hindus were honoring Yahveh many centuries before Abraham and Isaac were born. (The name Ila, which linguists say is etymologically identical to Allah, occurs too.) If God's grace truly is limitless, couldn't his Holy Spirit be working through the Hindu tradition too?

All Hindu prayers begin with the syllable Om, the most sacred mantra of all. It's the Hindu version of Yahveh's divine words in the Bible, "I am." When the Supreme God first uttered the sound Om, he announced his existence, and all the universe came into being to worship him. When we say Om with loving awareness, we align ourselves with the infinite source of all things.

Prayer to Agni

Prayers to Agni are recommended:

1. While you are running a Sun cycle.
2. If the Sun is poorly placed or afflicted in your Vedic chart.
3. For increased self-confidence.
4. To intensify your connection with your Higher Self.

Om. With loving reverence I bow to Lord Agni,
Who is the power of consciousness itself.
He fills the sky with splendor and the mind with insight.
Dispeller of darkness, protector of life,
Graciously light my way.
I bow again and again to the sacred fire.

Agni is cosmic fire, the transformative force of the universe. He turns matter into energy, annihilating form to release essence. He manifests on Earth as fire, in the atmosphere as lightning, and in heaven as the Sun. In our bodies he is digestive fire, in our minds he is the power of understanding, and in spirit he is the bright light people see at the time of death.

In the holy Veda Agni is especially honored as the High Priest who carries our prayers to heaven, connecting us with the source of our being. Ultimately, he is the energy of consciousness itself, the only force that can burn away karma.

Prayer to Uma

Prayers to Uma should be done:

1. While you are running a Moon cycle.
2. If the Moon is poorly placed or afflicted in your Vedic chart.
3. For a tranquil and illumined mind.
4. For a deeper sense of compassion.

Om.
With loving reverence I bow to the daughter of the mountain
Whose glowing face fills my mind with delight,
And whose sidelong glances melt the glaciers of my heart.
Sipping the nectar of Uma's loving smile,
My soul bathes in her soft radiance.
To the moon-faced one, again and again,
I offer the lotus petals of my devotion.

Uma, the mother of all beings, is also called Parvati, which means "the daughter of the mountain." According to legend, as a young woman she practiced spiritual disciplines in the Himalayas. Shiva, the divine reality, was so enchanted by her devotion that he asked her to marry him. Uma's dazzling beauty is represented by the full Moon, but when she merges with her husband at the time of the new Moon, she disappears into his solar light so completely you can't even see her.

In the same way, when our inner Moon (the mind) merges in the light of pure spirit during worship, meditation and selfless activity, we experience something greater than ourselves that illumines our actions and relationships.

Prayer to Hanuman

Prayers to Hanuman are indicated:

1. While you are running a Mars cycle.
2. If Mars is poorly placed or afflicted in your Vedic chart.
3. For energy, enthusiasm and an indomitable spirit.
4. For devotion to the Supreme Divinity.

Om.
I bow to the son of the cyclone
Who lovingly surrenders his irresistable might
At the feet of the Supreme Lord.
His very nature is unselfish service.
His stainless heart brims with devotion.
Hanuman easily lifts the mountain
For love of the Lord of Love.
I bow again and again to Hanuman,
Who embodies faith and strength.

Long ago an evil king kidnapped Sita, the devoted wife of Rama, lord of the universe. Sita is the human soul, abducted by material desires and concerns. But God loves the soul so intensely he will do anything to get her back. In an Indian epic called the *Ramayana,* the monkey king Hanuman helps Rama rescue his wife. When Rama needed a medicinal plant from a certain mountain, Hanuman brought the mountain itself back to Rama. To deliver a message to Sita, Hanuman leaped over the ocean. He is the son of the wind, one of the strongest forces in nature. He represents pure faith and passionate devotion, which make the impossible possible.

Prayer to Sarasvati

Prayers to Sarasvati should be done:

1. While you are running a Mercury cycle.
2. If Mercury is poorly placed or afflicted in your Vedic chart.
3. For intellectual power, mental clarity and the ability to use words brilliantly.
4. For enhanced artistic talent and inspiration.

Om. With loving reverence I bow to the Mother of the Universe
Who is the supreme creative force,
Who is the divine wisdom
And the universal intelligence,
Who is ever celebrating the Supreme Awareness,
Who is the matrix from which maya and moksha both emerge,
Who has infinite power, infinite glory and infinite majesty.
With awe, with adoration, and with rapture
I bow to the Mother of the Worlds.

Sarasvati is the goddess of creative energy who brought the universe into being. She's also the holy river Sarasvati that courses through the sky, which we in the West know as the Milky Way. Musicians, actors and other artists propitiate her before performances, speakers ask her grace before beginning a lecture, and school children appeal to her for help on their tests. She illuminates the intellect and is the source of all artistic inspiration. From her also emanate all worldly and spiritual knowledge. The word *maya* means the world we see around us, the expression of Sarasvati's majesty. *Moksha* means enlightenment.

Prayer to Indra

Prayers to Indra are especially good:

1. While you are running a Jupiter cycle.
2. If Jupiter is poorly placed or afflicted in your Vedic chart.
3. For strength, courage and capability.
4. For self-mastery and spiritual insight.

Om. With loving reverence I bow to the king of heaven,
The commander of angels,
Who casts his net over the worlds
And whose face is reflected in every knot.
Wielding the lightning, he shatters the darkness,
Unleashing torrents of joy.
The lord of thunder rules my heart,
He who gives strength, courage, and illumination,
Whose glance bestows victory.
I bow again and again to Lord Indra!

The chief deity of the ancient world was called Indra in India, Marduk in Iraq, Zeus in Greece, Jupiter in Rome, and Thor in Europe. In every culture his legend is the same: he is the dragonslayer who wields the thunderbolt and sends down rain. The yogis in India call him the masterful soul, because he mastered his senses and searched without ceasing till he found his innermost Self, conquering the serpent of kundalini. His net is maya, the force of cosmic illusion, yet his beautiful face—the face of limitless, creative awareness—is reflected in every atom in the cosmos.

Prayer to Lakshmi

Pray to Lakshmi:

1. While you are running a Venus cycle.
2. If Venus is poorly placed or afflicted in your Vedic chart.
3. For prosperity and well being.
4. For children and a harmonious family life.

> Om.
> With loving reverence I bow to Mother Lakshmi
> Whose very nature is harmony,
> Who is ever brimming with compassion, forgiveness and delight,
> Who is the source of all abundance
> And the ever flowing font of health, wealth, and happiness.
> I bow to the supremely beautiful one,
> Who is welcome in every home and in every heart.
> To that ever gracious one
> Who is the loving mother of all beings,
> I bow with respect, with gratitude and with devotion.

Lakshmi is the fantastically popular goddess whose image you'll find everywhere in India. She's the goddess of prosperity and source of all blessings, both spiritual and material. She makes everything beautiful and delightful. She is quick to help and to forgive. She is also notoriously quick to depart when we close our hearts to others. As she is generous to us, she expects us to be generous to others.

Prayer to Shiva

Prayers to Shiva may be prescribed:

1. While you are running a Saturn cycle.
2. If Saturn is poorly placed or afflicted in your Vedic chart.
3. For freedom from depression, sloth, feelings of ill will, sickness and unhappiness.
4. For enlightenment.

Om.
With loving reverence I bow to Lord Shiva,
Who is naked as consciousness itself,
Who is garlanded with space and time,
And whose overflowing bliss
Spills forth as galaxies.
The Supreme Lord is tranquil as the ocean depths
And active as the waves of the sea.
His grace is limitless.
I bow again and again to the lord of the universe!

Shiva, the Supreme Consciousness, is often pictured as a yogi meditating alone in the Himalayas. He is usually nude, with deadly snakes wrapped around his arms.

Otherwise he is shown as Nataraja, "the lord of the dance," his arms whirling while his hands form gestures of blessing, one foot gracefully raised, in the midst of a circle of fire. Shiva is both motionless absolute being, and the play of energy that manifests as the universe.

Though he looks intimidating and withdrawn, Shiva is famous for easily granting boons, because his very nature is grace.

Prayer to Kali/Durga

Prayers to Kali and/or to Durga are good to do:

1. While you are running a Rahu cycle.
2. If Rahu is poorly placed or afflicted in your Vedic chart.
3. When you need inner strength.
4. To overcome addictions or unhealthy cravings.

Om.
With loving reverence I bow to the Mother who removes ignorance.
With loving reverence I bow to the Mother who removes fear.
With loving reverence I bow to the Mother who bestows victory.
Homage to Mother Kali! Homage to Mother Durga!

Durga is the warrior goddess who rides a lion into battle against the selfishness and egotism within us and against injustice in the world around us. Although she's an invincible fighter, she is always serene. Kali is the frightening looking goddess projected from Durga's frown. Kali looks scary, like death, but in reality is the very essence of love. She assumes a wrathful form to protect us and to teach us to love others unconditionally, as she loves us. Her gift is not just knowledge about the blissful heart of reality, but the actual experience of it.

Prayer to Ganesh

Prayers to Ganesh are especially appropriate:

1. While you are running a Ketu cycle.
2. If Ketu is poorly placed or afflicted in your Vedic chart.
3. If you feel psychologically blocked or your life feels "stuck."
4. When you start an important new project.

Om.
With loving reverence I bow to Lord Ganesh
Who is commander of the constellations,
Who holds the orbits of the atoms
And the orbits of the galaxies
In the vast expanse of his awareness,
Who has infinite strength,
Infinite wisdom, and infinite compassion,
Who is the remover of obstacles
And the drinker of milk,
Who is the great hearted one,
Who is the ever delightful one.
I bow again and again to Lord Ganesh!

Ganesh is the elephant-headed deity who clears the obstructions on our path to material fulfillment and spiritual realization. As I mentioned in Chapter 13, on September 21, 1995, offerings of milk to Lord Ganesh began dematerializing in Hindu temples and homes throughout the world. Since that date the phrase "drinker of milk" has been added to his titles. Some traditions also associate Ganesh with Jupiter.

Prayer for the Three Worlds

Om.
May all beings be happy and well.
May all beings be happy and well.
May all beings be happy and well.
Om, peace, peace, peace!

In this traditional Hindu blessing you first visualize all the creatures in the world around you. When you repeat the blessing a second time you visualize all the beings in the astral realms, the souls who have passed through the gate of death into the immaterial worlds. When you repeat it the third time you send blessings even to the angels. As you say the prayer, engulf the entire universe in love.

Prayer for Enlightenment

Om.
From delusion, lead us to truth.
From darkness, lead us to light.
From death, lead us to immortality.
Om, peace, peace, peace!

This is one of the oldest prayers in the world. In Hinduism immortality doesn't mean that the body never dies. Hinduism has made peace with the fact that every material thing—even the universe itself—must perish. Instead it means that the focus of your attention shifts permanently from your mortal self (the body and lower mind) to the immortal part of your being, the Atman or Inner Spirit.

Prayers to the Planets

Prayer to the Sun
Om. With loving reverence I bow to the Sun
Who is the majestic lord of our world system,
Who is the ever flowing font of light, heat and life force,
Who is reverently worshipped by all creatures and all cultures,
Who is invincible,
Who is the illuminator.
Homage to Lord Surya!

Prayer to the Moon
Om. With loving reverence I bow to the Moon
Who is the lord of the mind and the maker of the month,
Whose cool radiance delights all creatures,
Who is ruler of the waters and husband of the stars.
Homage to Lord Soma!

Prayer to Mars
Om. With loving reverence I bow to Mars
Who is the fiery red one,
Who is full of courage and dynamism,
Who actively benefits all beings.
Homage to Lord Mangala!

Prayer to Mercury
Om. With loving reverence I bow to Mercury
Who is lord of the intellect and master of communication,
Who is full of wit and full of wisdom,
And source of our inspiration.
Homage to Lord Budha!

Prayer to Jupiter
Om. With loving reverence I bow to Jupiter
Who is the living exemplar of goodness,
Who is full of wisdom and benevolence
And whose gracious glance is desired by all beings.
Homage to Lord Guruji!

Prayer to Venus

Om.
With loving reverence I bow to Venus
Who is the diamond of the sky and the lord of delight,
Who is highly intelligent and ever benevolent,
Who is the ever flowing font of wisdom and protection.
Homage to Lord Shukra!

Prayer to Saturn

Om.
With loving reverence I bow to Saturn
Who is the lord of time and the keeper of karma,
Who gives self-discipline, self-reliance,
Endurance and lasting success,
Who is the protector of longevity.
Homage to Lord Shani!

Prayer to Rahu

Om.
With loving reverence I bow to Rahu
Who is the powerful one,
Who grants fame and fortune
And gives worldly success.
Homage to Lord Rahu!

Prayer to Ketu

Om.
With loving reverence I bow to Ketu
Who is the great ascetic,
Who is the harbinger of liberation
And the bestower of spiritual success.
Homage to Lord Ketu!

RX PRAYER

In the morning before you begin work, and again in the evening before you go to bed, spend at least five minutes in heart-felt prayer. Make this a life-long practice.

DEVOTIONAL MUSIC

Devotional music is the one upaya I'd recommend without reservation to everyone. Indian saints have said it's the perfect upaya for the present world cycle because it's so easy and so joyous.

Many people are severely resistant to spiritual disciplines because they feel that they work hard enough in life, why take on the additional work of an upaya? Kirtan is the one remedial measure that no one experiences as work—it's pure pleasure. Kirtan means chanting the names of God or Goddess and singing hymns of praise. Until very recently most Hindus did not own televisions. Instead of watching TV or DVDs, people would get together in the evening to sing to God. Watching Baul villagers in North India holding kirtan, I was blown away by the intensity of the passion with which they sing. These people have tremendous feeling for God, and express it freely and fully in their music.

There are two ways music can be used as an upaya.

1. Set aside an evening every week for singing to God. If there are hymns you particularly love, indulge yourself in this divine music. In California where I live, *bhajans* (love-saturated Hindu hymns) have recently become immensely popular, and public events featuring bhajan singers like Krishna Das, Jai Uttal or Bhagavan Das are invariably standing room only. Sing alone at home if you feel more comfortable, or invite friends over for a sing-along. These are lots of fun, especially if a few participants can play musical instruments.

If you're singing by yourself or would like some instrumental accompaniment, you may want to put on a tape or CD of devotional music. Here are a few CDs I recommend. These beautiful Hindu chants have been Americanized enough to make them accessible to the Western ear.

- *Breath of the Heart* by Krishna Das
- *Live on Earth* (For a Limited Time Only) by Krishna Das
- *Best of Both Worlds* by Ragani

You can purchase Krishna Das's music, as well as his DVD introduction to kirtan called *The Yoga of Chant,* at www.KarunaMusic.com. Ragani's CD is available at www.RaganiWorld.com. All are available through Yes International Publishers at www.yespublishers.com.

Don't worry if you can't hold a tune. Sing out with your whole soul anyway. Remember, it's the music from your heart, not from your lips, that God enjoys most.

2. If you can play an instrument, spend an evening every week consciously making music for the divinity within you. It doesn't matter whether there's anyone else there to hear you or not. Play for God. You may wish to practice beforehand so that you can play for God as perfectly as possible.

In India, musicians and dancers sometimes perform simply for their creator, with no one else present. It's their offering to the divine artist who did such a beautiful job crafting the world.

Soon you'll find that you're singing while you're washing the dishes, driving to work, or waiting in line at the supermarket. My husband and I often play bhajans for hours a day. I catch myself doing kirtan even in my dreams. This divine chanting is an effortless way to keep God in the forefront of your consciousness. St. Paul said, "Pray without ceasing." I always thought that was impossible until I was introduced to kirtan.

Devotional music has a tremendously purifying effect on the soul, much like mantras. Meditations immediately afterward are extraordinarily powerful. It's as if the music pouring forth from the divine awareness inside you effortlessly pulls you back to its source.

Rx MAKING MUSIC
Once every week for the next year, spend 1 1/2 - 2 hours singing or playing music for the Divine Spirit.

SILENCE

Lots of people recognize the need to develop spiritually. However, Western culture is almost exclusively geared toward drawing our attention outward toward the people and events around us—and the products those people are selling. Learning to redirect our attention to our inner states is difficult for most people raised in such a materially oriented climate. For us, practicing *mauna*, silence, is a perfect introduction to the interior life.

Jyotishis will prescribe silence for clients whose charts show they're ready to begin the inner journey or who need to learn to be more sensitive to the needs of others. It creates the mental room necessary to reflect on one's inner states. It also helps clients be more conscious of what other people are doing and saying. When the opportunity to speak is closed off, the opportunity to listen opens.

People have no idea how much energy it takes to constantly engage in conversation. In this respect, practicing silence is often a real revelation. You'll have so much more energy and clarity of consciousness at the end of the day, you'll be amazed.

The first step in keeping silence is to arrange a day in which you don't have to talk to anyone. Notes can be passed when offering information is critical, but this should be kept to a minimum.

Usually when people first engage in this practice they become intensely aware of the noise in their minds. The mind is a veritable chatter box, a constant stream of judgments, recriminations, ruminations, fantasies and inner gossip. The second step in keeping silence is to begin letting go of some of this inner garbage and cultivating inner stillness.

Rx SILENCE

One day a week for the next four months, practice silence.
Arrange the day so you don't have to speak.
Cultivate inner stillness as well as outer silence on that day.

Another form of this upaya, which for some people is more difficult, is to consciously practice kind speech. May a vow that for a certain number of days (perhaps one week each month) you will not say anything dishonest, spiteful, sarcastic or cynical. Monitor your speech; ensure that it's constructive and supportive. For those few days the part of you that mocks and criticizes others will remain silent.

The point of this practice is not to turn you into an insipid goody-goody. It's just to make you more conscious of the quality of energy you put out to the world. According to the law of karma, everything you project outward will ultimately come back to you. It also affects the psychic atmosphere around you, the collective karma, whether you're aware of this or not. Becoming more aware of the quality of your speech is one of the best ways to gauge your level of spiritual maturity. Your speech is a prime indicator of the karmic patterns at play in your subconscious.

Keep in mind that every opportunity for authentic self-awareness, such as that provided by keeping silent or monitoring one's speech, is a chance to untie knots of karma that bind us to unhealthy habits and unhelpful attitudes, and to clear out the karmic debris that litters our unconscious.

Rx KIND SPEECH

One day each month for the next four months, keep all your critical thoughts to yourself. On that day make sure all your comments are positive and supportive. Focus on remaining emotionally centered. Find the place in your heart that genuinely likes and appreciates other people. When others speak to you, move your awareness to that place inside yourself and respond to them with a smile.

17

Vedic Astrological Prescriptions II: Mental Upayas

The next set of astrological remedies use special mental techniques to help you see through your problems and frustrations to your inherent spiritual power. They also engage your emotions in order to put an end to conflict and dissatisfaction you may feel. They use your mind to take you beyond your mind to the unfettered part of your being that's the source of the healing energy and creative power you need to make the most of your time on earth.

Mental upayas that engage the intellect are designed to amplify a person's level of self-awareness. In the Vedic tradition, self understanding is considered a panacea in dealing with karmic entanglements. Mental upayas that also engage the emotions are designed to cleanse the *karmashaya* (karmic traces in the causal body), open the heart and purify the channels of intuition.

Indications: Some of these upayas are superb for people with enlivened, inquisitive minds. Others are ideal for people with a deep emotional nature.

Contraindications: Like mantric prescriptions, mental upayas have a strong inward focus. They should not be practiced by people who are mentally unstable or who may be frightened by the contents of their inner world. (These people should be assigned physical upayas.) Self surrender is not appropriate for extremely passive personality types, who need to practice a more self-directed method. In some cases, people who are extremely intellectually focused will experience more personal growth performing non-mental *upayas* such as selfless service or devotional practices.

SPIRITUAL STUDY

Taking time every day to read from the Bhagavad Gita, Bible, Koran, Dhammapada, Tao Te Ching or other scripture or inspirational book is an excellent way to keep yourself on track spiritually, to deepen and enrich your life, and to daily reconnect with your soul purpose. Can you spare fifteen minutes or a half hour that you would otherwise perhaps spend watching TV to read instead?

It may surprise you that reading spiritual biographies is considered an *upaya*, but I've found that many yogis recommend this one. In newspapers and on television we constantly see examples of how people should not live their lives. Criminal activities, self-destructive behaviors like drug and alcohol addiction, abusive relationships and neurotic and narcissistic lifestyles are on display night and day. Studying the lives of truly great souls, the saints, sages and authentic mystics of the spiritual traditions, sets a different standard. It shows us what we too can be when we live and love to our full potential.

There are two explicit purposes for reading this kind of material.

1. This activity redirects the mind away from other forms of entertainment that may be engaging, but aren't particularly helpful. Instead of watching TV or listening to CDs or reading novels that just keep our restless minds occupied, spiritual literature elevates the soul. It doesn't only entertain you, it also helps you grow as a person.
2. Reading about people who sincerely committed themselves to spiritual life helps you put your own life in perspective. Not all of us can be Mother Teresa, but we can use the models of these peoples' lives as an opportunity to reflect on our own, and to reevaluate our habits and goals. Reading scriptures, yoga books, and books on authentic mystical experience also challenges us to think seriously about our purpose in life. It provides us with vivid examples of how we can improve ourselves, and opens our hearts with inspiring stories and information.

A few spiritual biographies I'd recommend are:

- *Autobiography of a Yogi* by Paramahansa Yogananda
- *The Gospel of Sri Ramakrishna,* translated by Swami Nikhilananda (abridged edition)

- *Living with the Himalayan Masters* by Swami Rama
- *Shree Maa: The Story of a Saint* by Swami Satyananda
- *Walking with a Himalayan Master* by Justin O'Brien (Swami Jaidev Bharati)
- *Women of Power and Grace* by Timothy Conway
- *Daughters of the Goddess: The Women Saints of India* by (yours truly) Linda Johnsen

Of the countless excellent books on other spiritual topics I'd recommend:

- *Awaken Children!* by Mata Amritanandamayi (any of the first eight books in the series)
- *The Essential Rumi* by Coleman Barks with John Moyne
- *The Essential Kabbalah* by Daniel Matt
- *From Death to Birth* by Rajmani Tigunait
- *The Power of Now* by Eckhart Tolle

Rx: LEARN ABOUT SPIRITUAL LIFE

Every 2 weeks over the next year, read at least one spiritual book or watch a video about the life of a saint. Keep spirituality in the forefront of your consciousness. Allow your reading to inspire you to actively look for ways to spiritualize your life.

When you study a spiritual book as an upaya, you don't read as if you were cramming for a test. After the test, generally you forget everything you've just read. When you read as an upaya, you're riding the crest of the inspiration these books provide in order to change the things about your life that aren't working, to improve and transform yourself. Your reading becomes a catalyst for positive changes and personal unfoldment.

THERAPEUTIC MEDITATION

I mentioned mantra meditation in the last chapter. It releases the spiritual blessings inherent in a mantra and introduces you to your Inner Self. But when you use meditation for self-study, you focus explicitly on releasing unhealthy feelings nestled in your unconscious. When an "inner demon" is recognized and let go of in meditation, it loses its ability to wreak havoc in your life. Here's how to do it.

Cleaning Out Your Subconscious

1. Sit up straight on a meditation cushion or hard chair. Keep your back straight but not tense. Your goal is to be both comfortable and alert. Close your eyes.

2. Bring your full attention to the bridge between your nostrils. Feel the air flowing in and out of your nostrils. Focus on your breath for at least one full minute. Your breath should be slow, smooth, even and continuous, without any jerkiness. As you focus here, your breath and heart rate will gradually slow down. You'll start to feel physically relaxed but mentally lucid.

3. Bring your full awareness to the inside of your brain at a point several inches behind the point where your eyebrows meet. Keep your forehead relaxed.

4. Mentally repeat your mantra. You will keep mentally saying your mantra throughout this exercise. If you don't have a mantra, repeat *Soham.* (This is pronounced like "So hum a tune.") This mantra means "I am pure spirit."

5. Thoughts, images and feelings will enter your awareness. At first these may be trivial thoughts like some snatch of a conversation you overheard earlier or the memory of what you had for dinner a few hours ago. Then more powerful memories and desires buried in your subconscious may start to bubble up. Don't start thinking about them or reacting to their emotional content; instead just calmly observe them. Keep the mantra going.

6. Watch the thoughts and images that arise dispassionately. Position yourself as the observer, not a participant. It's as if you were watching a lousy TV show, or as if you were watching the traffic passing by outside. Thoughts are passing before your awareness, but don't engage your focussed attention.

7. If you find yourself starting to get drawn into the melodrama of your thoughts, return your attention to your mantra. Your mantra is the anchor for your mind. If particularly stormy feelings or distressing thoughts arise, turn your attention to the sound of your mantra. Breathe slowly,

smoothly and evenly. You are the tranquil observer who acknowledges these thoughts and feelings, and then releases them.

8. After a minimum of 15 minutes, whenever you feel finished, return your full attention to your breath. Breathe slowly and smoothly for another moment or two. Then mentally scan your body to see where you are holding any tension. Relax your head, arms, torso, abdomen and legs. Open your eyes.

This is a powerful technique for acquainting yourself with the contents of your subconscious. The point is to be aware of what's in there, but not controlled by it. So as thoughts arise, don't dwell on them, or judge or reject them. Just note that they're there and let them fade away. You are defusing the emotional charge of the unconscious feelings that dominate your life, often without your awareness.

You may find that one or two thoughts keep coming back to you with obsessive force, the memory of a person who particularly irritates you, for example. This is called a *vasana* in Sanskrit, a mental image that packs an emotional punch for better or worse, and therefore has formed a deep groove in your mind. If you get caught in the groove during your meditation, you'll start thinking more angry thoughts about that individual and feeding the vasana. But if you just keep releasing the thought of him, even if this takes numbers of meditation sessions, you'll find that your anger at this person starts to dissipate. The karmic connection between him and you—which you have created by your strong reaction to him—begins to evaporate. That person's annoying qualities lose their power over you, and one more knot of karma has been untied.

This process, correctly done, is like spring cleaning for your mind. People who are very fearful, emotionally immature, or mentally unstable should not do this practice, however.

Rx: THERAPEUTIC MEDITATION

Make a commitment that every day for the next three months, you will meditate for 15 - 20 minutes. Use breath awareness and your mantra to anchor your awareness. Then simply watch your thoughts and feelings arise. Don't engage with them; just let them come and go. You are pure consciousness, the inner observer. Become conscious of what's going on in the deeper layers of your mind.

PSYCHOLOGICAL COUNSELING

Self-study is called *svadhyaya* in Sanskrit. It's one of the most important upayas you can do because it leads to self-understanding. When you begin to study yourself you start to see how you are actually creating your destiny moment to moment, how the way people respond to you is triggered in part by your own unconscious behaviors, and how unexpected events in your life may actually have been invoked by your own thoughts, fears and expectations.

Sometimes the horoscope tell us things we aren't happy to hear, things that aren't particularly flattering—things we may recognize are true but would prefer not to face. One of the main purposes of Vedic astrology is to make the unconscious conscious. Only when we see what we're really doing, acknowledge our feelings and clarify our thought processes can we take command of the flow of our karma. Self-study requires us to take a long, honest look at our shortcomings and the areas in our lives where we feel frustrated and unfulfilled. We search for the roots of these problems in our own attitudes and actions, and make a sincere effort to change the things it is possible to change.

However, sometimes self-study is just too hard to do on our own. It's very difficult to be dispassionate when we try to evaluate ourselves. A mentor can be immensely helpful in offering an objective perspective on those parts of our lives where we are karmically "stuck."

In India, a person's guru often forces a disciple to confront negative and obstructive aspects of their karma, not just mentally or verbally but by putting them through real-life crises which can make a person painfully aware of their shortcomings. The guru's love and firm guidance push and pull the disciple to a greater state of clarity and more healthful habits.

Here in the West, a counselor can also be very useful in helping us develop deeper insight into our problems. Therapy is a wonderful upaya that fits the Western personality well. Sometimes issues it may take us years to work through on our own can be faced and released in a few months with a skilled counselor.

If there are numerous malefic aspects to the 7th house in your horoscope, for example, you may have difficulty getting along with other people or you may attract partners who take advantage of you. It's important to resolve these sorts of issues now, rather than dragging them with you into still another incarnation. A therapist can help you see the issues more clearly, offer a valuable outside perspective, and recommend different behavioral strategies that may work better for you in future relationships.

Rx: THERAPY
Commit to a course of at least six sessions of therapy with a counselor or psychologist you trust. Sincerely try to come to terms with the attitudes and behaviors that may be sabotaging your happiness.

SELF-KNOWLEDGE

Jnana yoga or the path of Self-knowledge is often called the single most powerful upaya of all. This is the practice that, when fully mastered, can fry all your karmas at once. It's the ultimate method for recognizing and continually aligning ourselves with our Highest Self, the divinity at the root of our soul, which is utterly beyond the grip of karma. This technique requires the ability to concentrate uninterruptedly as well as real spiritual maturity in order to practice it perfectly, though.

Here I'll describe two classic paths to Self-knowledge which are accessible to any person who has the ability to draw his or her attention inward. The first is the gradual path up the mountain outlined by Shankaracharya, a very famous yogi who lived (according to the Indian tradition) some five centuries before Christ. The second is the direct climb to the summit, so well articulated by the enlightened master Ramana Maharshi in the 20th century.

According to Shankaracharya, there are three steps in the process of Self-knowledge.

1. Study. Learn all you can about the nature of your mind and the nature of reality itself from scholars, scientists and saints who've already carefully investigated them. Educate yourself about spirit and nature.

2. Contemplate. Once you have a broad general knowledge about God, the soul, and the nature of the world, choose a central truth to contemplate deeply such as, "Everything that exists is divine" or "God is everything and I am part of God." Don't just accept it as a truism. Really think about it.

3. Experience. It's not enough to know a spiritual truth intellectually, to simply think, for example, that your innermost soul is one with the Divine Being. It's one thing to know the king lives in the castle; it's quite another to meet him. Dive deep into the truth you've been contemplating. Carry it with you into meditation. Live with it till it becomes your living reality—till you directly experience it as the actual truth.

When you truly experience yourself as the immortal spirit you are in reality, unfettered by time or space, then karma no longer binds you. Karma only controls the things that exist within time and space. Karmic law cannot follow you into spirit. The greatest masters experience themselves as pure spirit, and become conduits for healing and blessing energy through the force of this Self-realization. Ramana Maharshi recommended the process of Self-inquiry to make this experience a living reality in your life.

Self -Inquiry

1. Sit comfortably in an upright position. Close your eyes, withdrawing your awareness from the sights and sounds around you, from everything that's not truly you.

2. Bring your full attention to your head and shoulders, chest and waist, back and abdomen, arms and legs. This is your physical body, but it's not really you. At death it passes away, but you will go on. Who are you really?

3. Pay attention to the energy surging through your body. It's making your heart beat, your lungs expand and contract, the blood course through your veins, your stomach gurgle. The force orchestrating this movement is your prana, your vital force. It belongs to you, but it's not really you. Who are you really?

4. Shift your awareness to your thoughts and feelings. This is the intimate part of your nature you usually identify as yourself. Yet, if you pay close attention you'll find that you have thoughts and feelings, but those thoughts and feelings aren't really you. They change from moment to moment, yet you remain the same. Who are you really?

5. Ask yourself, "Who am I really?" Contemplate deeply, searching inside for the one who is not your thoughts but thinks your thoughts, the one who manifests through your body and vital energy and mental states.

6. Simply be aware of your own awareness. This is the pure consciousness that is having the experience of your life, yet lies beyond this experience. It's not your thoughts and feelings, but the one who observes them. This is your true Inner Self, your immortal being. This is the pure witnessing consciousness that neither death nor karma can ever affect. Rest in your own pure awareness for as long as you can hold your attention there.

7. Return your attention to your physical body and open your eyes. Take a moment to relax and absorb this experience before you get up.

You are a multi-dimensional being. Your awareness manifests on many different planes. Once you become intimately acquainted with your innermost being you can draw on its infinite resources to help you overcome any obstacle or shortcoming shown in your Vedic chart. The yogis say that all karma is incinerated in the fire of Self-knowledge. The famous inscription over the temple at Delphi, the center of the ancient Greek world, said, "Know Thyself." People arrived at Delphi from all over Europe hoping to consult the oracle there. Yet the greatest advice it had to offer was that inscribed over the entrance where anyone could read it for free. Know Thyself.

Self-knowledge is the greatest of all cures for what ails us. Ultimately, though, the "Self" referred to here is not the mind and its incessant chatter (we may already know our own minds quite well and that hasn't helped us much at all), but the Higher Self or immortal spirit at the center of our being.

Rx: SELF KNOWLEDGE
Every day without fail for the next three months, spend at least ten minutes practicing Self-inquiry. Make contact with your innermost Self. Spend time there. Get to know your Self.

VISUALIZATION

Sometimes, it's just not possible to physically accomplish an upaya you really want to do. Perhaps you'd like to make a pilgrimage to Mount Calvary in Palestine or to Mount Kailash in Tibet, but your Vedic chart shows you don't have the money for airfare, or you're not healthy enough to travel. Perhaps you sincerely wish you had millions of dollars to donate to the poor, but your chart is full of daridra yogas (planetary combinations which signal poverty) and you don't have a dime to spare. In the Hindu and Buddhist traditions, you are encouraged to do good deeds in your mind if you are unable to do them physically. Instead of fantasizing about a trip to a luxury resort in Hawaii, fantasize about visiting Jerusalem, the Himalayas, or some other place that's sacred to you. Imagine the saints you would meet there and what you would learn from them. Or visualize all the wealth you can hold in a single mental image and offer every bit of it to God. Yogis use the power of imagination to reshape their attitudes, to cultivate qualities like generosity and to educate themselves. By powerfully energizing an image of yourself as, for example, a pilgrim or a prosperous donor, you can set in motion the karma that will actually make these events occur for real in your next life, or possibly even later in this life.

Visualization is an important tool in the astrologer's kit of upayas. In the Vedic tradition, our thoughts and daydreams are not just idle fantasies but form an actual alternate reality. This concept is part of the Christian tradition, too. Remember how Jesus said that if a man even fantasizes about committing adultery, as far as God is concerned, he's actually done it? That sounds harsh to us today, but there is an important teaching here about the karmic impact of our thoughts.

Many Vedic upayas harness the positive power of the imagination and use it to work through karmic complexes symbolically rather than literally. If you can't get your boat loose because it's tied to the pier, you have to get out of the boat and physically untie the rope. But karmic bondage consists of knots in consciousness. These can be untied through symbolic physical acts or through movements in consciousness itself. You can anthropomorphize your problem, by imagining it as a planet for example, and propitiating that planet. In this way, you mentally make peace with the troubling qualities it represents.

Here is an example of using the power of visualization as an upaya.

Burning Bad Karma

1. Sit comfortably with your head, neck and trunk straight. Close your eyes.

2. For a minute or two, simply watch your breath. It will spontaneously slow down and become smoother and lighter. Keep your awareness on your breathing cycle until you feel tranquil and mentally clear.

3. Now shift your full mental concentration inside your brain. Focus on the point several inches behind the junction on your forehead where your eyebrows meet. Then shift your awareness upwards a little bit more, though not to the very top of your skull. This point above your ajna chakra or "third eye" is the jnana chakra, a center of consciousness associated with discriminating wisdom. If you experience a sensation of deep pleasure, which may be associated with a cool, milky light, you've arrived at the *soma* chakra. Move past this till you find the jnana chakra. Its quality is a vivid sense of intense, focused intelligence.

4. At the jnana chakra, imagine a searingly hot bonfire burning with intense brightness. Visualize it so vividly that you can virtually feel its heat and hear the crackle of the flames. Now visualize a painful situation you want to grow out of, or qualities in your personality you want to be rid of, as a very dry, brittle log. Throw the log into the fire of consciousness and watch it slowly burn to ashes.

5. Now picture the bonfire transforming into a pure white light that completely fills the field of your awareness. It is the very embodiment of wisdom and blessing power. Feel its living energy surge through you, purifying your body and mind. Sit for a moment surrounded and permeated by this light.

6. Return your attention to your breath. Breathe slowly and evenly for a few moments, then open your eyes.

People with vivid imaginations can benefit immensely from this type of practice. Merely fantasizing that your inner or outer obstacles are being incinerated, however, is not the same as focused yogic visualization and is unlikely to give you much relief. A fantasy is transformed into an upaya that has real power when you apply intense focus of your will coupled with an absolutely sincere desire to improve your life. There must be complete, uninterrupted focus. You must repeat the visualization every day without fail until the inner work is done. Ten minutes of laser-like focus will do 100% more good than an hour of listless fantasizing.

Rx: VISUALIZATION

Spend at least ten minutes every day for the next three months in meditation, offering your problems and shortcomings into the fire of consciousness. Vividly imagine this literally occurring. Knots of bad karma are incinerated in the purifying flames of inner intelligence.

Visualizing the Planets

Another powerful way of working with visualization is to vividly imagine yourself in a reverent relationship with the planetary intelligence who represents an imbalance in your Vedic chart. In the last chapter, I described five different levels of Self-consciousness. The third level was *pashyanti,* the level at which consciousness communicates with itself through symbolic images. This reflects a deeper dimension of reality than spoken words or thoughts. Learning to work constructively with this level of your awareness is a positive way to channel the mental energy usually frittered away in daydreams.

In this technique, we create a visual symbol or an anthropomorphic form of the planet causing problems in our chart and worship it. By honoring the planetary energy we begin to heal the imbalance in our psyche that's playing out as problems in our outer world. There are four ways to visualize a planetary intelligence.

1. Visualize the physical planet itself. Find a color photograph of the planet and memorize the image in detail. However, when you're doing the upaya you will need to keep in mind that it is the living intelligence of the planet, not its physical crust or gaseous atmosphere, that you're entering into a relationship with.

2. Visualize a symbol that represents the planet. In India, you would visualize the first two letters of the planet's name. The beautiful Indian scripts lend themselves very well to this process, but the plainer looking English letters are less psychologically appealing. Better to use the classical Western glyphs:

☉	Sun	☽	Moon	♂	Mars
☿	Mercury	♃	Jupiter	♀	Venus
♄	Saturn	☊	Rahu	☋	Ketu

3. Visualize the classical deity associated with the planet. Page through a book filled with color pictures of Greek statues or Roman paintings till you find an image of the appropriate god that strongly appeals to you. Use an image of Apollo for the Sun, Diana or Artemis for the Moon, and so on. If you already have an extremely vivid image in your mind for a deity like Zeus (Jupiter) or Aries (Mars) or Aphrodite (Venus), use that instead. For Rahu and Ketu, use an image of a potentially dangerous snake. The raised head of a cobra with its fangs extended is ideal for Rahu. The full, coiled body of a cobra or rattlesnake is best for Ketu.

4. Visualize the Indian deity associated with each planet.

Sun Lord Surya is an extraordinarily handsome, well-built, mature man with blond hair. He is dressed like a great warrior in splendid armor, and wears a breathtaking crown and many exquisite, shining gems. His whole body is radiant. His face is lit with a beautiful smile.

Moon Lord Chandra is an extremely handsome young man with a light complexion. He has a round face, beautiful eyes and a soft body.

Mars Lord Mangala is a young man with a slim, muscular body and quick, angry eyes. He looks impatient and physically powerful, but also noble and generous.

Mercury Lord Budha is a thin adolescent boy with beautiful features. His eyes sparkle with lively intelligence. He is quick to smile, and seems young and impressionable.

Jupiter Lord Brihaspati is a handsome, heavy-set, middle-aged man. He looks calm, serious, kind and well educated. He is deeply spiritual and sincerely wants to help others.

Venus Lord Shukra is stunningly good-looking and elegantly dressed. He projects breathtaking sensuality, keen intelligence, deep spirituality.

Saturn Lord Shani has a tall, lean, aged body. He wear a dark, ragged cloak. His eyes are dark and hard. He looks pitiless, but also wise and completely honest.

Rahu Lord Rahu is a scowling mature man with a dark complexion, and a thick black moustache and heavy eyebrows. He is dressed in pricey but tasteless clothes and wears too much flashy jewelry.

Ketu Lord Ketu is a wandering mendicant of indeterminate age. He is very thin, and wears the robe of a renunciate and a mala. His expression is difficult to read; he looks either insane or enlightened.

If you feel uncomfortable using planetary archetypes as a tool for visualization, you may want to use instead a vivid image of Jesus, Mary or some other saint or teacher of your religious tradition. Otherwise, simply imagine a living ball of dazzling white light that emanates wisdom and benevolence. However, because of the way our human brains are wired, imagining a deity in human form usually has a much quicker and more profound effect.

How do you work with these images? Let's say Jupiter rules your 7th house and is badly afflicted. This may have led to a series of unsuccessful marriages, or frustrating business partnerships. Or Mercury rules your 11th house and is exceptionally weak, so you have intense difficulties achieving your goals in life, or perhaps even defining your goals in the first place. Maybe Mars and Ketu both afflict your 5th house and you're having trouble getting pregnant. In these cases, an astrologer might recommend that you enter into a reverent relationship with Jupiter or Mercury, or with Mars and Ketu, in order to symbolically repair the karmic dysfunction revealed in your chart. Here is a sample visualization for that purpose.

Honoring a Planetary Energy

1. Sit comfortably with your head, neck and trunk in a straight line. Close your eyes.

2. For a few moments simply watch your breath. It will slow down, becoming more smooth and light. Focus your awareness on your breath until you feel tranquil, yet mentally alert.

3. Vividly imagine that your chosen planetary deity is standing in front of you. In your mind's eye see him (or her) as clearly and three dimensionally as if he's actually physically present.

4. Offer the deity (or the symbol of the deity) your deepest respect. Mentally bow to him, and visualize yourself offering him a comfortable chair and something delicious to eat and drink, as if he were an honored guest in your home.

5. Imagine yourself sitting directly in front of your divine visitor. Now bring your full awareness to your heart center. Vividly feel the deepest love, respect, and gratitude emanating outward from your heart to the

deity. Remain mentally silent (no mental chatter) while you offer your devotion with heartfelt sincerity.

6. Vividly imagine the deity smiling lovingly at you. Watch him (or her) raise his hand in blessing. Actually feel his blessing power washing over your body.

7. Return your awareness to your breath. Breathe slowly and evenly for a few moments, then open your eyes.

Rx: VISUALIZING A PLANET
Spend a minimum of 10 to 15 minutes each day for the next 3 months visualizing that the living intelligence of a planet is a guest in your home. Extend your sincerest hospitality, and imagine receiving the deity's blessing. Vividly picture this actually occurring.

Visualization techniques like those given here are meant for people who are reasonably mentally and emotionally balanced. People who are mentally disturbed or severely neurotic should not work with this type of powerful internal practice.

FORGIVENESS

One of the most critically important of all upayas is forgiveness. Sometimes you'll run into people who, although you've never met them before, you instinctively dislike. Or you'll meet someone who, for no apparent reason, is intensely hostile toward you. From the Vedic point of view, this may be because there is unfinished business between you from a previous life. Often this sense of unease actually shows up when you compare your horoscope with theirs: you'll find tight malefic aspects between your planets.

In the multi-incarnational journey of the soul, any burden you don't lay down you'll have to carry with you. It's important to let go of your grudges and repay your karmic debts in this life, so that you're not burdened with them in the next.

Forgiving

1. Sit comfortably with your head, neck and trunk straight. Close your eyes.

2. Bring your full attention to the bridge between your nostrils. Feel the air flowing in and out of your nostrils. Spend at least one full minute feeling the cool air enter your nose and warm air flow out. Your breath should become slow and smooth, deep and even. Don't go on to Step 3 until you feel deeply tranquil. It is important that you do this exercise in a serene frame of mind.

3. Shift your full awareness to your heart area. Imagine the people or things you love most. Feel your love for them glowing warmly in your heart.

4. Now imagine the person who has hurt you. Extend the same love you feel for your most beloved friends to this person also. If it's not possible for you to think of the person without becoming angry, then don't imagine their body or personality. Instead imagine their soul as a glowing ball of peace and light. Extend your love directly from your soul to theirs. It doesn't matter whether the person is still alive or not. Your two souls touch in mutual acceptance and understanding.

5. Bring your awareness back to your breath. Spend at least two or three more minutes watching your breath and remaining serene and loving. If angry or spiteful feelings start to arise, relax and watch your breath, then try this exercise again.

There is another equally important component to this upaya: Asking others to forgive you. If you too have caused a wound, try this upaya.

Asking Forgiveness

1. Sit comfortably with your head, neck and trunk straight. Close your eyes.

2. Watch your breath for a minute or two. Your breath should be slow and smooth, without any jerks or pauses. Don't go on to Step 3 till you feel calm and mentally clear.

3. Shift your full awareness to your heart area. Imagine the person you've hurt. Send them your deepest love and sympathy. Do not speak to them mentally. Instead, focus on your sincere good wishes for that person. Imagine your good will radiating out to them. Feel this very vividly.

4. Return your awareness to your breath and open your eyes.

5. When you have the opportunity, go to that person and apologize. If that person is no longer alive or isn't receptive to your overtures, mentally send your very best wishes for their welfare directly to their soul.

6. Make amends if at all possible. At the least, send a thoughtful gift or, if there's no way to contact the person, make a donation in their name.

7. Seriously try to avoid hurting them again.

Forgiveness is an amazing upaya that instantly short circuits the karmic process. It can erase huge masses of karma instantaneously. It's as if you owe the bank $10,000, but your banker writes off the debt. This packet of karma now has no more power than a cancelled check. Note that this only occurs when forgiveness comes from the depths of your heart. You have to reach into your karmashaya, the depository of karma stored in your causal body, to nullify a karmic debt. Words of forgiveness that come only from your mouth (physical body) or superficial thoughts (subtle body) don't come from a deep enough place to overturn reality, which is what you're doing when you truly forgive. You have to come from the part of your being that's beyond cause and effect to negate karma, the very principle of cause and effect itself.

When we pray to God for forgiveness we are asking for his grace. When we sincerely forgive others, we are connecting with a divine place in ourselves to generate a flow of grace that shatters the negative connection between our debtor and ourself.

Forgiveness is a task that has to be done in this lifetime or the next, no matter how hard it seems. Might as well do it now.

Incidently, forgiving others does not mean accepting unacceptable behavior. If someone has seriously injured you they will need to deal with the karmic consequences, in this life or the next. You, however, do not need to carry the burden of your anger and sense of having suffered an injustice even one moment longer. Lay your anger down and let the law of karma (or the law of the land, if a crime is involved) finish dealing with the situation. You are now karmically free. It is no longer your problem.

Rx: FORGIVENESS
Let go of your grudges. Do not analyze or justify them; simply release them. Work with the Forgiving Meditation on a daily basis until you feel your ill will easing. Try to replace your anger with understanding. When resentful thoughts toward the person you need to forgive no longer arise in your awareness, the upaya has been completed.

SELF-SURRENDER

In Indian ashrams you'll often hear the story of the cat and the monkey. The baby monkey clings to its mother with all its might as she swings through the trees, seeking food and shelter. The newborn kitten is so helpless it's not able to hang on to its mother, yet it isn't afraid because it knows its mother will pick it up and carry it to safety without the kitten having to make any effort at all. Effort is called *sadhana*, or spiritual practice, in India. Simply trusting in the grace of the Mother of the Universe is called *Ishvara pranidhana,* surrender to God. Actually, both effort and surrender are needed on the spiritual path.

"It is an unavoidable fact of life that we must experience prarabdha karma, the results of our past actions. Yet 75% of the suffering can be avoided through self effort and surrender to God," explains Ammachi, one of the most loved saints in India today. "Once we take a body, we all have to suffer some. Even the greatest yogis once they incarnate in a body have to undergo physical suffering, for suffering is inherent in embodied life. Just as the nature of the Sun is to shine and the nature of a river is to flow, so the nature of the body is to fluctuate between pain and pleasure.

"What you must keep in mind is that you are not the body, but the Inner Awareness. The reflection of the Sun in the sea appears to rise and fall with the waves, yet in reality the Sun is completely unaffected by the waves. In the same way, the body undergoes the turbulence of pleasure and pain, yet nothing ever disturbs the supreme bliss of the Inner Self. Spirituality teaches us how to remain established in our true Self, and thus never overpowered by outward circumstances. When we give in to fear, the mind becomes agitated, making our outward circumstances even worse, but when we take refuge in the Supreme Self, the mind will remain calm and peaceful, even in the midst of external traumas."

"In a way, these karmas are blessings," Ammachi said on another occasion. "They make us remember God. When people undergo difficult times, even those who have never once uttered God's name will begin to call Him earnestly. By wholeheartedly turning to spirituality, one becomes freed from these karmas to a major extent."

When we surrender to God, we stop worrying about our horoscope or trying to control our fate. Instead, we trust that everything that happens to us is for the best. It doesn't mean we then go on our merry way. It means we sincerely direct our thoughts and prayers to God, and accept both the grief we experience in life, as well as the joy, as gifts from the divine meant for our growth and happiness, respectively. This upaya takes us beyond propitiating the planets to invoking the grace of the One who created the planets in the first place.

In India, divine being is not just thought of as a transcendent abstraction. It's visualized in a number of different concrete forms so that people can easily enter into a living, loving relationship with it. In the *Tripura Rahasya* the Goddess says, "I love you more than you can possibly imagine. Yet what I am in reality is impossible for your mind to conceive. Therefore imagine me in whatever form appeals to you, and I promise in that very form I will come to you."

The Judeo-Christian-Islamic religions portray God exclusively as a divine father and judge. In India, devotees are encouraged to picture God in whatever manner moves them most deeply. They may choose to imagine the divinity as their:

- Parent, either as the Divine Father or Divine Mother
- Beloved, the Divine Lover
- Child, like baby Jesus for Christians or Gopala and Uma in India
- Friend, one's closest, most intimate companion, like Arjuna's friend Krishna in the Bhagavad Gita
- Animal, like the elephant-headed Ganesh, or a totem animal of a tribe, or the Christian dove representing the Holy Spirit
- Savior, like Jesus to Christians, or Krishna, Rama and Durga to Hindus
- Teacher, one's guru standing in for the divinity.

Devotion to the Supreme Being in whatever form we choose is seen as tremendously purifying in India. Devotion washes away sin (i.e., bad karma) and inspires you to do better in the future since all your actions become offerings to God. In India, you'll often encounter people as devoted to God as they are to their closest relatives and best friends. Developing a living relationship with the divine takes the sting out of the problems karma throws our way and turns life into a love affair with a higher power.

K.N. Rao told me his own guru "encouraged surrender to the will of the Lord as the supreme path. There could be nothing superior to worship, in a simple, straight and guileless way, and I have found that to be the best, most effective and uplifting way of both propitiating the planets and making steady progress on the spiritual path.

"If you worship God with deep faith, don't bother to go to an astrologer. Then you are appealing straight to the person who controls the destiny of the astrologer and of the planets themselves, the emperor of emperors. When you are worshipping God, you are on the right path. As an astrologer I assure you that if you are leading a decent, good life and you are worshipping God, 90% you will have no problems, either mental or emotional or physical." Rao's comments astonished me. I had expected him to try to drum up business, not to discourage clients from patronizing his profession. But just as a true physician's greatest wish is that one day her office will be empty because no one suffers any illness, Rao wishes that one day no one will consult astrologers because everyone has found peace, purpose in their lives, and a deep sense of connection with the divine. The stars rule destiny, but God rules the stars. Therefore, go directly to God, Rao advises.

There are cases where you'll find fixed karma in a chart, which means there's an experience you'll have to undergo in this life whether you want to or not. For example, sooner or later everyone has to face death, your own or that of someone you love. In cases like this particularly, surrendering to God's will with trust and reverence is much easier said than done. Expecting us to have faith in him while our hearts are being ripped out seems like it's too much for God to ask.

Sometimes things happen in life—like good people suffering agonizing diseases, people falling victim to vicious crimes, betrayal by the people we trusted most, the death of innocent children—that are nearly impossible to accept. It's natural to respond with outrage, to resist reality with every fiber of our being. (I've been there!) Needless to say, these events can and should motivate us to work ceaselessly for a more just world, and to find cures for the afflictions that cause so much torment.

It's easy to be pious when things are running smoothly. But every part of our being is put to the test during a crisis. Responding to these awful events is a make or break lesson for us spiritually. No one said it would be easy. The great sages of the Hindu tradition, and saints of all other religions as well, have always called our attention to the fact that our life is here is fleeting, that it's the nature of the things in this world to ultimately decay and die. Because we live in a plane of reality where free will has full play, we are also constantly faced with genuine evil, and we're forced to make tough moral choices ourselves. The whole purpose for doing spiritual practice is so we can be prepared psychologically and spiritually to meet the tests we're going to have to face. This world is God's game, and we have to play by his rules. It's in our hands to learn to play as skillfully as possible. There is a game plan. The fact that the law of karma is a reality, as you'll directly experience when you begin working with your Vedic chart, proves this. For many of us, accepting the painful lessons life has to offer, not just the beauty and good fortune, is the greatest challenge and final triumph of our experience here.

When it comes to fixed karma, bowing to God's will and grateful acceptance of the loving wisdom behind it (whether we can see it or not) is certainly the best policy.

Rx: Self-Surrender

Cultivate a close, loving relationship with God. Learn to trust in His providence. Live your life in His service, doing your sincere best to treat others with respect and concern, as He would want you to do.

18

Vedic Astrological Prescriptions III: Physical Upayas

Physical remedial measures involve your body and your actions. These yoga techniques actively burn bad karma and kindle good karma.

Indications: These prescriptions are for extraverted people who would rather take action than focus inward. These are especially helpful for dynamic personality types, people who have little patience for techniques like meditation, or who have no confidence in mantras. Even if a person is doing a mental or mantric upaya, it's ideal to do a physical one at the same time. Physical actions anchor your inner efforts in external reality.

Contraindications: Health considerations may prevent a person from fulfilling a vigorously physical prescription. People with medical conditions should consult a physician before beginning a demanding physical upaya. Fasting should never be recommended to individuals with severe self- image problems; in rare instances it can contribute to anorexia.

STRESS REDUCTION EXERCISES

When I was manager of the Center for Holistic Medicine in Glenview, Illinois in the late 1970s, our doctors were considered medical quacks because they prescribed yogic breathing exercises instead of sedatives for people who needed to relax. Today these exercises, called *pranayama* in yoga, are the basic stress reduction techniques taught at medical clinics throughout the globe.

If a Vedic chart shows an irritable and impatient personality type, or a nervous, fearful one, or if it shows a cycle during which a person is likely to fall under a great deal of stress, then pranayama may be the most useful upaya of all. These centering techniques promote tranquility of mind and body, helping you gain perspective on your past karma and on future goals.

Centering

This is the most basic and important technique at the core of all yoga practice. It rests and rejuvenates your mind and nervous system through diaphragmatic breathing and a relaxed but attentive mental focus.

1. Sit comfortably with your head, neck and trunk in a straight line.
2. Bring your awareness to your breath. Watch it flowing naturally in and out through your nostrils for a half minute or so. Your breathing will naturally slow down as you begin to relax.
3. Feel your abdomen just below your ribs moving slightly forward and backward as you breathe. Your chest should not be moving. This assures that you're using your diaphragm, not your chest muscles, to breathe.
4. Your breath should be smooth, even, silent, without jerks or pauses. Inhalation and exhalation should be about equal in length. Avoid momentarily holding your breath between breaths. Your breathing cycle should keep moving in a slow, smooth, continuous flow.
5. Breathe like this for another five minutes. Keep your mental attention on the flow of air in and out of your nostrils. Notice how calm and centered you're feeling.

Rx: CENTERING
Three times a day for the next four weeks, do the Centering exercise for five minutes. If you find yourself feeling agitated, angry or anxious during the day, stop for a few moments and devote your full attention to centering.

The idea of "breathing your way to enlightenment" may sound silly to us, but it's not silly to the yogis. That's because the yoga masters of India have devoted thousands of years to exploring the breath and mind.

They noted that many of the problems we experience are due to the vrittis in our minds. When these modulations of consciousness are erratic, disordered or disharmonious, difficulties frequently ensue. By remaining calm and centered, we stop mulling over the past and fretting about the future, and move our full awareness into the present moment. When we are fully mentally present we can respond appropriately to events occurring around us, rather than reacting reflexively on the basis of our past conditioning (karma). We start dealing effectively with the reality of our situation rather than losing ourselves in fantasies or reverie.

According to the yogis I interviewed, Americans are addicted to thrilling experiences like extreme sports because they yank them sharply into the present moment and make them feel intensely alive. Yogic breathing techniques do the same thing without putting your life at risk. Alternate nostril breathing is a more advanced centering technique that actually purifies your *nadis* or channels of consciousness (think of them as the nerves of your subtle body). It's said that when the nadis are completely clean so that the energy of higher consciousness flows through them unimpededly, then karma simply falls away like ripe fruit falling from a tree. This is a very advanced state of consciousness, but alternate nostril breathing is one of the first steps toward attaining it.

Alternate Nostril Breathing

This technique, called *nadi shodanam* or "channel purification," relaxes your body and gently focuses your attention.

1. Sit up straight in a comfortable position. Breathe through your nose, never your mouth, during this exercise.
2. Bring your full attention to your breath. Simply watch your breath for a moment or two until your breath rate slows down. Allow your breath to flow smoothly, evenly, silently, without jerks or pauses.
3. Rest the index and middle fingers of your right hand on your forehead just above your nose. With your right thumb, gently apply pressure to the right side of your nose, blocking your right nostril. Exhale slowly and smoothly, in a relaxed manner, through your left nostril.
4. With your right ring finger, gently apply pressure to the left side of your nose, blocking your left nostril. Inhale slowly and smoothly through your right nostril.

5. Repeat steps 3 and 4 two more times.
6. You are about to begin your fourth exhalation. Leave your ring finger on your left nostril and exhale through your right nostril.
7. Block your right nostril with your right thumb and inhale through your left nostril.
8. Repeat steps 6 and 7 two more times.
9. Put your right hand down. Slowly exhale and inhale through both nostrils three times.
10. Use your ring finger to gently block your left nostril. Exhale slowly and smoothly, without jerks or pauses, through your right nostril.
11. Use your right thumb to block your right nostril. Inhale slowly and smoothly through your left nostril.
12. Repeat steps 10 and 11 two more times.
13. Now leave your right thumb on your right nostril and exhale through your left nostril.
14. Block your left nostril with your ring finger and inhale through your right nostril.
15. Repeat steps 13 and 14 two more times.
16. Put your right hand down. Exhale and inhale through both nostrils three times.

This exercise isn't as complicated as it sounds. Here are the same steps spelled out in tabular form.

Breath	Exhale	Inhale	Breath	Exhale	Inhale
1.	Left	Right	10.	Right	Left
2.	Left	Right	11.	Right	Left
3.	Left	Right	12.	Right	Left
4.	Right	Left	13.	Left	Right
5.	Right	Left	14.	Left	Right
6.	Right	Left	15.	Left	Right
7.	Both	Both	16.	Both	Both
8.	Both	Both	17.	Both	Both
9.	Both	Both	18.	Both	Both

Repeat the full process—Steps 1 through 18—three times. This constitutes one full session. Remember that your breathing should remain slow, smooth and even, with no jerks or pauses. Don't breathe so slowly that you feel like you're not getting enough air. You should be relaxed and comfortable throughout this exercise.

Rx: ALTERNATE NOSTRIL BREATHING
Do one full session of the Alternate Nostril Breathing exercise three times a day every day for one month. At the end of each week jot down the effects you've noticed from this practice.

PHYSICAL EXERCISES

Today, scientists are developing DNA tests that will give you advance warning whether you're a prime candidate for developing diabetes, Alzheimers, schizophrenia, certain types of cancer, or other genetically-transmitted diseases. The purpose of these tests is not to let you know you're "doomed" to get a disease. Rather, it's to alert you that there's a better than average likelihood a certain medical problem is headed your way. Then you're in a position to adopt preventive measures that could delay the onset of the illness or perhaps even prevent it from ever showing up at all.

Your Vedic chart contains information about the state of your health and the timing when major medical problems are most likely to occur. My horoscope, for example, shows the strong likelihood of adult onset diabetes. This is hardly surprising since almost every member of my mother's family suffered from this disease. Knowing that diabetes is not just in my family, it's in my chart, was a constant reminder to watch my diet and have my blood sugar checked regularly.

If you have a medical problem, or believe you may be a candidate for one, consult your doctor. At the same time there are several upayas that can help you get a handle on your health.

Hatha Yoga is an ideal upaya for people who need to begin dealing with health issues. In a Vedic chart, this can be seen from challenges to the 1st, 6th or 8th houses, certain planetary yogas and by transits and cycles that trigger health problems. Virtually anyone, provided they're not in a coma, can practice some level of hatha. "Gentle Yoga" classes are available for those who are very stiff or have medical conditions like high blood pressure, hernia, severe arthritis or an injured or missing limb.

Hatha is excellent for mentally oriented people who're completely out of touch with their bodies. It's also superb for people who want to start meditating but have difficulty turning their minds inward. Hatha not only tones and conditions the body, it teaches people how to focus inside themselves, unlike almost every other class you can take in the modern West, where you are constantly directed to continue focusing exclusively outward.

Rx: Hatha Yoga

Attend a hatha yoga class at your local yoga center. Practice the postures at home on days when you can't be in class. Spend a minimum of 15 minutes five days a week doing hatha. When you have time, increase the length of your sessions to 30 or 40 minutes per day.

Aerobic exercises, exercises that get your heart pumping rapidly and increase your respiratory rate, are optimal for promoting cardiovascular health. They help improve your mood too, studies have shown.

If the Ascendant in your Vedic horoscope is weak, exercising regularly is one valuable way to strengthen it. Not only fluctuating health but other 1st house indications like low self-esteem or preoccupation with an unimpressive physical appearance can be improved through daily physical exercise.

Rx: Active Exercise

Commit to a regular routine of physical exercise. Go for a brisk walk, or go hiking, jogging, swimming, bicycling, or engage in some other form of active exercise for at least 30 minutes five days a week. Be regular. Physical work like cleaning the house, shoveling snow, raking leaves or pushing the lawn mower counts. Exercise doesn't have to be a chore. Put on some music you love and dance. Enjoy yourself.

If you have a serious medical condition or are pregnant, you must check with your doctor before starting an aerobic or hatha yoga routine.

SELF-DISCIPLINE

Now we come to the least popular of all astrological prescriptions and one of the most effective. *Tapas* is often translated by that awful sounding word "austerity," but it really just means practicing self-control. In ancient India, it was one of the most highly prized of all the remedial measures. When it's done correctly, it directly stops the flow of negative karma. That's why it's considered so powerful.

Through the carefully prescribed practice of self-discipline, karmic complexes involving overindulgence can be overcome. It's recommended, for example, when a chart reveals a person who's likely to contract a venereal disease, or when the horoscope shows that a habit such as smoking, drinking, drug use or overeating will lead to dangerous medical problems later in life. It's also recommended for people who simply feel their lives are out of their control, because it helps develop will-power and a sense of self-mastery. When it's done right, it promotes a tremendous feeling of karmic cleansing.

The downside of tapas is that it can lead to suppression or increased tension if it's not approached in the right spirit. Self-discipline should be entered into with enthusiasm and full appreciation of its positive purpose and final goal. If you look at it as self-mortification, I'm not so sure it will be helpful. This upaya is prescribed not to punish you, but to make you stronger. It helps free you from karmic compulsions. A simple example would be a client who keeps gaining weight in part because she eats rich pastries every day. Okay, the prescription is for the next four months, no pastries. She is now reorganizing her karmic tendency to seek gratification through fattening foods into a new karmic vector of seeking gratification through feeling better and getting healthier.

Tapas doesn't just mean stopping unhealthy behavior. It can also mean adding a difficult behavior that's good for you. Tapas literally means "heat," because your practice should make you sweat. That is, it should be a bit of a stretch for you. Start doing a dozen Sun Salutations (a series of Hatha Yoga positions) before your meditation routine in the morning. Take a class in *yoga nidra* (the yogic control of sleep) and start reducing the amount of time you spend in bed, as you learn to remain conscious and clear while your body rests deeply. Commit to eating at least one large salad full of mixed greens every single day.

Olympic champions win medals because of self-control and self-discipline. Budding artists became great artists because of tapas. The luxuries of life are sacrificed and hardships are willingly embraced so that you can achieve a cherished goal. If your chart reveals an imbalance due to some type of excessive behavior or to the lack of a healthy behavior, consider undertaking a course of self-discipline. But only do this if you recognize in yourself the maturity to understand the purpose of the exercise and to follow through.

Rx: SELF-DISCIPLINE

Commit to a course of karmic self discipline such as:

- Place a symbol of God, Goddess or a saint you especially love on an altar in your home. Prostrate before it, moving from a full standing position to a full lying position, 100 times each morning for the next six months.
- Fast on water, fruit juice and vegetable broth one day each week for six months.
- Take no alcoholic beverage whatever for the next six months.
- Give up eating meat for the next six months.
- Three days per week for the next two months, instead of filling your free time with entertainment like TV or CDs, sit for an extra, longer session of meditation.

Self-discipline always gives results. It's an excellent remedial measure. Self-discipline isn't helping if you make yourself sick doing it. Always use common sense in undertaking a karmic discipline.

SELFLESS SERVICE

An Indian astrologer told me that a person who practices *seva,* selfless service, can throw their birth chart away because the good karma they're creating is completely reshaping their destiny. This is an exaggeration, but there's a kernel of truth in it. Selfless service burns away the evil effects of lifetimes of bad karma.

Seva can entail volunteering your time in a community, national organization, or a wholesome outlet to which you may devote your energies. It can involve serving family or friends who really need you. True service means not expecting anything back, whether financially or in terms of appreciation. "When you give with complete freedom, and without any expectation, you're giving the way God gives," the jyotishi told me. "Then it becomes difficult for your negative karmas to attack you. They stand back and say, 'This person is acting like a saint. Instead of attacking him, let's support him.'"

When you have this attitude, situations in life that seem difficult or unfair suddenly transform themselves into opportunities to help others who are suffering too. Life no longer seems depressing or disappointing but fills with a joyous sense of purpose. Your heart begins to glow.

This is called Karma Yoga, sacred activity, in India. When we no longer claim any benefits for our efforts we are karmically free, because no new chains of unfulfilled expectations or desires are being created. At the same time, ethical and compassionate activities performed out of sheer love, with no expectation of reward, help to "cancel out" unwholesome actions we may have performed in the past. Our karmic bank account, in effect, becomes "balanced."

Remember, you don't have to join the Peace Corps to serve others. Supporting your own family, financially or emotionally, is a form of sacred duty. Even housework, when performed cheerfully, is a form of seva. Church work, social service, environmental work and cultural activities can all be transformed into seva. So can your present job if you approach it sincerely as a chance to help other people rather than merely as a way to make money or gain public recognition.

Rx: SELFLESS SERVICE

Commit to a course of selfless service such as:

- Once each day, secretly do something to help someone else. Don't let anyone else know and don't inwardly gloat about it. Just get in the habit of serving others even when there's nothing in it for you.
- For the next six months, devote one afternoon each week to community service.

THE GREAT VOW

Many centuries ago the illustrious sage Patanjali said there is one universal upaya everyone can and should keep all the time. It involves making five unwavering commitments.

- *Ahimsa:* Not to harm others or yourself.
- *Satya:* To always speak the truth.
- *Asteya:* Not to take what doesn't belong to you.
- *Brahmacharya:* To avoid overindulging yourself.
- *Aparigraha:* To stop craving things you don't really need.

"These ethical commitments are valuable at any time, in any place, under any circumstances. They are called the great vow," says Patanjali in his classic work, *The Yoga Sutras.* This promise to yourself is the very foundation of spiritual life whatever your religion. It's a huge commitment that involves living each moment consciously, cultivating selflessness and contentment and making spiritual growth your top priority. Please don't take ethics for granted. Most people consider themselves basically moral, yet their moral standards often contain significant loopholes.

One of the most common examples of this is the church-going man who might never hit his children or cheat on his wife, yet is callous to his employees and dishonest with his competitors. I'm still hunting for the verse in the Bible where Jesus says, "Love thy neighbor as thyself, except at work. After all, business is business."

Among hundreds of reports of near-death experiences, I've never heard of the shining white light at the end of the tunnel demanding, "How much money did you make? How successful was your business?" According to Jesus, the question we'll have to face when we meet our Maker is "Who did you serve?" (Matthew 25: 31-46.)

One of the great classics of Vedic astrology, called the *Phala Dipika,* states that the person who lives consciously and ethically, the planets will trouble the least. In very early Christian texts found at Nag Hammadi in Egypt, Jesus himself explains that if our thoughts and actions aren't truly pure, after death, the planets catch hold of us and heave us back into a physical life filled with suffering rather than allowing us to pass higher into the kingdom of heaven. What an interesting image.

Rx: ETHICS

Make an earnest commitment to live your life ethically, both when it's convenient and when it's not.

CHARITY

Charity *(dana)* is one of the most commonly prescribed remedial measures in India, and one of the least commonly used ones in the West. The immensely powerful karmically cleansing effect of giving in charity should never be underestimated. Much bad karma is the result of debts we have incurred in previous lives. Making generous donations helps us balance our karmic accounts. In fact, our word "donate" can be traced back to the Sanskrit term *dana*.

Charity is not about negotiating with destiny or buying off fate. Fund raisers for churches or ashrams sometimes claim that if you give $10, God will give you $100 back. First, that's not necessarily true, especially if you already have $100,000 in karmic debt you need to pay off. But more importantly, selfish motivation disqualifies a donation from being true dana.

The real purpose of practicing charity is to develop generosity of spirit, so it's particularly appropriate for people whose charts reveal Saturn-related problems like greed, avarice or miserliness, or for people with Venus or Jupiter dysfunction who waste their resources.

How much you should donate depends on your circumstances and the severity of your karma. The old Christian model of tithing 10% throughout life is a good ideal. Another good prescription is that one month each year, you should note down everything you're planning to spend on yourself, other than necessities, and then not buy those things. Instead, at the end of the month tally up the amount of money you were going to fritter away on exercise equipment, delicacies, movies or another tube of mascara when you already have three tubes at home. Then donate that amount of money to your favorite charity.

People with health problems can donate to an organization that does research to find cures for diseases like the American Cancer Society or to a local free clinic or hospice. People who're lonely or who tend to alienate others can donate to homeless shelters, food banks or schools. Focusing on these charities helps redirect their thoughts towards assisting other people rather than dwelling on their own misery. People having problems with children, either because they don't have any or because they do, can donate to orphanages or children's clubs.

Again, this is not buying off fate. You are trying to create a sense of generosity, a sense of flow, a sense of connectedness with others, an altruistic impulse. Don't just write out a check and drop it in the mail. Sit with the check for a couple of minutes imagining how others are going to benefit from this donation. Send your blessings along with the money.

If you don't have money to share, donate your time. Be a mentor, volunteer at your local library or hospital, participate in outreach programs at your church or synagogue that involve visiting the sick, disabled or elderly. Please don't volunteer with the expectation that other people will admire or even thank you. Give solely for the sake of giving, because it's the right thing to do. Then your donation is completely karmically clean.

Learn to let go of what you value, whether it's money or time, and offer it to others. For many people, mastering this one spiritual lesson can untie more knots in the flow of karma than virtually any other practice.

Rx: CHARITY

Commit to a course of charitable action such as:

- At the end of each month, make out a check for 10% of your takehome income, and send it to charity.
- Donate one evening every week for the next six months to an organization that benefits others.

If you have a favorite charity, please given generously. If you are looking for an outstanding charitable organization to support that's managed honestly and run with the highest humanitarian ideals, please consider the Mata Amritanandamayi Math, based in Kerala, India. It's one of the most extensive charitable trusts ever established in India, serving a population of nearly a billion South Asians of all castes, colors and religious backgrounds. The Math has been honored by the Indian government as one of the best run and most effective such organizations ever launched in their country.

The Math helps with disaster relief, provides pensions for destitute women, and sponsors hospices, care for the elderly, refuges for battered and abandoned women and their children, special programs serving India's tribal peoples (the poorest of the poor), vocational training centers, orphanages and over 45 schools for children. In addition, the Math supports numerous hospitals and medical clinics with free care for the indigent, as well as offering professional medical training. It also is extremely active in the environmental protection movement. In addition, the Math is building 10,000 homes a year which are given away free to impoverished families. The array of services the Math offers is truly mind boggling, and it's run for the most part by deeply committed volunteers. The Math's work is inspired by Ammachi—one of the greatest saints living in India today (one of the greatest saints in world history, in my opinion). The United Nations recently acknowledged her extraordinary work with its highest honor, the Gandhi-King Award.

To learn more about these charitable programs or to send a contribution, contact:

Mata Amritanandamayi Center
P.O. Box 613, San Ramon, CA 94583-0613 USA
Phone: 510-537-9417 (in northern California)
Website: www.ammachi.org

Please keep in mind that Western currencies are very strong against the Indian rupee. This means that a $50 contribution to an Indian charity can provide as many goods and services as a $150 donation in most Western countries.

PILGRIMAGE

Pilgrimage is a valued spiritual practice in every religion. Since time began, pilgrims have visited sites associated with great saints and bathed in holy rivers. Today we hop on a plane, then catch a tour bus for Medjugorje or Mother Meera's ashram in Germany, but in medieval times, as in India to this day, people made long and difficult journeys to sacred sites on foot. The journey itself was a form of spiritual practice, purging the personality through the privations the pilgrim experienced on the trip, and strengthening their faith and reliance on Spirit to see them safely through to the journey's end.

I've been on a number of pilgrimages (called *yatras* in Sanskrit) myself and can personally attest to their tremendous transformative power. Traveling through rural Bengal to see the villages where the great saints Ramakrishna and Sarada Devi had been born, I actually got cholera. Traveling to Prayag for the Maha Kumbha Mela spiritual festival (attended by 70 million devotees) in January 2001, I had my first taste of hypothermia when the winter temperatures unexpectedly plummeted to record lows and we had no way to heat our tent. Yet I have to say that difficult as these pilgrimages were, they were among the greatest spiritual experiences of my life.

I am not recommending that you risk your life going on a pilgrimage. Perhaps it's our good karma that we live in a time when we can visit holy sites, especially in Europe, in comfort and safety. But I encourage you to consider making a physical journey part of your spiritual journey in life. Any special place you can reach that elevates your mind and exalts your spirit is helping you to empty the trash containers in your subconscious and to realign yourself with something truly sublime.

You don't need to visit a site connected with any religion to go on pilgrimage. Places of extraordinary natural beauty like Yellowstone Park, Mount Shasta, the Grand Canyon, or Carlsbad Caverns in New Mexico, will do as well. Just keep in mind that you're traveling there as a pilgrim, not a tourist. Use your time to sit quietly, to read inspirational stories, or to chant your mantra. Beautiful natural sites like these were preferred by many aboriginal peoples as places where they could most readily make contact with the Great Spirit. A spiritual retreat, like a stay at a monastery or ashram, can serve a similar purpose.

In Vedic astrology, the 9th house is particularly associated with pilgrimage. Your jyotishi can advise you whether this upaya is especially indicated in your chart, and suggest the most auspicious times for the trip.

One rule for the road: Pilgrims don't grumble. Please don't squander this opportunity for spiritual growth by complaining about the food, the uncomfortable seats in the bus or the irritating people you're traveling with. Welcome them all as opportunities to burn off more karma.

Rx: PILGRIMAGE

Spend a week this year on pilgrimage or a spiritual retreat. Instead of vacationing in Las Vegas or Disneyland, choose a sacred site you've always wanted to visit, and go there instead. Use the time to focus on Spirit, within you and all around you. While you're there, make a generous donation for the upkeep of the site.

19

Vedic Astrological Prescriptions IV: Tantric Upayas

The most important part of your Vedic astrological reading is not the information about your future itself, but recommendations for what you can do to ease the impact of difficult upcoming cycles or to enhance the qualities of potentially positive cycles. Yet a frequent despairing comment I hear from Vedic astrologers is that Western clients refuse to do upayas, even when it would benefit them tremendously. In some cases this is simply due to lack of faith. We in the West don't have an astrological tradition many thousands of years old in which we have implicit trust, as Hindus do. But another reason is that Westerners are often suspicious of Eastern techniques like mantras, or they feel they're just too busy to do a lengthy and demanding spiritual practice.

The question Vedic astrologers ask themselves is, "How can we help these people?" Some decide to recommend tantric upayas, which are often comparatively easy and sometimes actually involve having other people do the work for you. Sometimes it's just less effort to prescribe a gemstone than to educate people about the mechanics of karma, urging them to really look at the ways they're unconsciously sabotaging themselves, and then inspire them to make a sincere effort to change. However, Vedic astrology was designed to benefit everyone, and that includes even the least motivated souls. Tantric upayas may be their best bet.

Tantric upayas work with the subtle laws of nature, such as "like influences like." Saturn, for example, represents (among a million other things) black sesame seeds. So a client may have a priest do a special fire ritual in which black sesame seeds (here representing the seeds of one's bad karma) are offered to Saturn. In very ancient cultures like India, these subtle connections are intuitively understood by masses of people. Tantric techniques, like offering a gift to the spirit who lives in a tree near your home, makes perfect sense in their cosmology.

Indications: These upayas generally involve less effort than mental, mantric or physical ones so people disinclined to make a sustained effort on their own behalf can still benefit to some degree from a Vedic prescription. People attracted to "magic" may also especially appreciate the inherently magical qualities of these methods.

Contraindications: These techniques are not advisable for people more than usually superstitious because they may actually aggravate this quality in their personalities. In some cases, people with very weak 5th and 9th houses (the houses of luck) or a badly afflicted 8th house (house of occult practices) sometimes benefit less than others from these upayas.

RITUALS

Since the planets are believed to be living intelligences, Indians often perform religious rituals to planets controlling trouble spots in their birth charts. In this way, they properly integrate the disturbed qualities that malefic planet represents into the field of their higher awareness. In the West, of course, most of us have been taught from childhood to sneer at "ritual magic," and to believe that the divine can have only one face, usually a white male one. Nevertheless, the well-known Vedic astrologer James Braha enthusiastically describes the powerful impact these pujas, or yajnas as they're also called, can have even for Westerners. He frequently recommends them to his clients, and often sees dramatic positive changes in a person's life within several days and sometimes within several hours after the yajna is completed. "Of course we deserve the bad karma that's coming," Braha admits, "but when we pray to the planet related to the problem, it's like asking for grace."

Propitiating the planets with an offering helps us make peace with their energies. The items we offer into the sacred fire represent the bad karma we wish the fire to burn away.

"*Graha shanti* (making peace with the planets) does not give you license to go out and commit the sin again," K.N. Rao admonishes. "Your moral conduct must improve."

I've already told several stories about my experiences with rituals. But let me also mention a woman I know who desperately wanted to be an artist. She asked a priest to perform a yajna for her. Incredibly, within 24 hours, she got a phone call out of the blue from an art dealer looking for works for an exhibit. The woman was ecstatic but today, several years later, she still hasn't done the paintings. The wonderful opportunity simply came and went. Here's the point I want to strongly emphasize: ritual magic may be able to smash a gateway through your bad karma, but if you don't make the effort to step through the door it's created, what good has it done? Tantric methods like yajnas can offer karmic reprieves, but it's up to you to use them wisely.

Like James Braha, I've had spectacular results with yajnas myself, but the results may be less dramatic if very strong karma is involved or if the condition of your 5th, 8th or 9th houses blocks the flow of shakti through pujas for you. Your astrologer can help you determine if this upaya is likely to be effective in your case.

The ideal is to do a series of rituals yourself, but few Westerners are adept at this and most have psychological blocks due to cultural conditioning that prevent them from enacting a puja with full faith. So the next best bet is to have a *pujari*, a ritual specialist, perform the yajna for you. India has always had an entire class of society—the brahmins—who devoted themselves to making rituals work. Unfortunately, as the Kali Yuga deepens, it's getting harder to find truly pure-minded brahmins who do the pujas in the traditional manner. Some pujas are quite expensive too; they can cost thousands of dollars due in part to the number of priests involved and the quality of the materials being offered in the sacrifice. However, if you'd like to experiment with pujas at a very affordable price (between about $40 and $250), I would recommend that you check the M.A. Center website at www.ammachi.org or contact the center at puja@ammachi.org, or call 510-537-9417 (this number is in the San Francisco Bay Area). The pujaris associated with this center are supervised by Mata Amritananadamayi (Ammachi), and are the genuine articles. The prices are comparatively low because Ammachi wants to ensure that everyone who would like to perform a puja can afford to do so.

Pujas are available for each of the nine planets or all nine at once, and also for specific purposes such as opening a new business, harmony in the home, blessing a marriage or one's studies, prosperity, improved health, mental peace, spiritual growth and for a blessed release for those who are dying.

Even when someone else is doing a yagna for you, the experience should be interactive, not passive. On the day the puja is performed, bathe and put on fresh, clean clothes. Fast all day on water and juice. Sit for a least one session of meditation that day, even if you never meditate otherwise. If you're not sure exactly when the puja is being conducted (for example, if a priest in India is doing it for you), select a time when you can sit down, still your mind, and open yourself to the blessing forces the yagna is generating for you.

After the yagna, the pujari will offer you sacred ash from the fire pit or other materials from the ritual. These are imbued with the blessing energy of the mantras chanted on your behalf. Keep this packet of ashes on your home altar or some other special place in your house, and rub a little on your forehead when you do your spiritual practices.

Note: When you contact a brahmin about doing a puja, he or she will want to know your birth star. This does not mean your Sun sign, as it does in the West. It means the nakshatra your Moon was in at the moment of your birth. If you're unsure about it, give the pujari your birth data and he or she will calculate your birth star for you.

Rx: RITUALS
Ask a pujari (ritual specialist) to perform a puja for you or to teach you how to do your own pujas. If you are working with deeply set karma, plan to do a series of pujas to help uproot that karma.

THERAPEUTIC MYTHS

When I was in my late 20s, I went through an extremely painful life crisis that involved leaving my job, my home and the man I was with at the time. It felt like starting my whole life over from scratch, and absolutely nothing I tried to do was working out. I had a very basic knowledge of Western astrology then, and finally decided to check my transits. Sure enough, it turned out I was having horrendous planetary transits, and they would continue for the next year and a half. Needless to say, finding this out made me even more depressed.

One evening I was in so much distress, I deeply wanted to connect with the Divine Mother. I stopped by the local library but the only book on the Goddess I could find was the *Chandi,* a Hindu text describing in lurid detail the gruesome battles between the warrior goddess Durga and various demons. I had taken a look at this book some years earlier and had been repelled by its brutal imagery. This evening I was so desperate though, I took the book to bed with me and read it all the way through. It was amazing; I could actually feel Durga's battle taking place inside my chest as if she were attacking all the demons, negative emotions, I was experiencing. At the very end of the text I was astonished to find a verse that said, "The malefic cycles of the planets lose their power against those who recite the *Chandi* with an open heart."

I woke up the next morning feeling absolutely wonderful. The sense of grief and despair I'd been going through for weeks vanished as totally as rain clouds after a storm. I barely finished getting dressed when I received a phone call—completely out of the blue—offering me a fabulous new job. I was totally stunned.

Years later, I learned that therapeutic myths like the *Chandi* are often prescribed as upayas for negative planetary cycles in India. In fact, whole communities will turn out to listen to the recital of deeply moving epics like the *Ramayana,* which tells how the prince Rama (representing God) rescued his wife Sita (the human soul) from the clutches of Ravanna (greed and desire), or the *Mahabharata,* which relates how Krishna (God again) helps his dear friend Arjuna (the human soul) win the war at Kurukshetra (the painful battles of life). These stories are deeply symbolic and have a profoundly cathartic effect on the hearts of villagers listening to them.

If you're interested in working with myths this way, I'd recommend that you pick up Robert Svoboda's wonderful book, *The Greatness of Saturn,* which explains the psychological and spiritual effects of this type of upaya. The book also includes Dr. Svoboda's translation of *Shani Mahatmyam,* the perfect text to work with if Saturn is the planet in your chart representing the problem.

Many of the great works of Indian literature were specifically written to purge the mind of cynicism, selfishness and hatred, while increasing faith and a sense of connection with spirit. In this way they clear out bad karma and refresh the soul. Finding literature in the West with similar impact isn't always easy. Here are a few Western works you might try.

- The Book of Psalms in the Bible. It represents a soul crying out to God with both love and despair.
- The books Matthew, Mark, Luke and John in the Bible. These recount the life and teachings of Jesus.
- *Trustful Surrender to Divine Providence* by Father Jean Baptiste Saint-Jure, S.J. and Blessed Claude de la Colombiere, S.J. Classic advice for Christians on trusting God and coming to terms with his will.
- *The Consolation of Philosophy* by Boethius. This is a mythic conversation between the Goddess of Wealth, the Goddess of Wisdom and a condemned man. It's especially appropriate for periods in your life when you're overcome by a sense of meaninglessness or injustice.
- *Phaedo* by Plato. This is a fictionalized account of the last day in the philosopher Socrates' life. It's excellent for deepening your living experience of the soul.
- *The Odyssey* by Homer. Odysseus thinks he doesn't need God's guidance, that through his own efforts he can find his way home. He does finally get home, but only with God's help.
- *Faust* by Goethe. This is the myth of a man who risks damnation to satisfy his lust, but is rescued by God's limitless grace.

In my opinion, reading the Bhagavad Gita, which recounts Krishna's conversation with Arjuna just before the start of a mythic battle, is one of the best upayas of all time. Numerous translations are available. For newcomers to the Eastern tradition I'd recommend *The Song of God* by Swami Prabhavananda and Christopher Isherwood or *The Bhagavad Gita: A Walkthrough for Westerners* by Jack Hawley.

Someday, as Westerners become more savvy at working with therapeutic myths, perhaps the ancient Gnostic myth of the lost pearl will be rewritten specifically as an upaya for the Sun, the tale of Adonis will be redeveloped as an upaya for the Moon, the legends about Hermes Trismegistus or Merlin may provide the basis for an upaya for Mercury, the descent of Innana will be recast as an upaya for Venus, and the story of Gilgamesh will appear as an upaya for Mars. Percival's quest for the Holy Grail might serve as a myth to heal the wounds of Jupiter, while the tragedy of King Lear could be reshaped to help heal Saturn. Thor's struggle with the Midgard serpent could be used as an upaya for Rahu, while Alexander the Great's famous encounter with the yogi Dandamis could be rewritten as an upaya for Ketu.

Myths and literature work as upayas only when you feel their power stirring your soul. If something deep inside you doesn't feel purified or transformed after encountering a myth, try another upaya.

Rx: THE MYTHIC ENCOUNTER
Select a mythic story that symbolizes the struggles you're going through and ends with victory. Find a modern retelling that speaks to you deeply. Read the myth, projecting yourself into the characters and events, and allow them to resolve your conflict for you symbolically.

GEMSTONES

When Americans come to me asking for astrological advice, they almost invariably ask what gemstone they should purchase as an upaya. This shocks me since in the tradition in which I'm trained, gems were prescribed very rarely and only for specific purposes. Of the top Indian astrologers I've interviewed, not a single one prescribes gemstones on a regular basis. Yet in the West, prescribing gems has become almost synonymous with practicing Vedic astrology.

Of the Vedic gemstone suppliers I've had the privilege to meet, every one is an ethical person who does his or her best to offer the finest quality jewels prepared for you with care and respect. Yet I still feel very queasy about the casualness with which gems are often prescribed in the Western Vedic community. If a client walks out of a Vedic astrologer's office believing that simply by putting on an expensive ring or pendant all their bad karma is going to vanish forever, that astrologer has done their client a serious disservice.

Parashara, the father of Vedic astrology, did not recommend gems, nor did a single one of the other major ancient astrological treatises. This is because the sages understood that remedial measures which work directly with consciousness such as mantras, good deeds and sincere and loving devotion are always preferred to external measures such as gems. Gemstones are like prostheses; they may temporarily improve the symptoms, but they don't always cure the underlying karmic condition. Only your own sincere, conscious effort will do that. No gem can do your inner work for you. Remember that at the time of death you cannot take your astrological ring or bracelet with you. What will travel with you into the next phase of existence is the blessing power of your mantra and the protective force of your good thoughts and deeds.

Gemstones can cause problems if they're not properly prescribed, so please don't select a stone for yourself if you're not familiar with Vedic astrological principles. For example, for a person with Cancer rising, Mars rules the 10th house of career. If Mars is placed in the first house (Cancer), it's "fallen" or very weak. Strengthening Mars' influence by wearing red coral in theory will empower your 10th house, allowing you to experience advances in your career. But now that Mars is much stronger, its challenging aspect to your 7th house of marriage will also be felt much more keenly. So while your professional life is improving, your marriage may be disintegrating. Mantras, when chanted correctly, do not have this kind of problematic side effect.

Another reservation I have about gems is that they can be extremely expensive. If you can't afford a gemstone, never let any astrologer pressure you into purchasing one. In India today, unfortunately, a few unscrupulous jyotishis will prescribe several pricey gems for you, whether your chart calls for them or not, and then collect a hefty kickback from the jeweler they send you to.

Vedic astrology was a free gift offered by the ancient sages for the welfare of all humanity. It's designed to benefit the poor as well as the rich. It is absolutely mistaken to believe that if you can't afford a gemstone, you're not able to fully benefit from Indian astrology. A great Assamese saint told me that a $10 mala (string of beads) does far more to improve your karma than a $10,000 diamond necklace, if you use it to chant the names of God.

Nevertheless, in the United States today it's popular to prescribe upayas such as jewelry, certain types of metals rings or bangles, amulets inscribed with sacred letters or numbers or herb packets. Let's assume your astrologer is deeply knowlegable and has prescribed this remedy correctly. How do you work with it?

Your gemstone is assigned on the basis of the *bandhas* or subtle connections between the stone and the planet it represents. Following are the gems most commonly used for astrological purposes.

PLANET	**GEMSTONE**
Sun	Ruby, garnet
Moon	Pearl, moonstone
Mars	Red coral, carnelian
Mercury	Emerald, jade, green zircon
Jupiter	Yellow sapphire, citrine
Venus	Diamond, white sapphire
Saturn	Blue sapphire, lapis lazuli
Rahu	Hessonite
Ketu	Cat's eye

Always get the absolute best quality stone you can afford, as the purer the gem, the more shakti or energy of consciousness it holds. The gem needs to be set so that it touches your skin. Most rings in America are not designed this way, so you'll have to have yours specially prepared. Your astrologer can recommend a jeweler who specializes in filling Vedic gem prescriptions.

To get the maximum benefit from a stone, you will need to empower it in the tantric fashion. According to Tantra, it's the *chintamani*, the "wish fulfilling gem of consciousness," that is the primary source of a gem's power, not the rock itself. So when a jyotishi prescribes a gem for you, be sure to get the following information:

1. How should the gem be potentized?
2. What are the best dates and times for potentizing the gem?
3. How often does the gem need to be re-empowered?

Both first potentizing and then routinely re-empowering a gem usually entail cleaning it, chanting a mantra to the appropriate planetary deity several thousand times, visualizing your goal in using the gem very clearly and specifically and offering a heartfelt prayer. In the *sampradaya* (orally-transmitted lineage) in which I was trained, if you choose to work with a gem, you must recharge it a minimum of once every seven days. Astrologers in other sampradayas may have differing opinions.

Because the ancient wisdom tradition has been almost completely extinguished in the West, most people here don't know how to do magic anymore. They assume you can buy a special ring and immediately start getting magical effects. If this were true, why isn't the jewelry you already own producing magic?

You need to consciously activate the bandha between the gem and its planetary ruler, or have a saint or tantric do it for you. Magic happens where there is focussed awareness. The Bible says God "brooded" on the cosmic waters and in this way produced the universe. And it says we were created in his image. We also have the ability to create a new reality through our focussed attention, though obviously on a much smaller scale. Some tantrics say you can use mantras, meditation, prayer and visualization in conjunction with a gemstone to produce changes in your life. Respect your gemstone as a living connection with the highest energy of the planet it represents. But don't expect a rock to drain the negativity out of your karmashaya (the repository of karma in your subtle body). Only your own sincere good thoughts and deeds can do that job.

Rx: ASTROLOGICAL GEMS
Wear a carefully prescribed astrological gemstone next to your skin in the form of a pendant or ring. It will need to be energized with mantras before you first put it on, and recharged on a weekly basis.

DIVINE IMAGES

There's a remarkable story in the 28th chapter of the biblical book of Genesis. Jacob has just had a dream in which God appears to him and assures him of his blessings. Jacob wakes up and cries out, "Surely the Lord is in this place, and I did not know it. How awesome is this place. It is none other than the house of God, and this is the gate of heaven." Jacob pours oil over the stone he had used for a pillow, saying, "This stone, which I have set up for a pillar, shall be God's house." This identical ritual is still performed daily throughout India. The stone pillar, called a Shiva lingam, is anointed with oil (usually clarified butter) and honored as a physical dwelling place of the Divine.

Today, this practice is condemned by the monotheistic religions which have forgotten that inanimate objects can indeed serve as a "house of God." This has led to the wildly inaccurate claim that Hindus "worship idols." I have traveled from one end of India to the other and I've never seen a single Hindu worshipping an "idol." Hindus worship God.

You don't have an electrical power plant in your house. There's no way it could fit in your house even if you wanted one. But you do have outlets in your wall that allow you to connect with the power constantly surging from the power plant. In the same way, no house, no temple, indeed no planet or star, is large enough to contain God. Recognizing this, the ancients used images (called *murtis* in India) that serve as continual reminders of God's living presence and as outlets for his grace. The images of God or Goddess which Hindus keep on their home altars serve as concrete objects on which they can focus their minds when they worship. Not everyone finds it easy to enter into a loving relationship with an abstract, immaterial deity. The statue or painting of God in the home or temple helps the devotee "hook up" with the inconceivably vast intelligence from which the universe emanates.

Hindus understand that the image in the temple is not God. In fact, if it cracks or wears out, they cart it away and dump it in the river. But when a priest or devotee performs the *prana pratishtha* rite, inviting God's living presence into the image, from that point on God really is fully present in the image, just like an outlet really supplies live electricity when you plug into it. On a number of occasions I've felt the energy blasting from a murti as strongly as a force field.

Many such murtis have human-like shapes, depicting Divine Being in the form of the gods Vishnu or Krishna or the goddesses Lakshmi or Parvati, for example. Other murtis like the Shiva lingams or Jacob's stone pillar are unshaped or abstract forms. Sometimes yantras are used instead, which are geometric shapes inscribed on metal or some other material, representing the powers and qualities of God or Goddess.

In India, tantrics will invoke the sacred power from the core of their being and project it outward into specially designed yantras, murtis and talismans. These objects then take on extraordinary protective power. I don't recommend that Westerners work with images that have actually been ritually empowered because most of us aren't willing to do the daily worship required to keep the image alive. In India, these images are taken very seriously because they literally embody God's presence. Therefore food, water, flowers and other offerings are presented to them throughout the day, along with the chanting of appropriate mantras. I personally find this a wonderful practice, which creates the vivid sense that God is a permanent guest in one's home, and that one should speak and behave appropriately at all times.

For Western people who're open to working with a visual symbol of God, simply having a picture or statue of a favorite deity in the home is an excellent beginning level version of this upaya. In one room in your home, perhaps your living room or bedroom, place an image of the deity you love most, or of a deity recommended by your astrologer. Don't keep pictures of yourself, your relatives or friends in the same room. The only other images it is appropriate to keep nearby are of other deities or saints. All images in that room should direct your mind toward something higher than yourself. Every time you see the picture or statue, consciously or unconsciously your awareness is lifted to a greater reality.

Rather than using pictures of the planets or planetary deities themselves for this purpose, it's preferable to use an image of a saint or divinity connected with the planet whose energy you are propitiating. For example, if finances are a problem for you because your Venus is afflicted, your astrologer may suggest that you keep a picture of Lakshmi, the goddess of good fortune and prosperity, in your home. This is because the planet itself is not the ultimate source of the blessings you're seeking. The real source is God or the Goddess, divine consciousness itself.

Try not to think of the image as just a decoration in your house. It should be more to you than just a piece of art. Electrical transformers can change a 440 volt current to 220 volts. Let the image transform your mind from a material voltage that constantly dwells on your problems to a spiritual voltage that sees the solutions. Align yourself with the blessing power symbolized by the image. Allow it to raise your consciousness.

If you choose to work with an image of a Hindu deity, here again are the deities whose blessing force is most commonly associated with each planet in India today.

PLANET	DIVINE IMAGE
Sun	Shiva, Rama
Moon	Parvati, Krishna
Mars	Skanda, Hanuman
Mercury	Vishnu, Sarasvati
Jupiter	Brahma, Ganesh
Venus	Lakshmi, Lalita
Saturn	Shiva, Kali
Rahu	Durga, Sarpa
Ketu	Ganesh

Rx: DIVINE IMAGE

Place the image of the deity whose blessings you would like to invoke in a prominent place in your home. Honor that image by mentally offering it your respect or by pressing your hands together in the "Namaste" prayer position each time you enter that room. Think of it as an honored guest who is living with you.

FEEDING OTHERS

A very common tantric prescription in India is to feed others. In some villages you'll see a tulsi plant in front of nearly every home, which is lovingly tended every day. Caring for that plant represents the family's respect for the divinity in all nature. Unfortunately, tulsi doesn't grow well in North America; I've tried it. But tending to a garden, or to potted plants if you live in an apartment, is a time-honored way to align yourself with the forces of nature.

Sometimes an Indian astrologer will recommend that a person donate a cow to another family. This is a very expensive gift for most Indians. The family that receives the cow doesn't eat it, incidentally. Heaven forbid! They use its milk both to drink and to make products like yogurt, butter and butter oil. In this way the astrologer's client is helping to feed other people.

Depending on which planet is weak or afflicted in your chart, your astrologer may recommend that you offer food to other people or creatures. Feeding in this case means actually preparing the food yourself and offering it to others in person, not just writing a check to pay someone else to do the work. If Jupiter is weak for example, you may be asked to cook for people Jupiter represents, such as priests, pastors, teachers or their families, one day a week. If Saturn is afflicted, you may be asked to serve the elderly. If it's Mercury, you can feed students, while if it's Ketu, you should help feed the homeless. Animals are associated with each planet too, such as horses and the Sun, crows and Saturn, dogs and Ketu, snakes (and boars) and Rahu. The type of food you offer may be astrologically determined too. For example, if your Moon is afflicted you may be asked to offer some milky treat like rice pudding (the Moon rules milk) to women who are mothers, or to the women you work with at your job (the Moon symbolizes women).

There's a very beautiful custom in India that when you go to visit a saint, you bring oodles of delicious home-cooked food. The saint doesn't eat it though. Instead she takes a bite, then distributes the rest of the food to the devotees who have come for her blessing. What a delightful way, what a tasteful way, to earn karmic merit.

I have a good friend who very much wants to become a Vedic astrologer. He's studied for years but so far hasn't shown much aptitude for seeing into the heart of a chart. A master jyotishi recommended a practice for him that involved months of chanting a particular mantra at the exact same time every night, then preparing with his own hands sweets made of sesame to offer to people who are spiritually inclined (or brahmins, we would say in India). Finally he was supposed to offer the leftover sesame treats to crows. He spent months carefully following every detail of the prescription. When he finally came to the very last step, he was absolutely unable to get any crow anywhere to taste a single crumb of his offerings, even after weeks of trying. He finally decided the universe was telling him something about his prospects as an astrologer.

Rx: Feeding Others
One day each week for the next six months, prepare some wholesome vegetarian food and offer it to people whom you wouldn't ordinarily feed, like fellow employees at work or your church group. If you live in a rural area, consider offering food to the wildlife around you.

REWRITING YOUR HOROSCOPE

If you're not satisfied with your birth chart, can you completely rewrite it using the techniques of Vedic astrology? Not really, but to some extent you can modify the way your chart's patterns manifest in your life. A technique already well-known in the West is relocational astrology. When you move to another part of the country you can draw a relocated chart, using your original birth time but calculating it for the longitude and latitude of your new home. Your relocated chart won't replace your birth chart, but it may reveal fresh directions your planetary energies can flow in at this new location.

Another technique for modifying the influences of the birth chart is taught by Prince Hirindra Singh, a Sikh who practices Vedic astrology. In

India some astrologers actually worship their own birth charts during their morning ritual practices. Their horoscope is inscribed on a consecrated metal plate or some other sacred material, and the planets in the chart are propitiated with offerings of flower petals, grain, and sacred powders or perfumes, which are dropped on the chart directly into the house the planet occupies. The astrologer then chants mantras to his or her planetary positions, thanking Mars in Virgo (for example) for the blessings he has bestowed, and requesting Mars' Virgoan energies to work in the best possible manner that day.

Prince Hirindra takes this traditional process one step further. Each morning he gets up and rearranges the planets. For example, if he is scheduled to lecture that day, he may move one of his natal planets into the 2nd house which governs speaking, carefully selecting a planet which will be most beneficial in the sign occupying the 2nd house. If the second house contains Libra, he would move his natal Venus (the ruler of Libra) there, where it can greatly enhance his speaking abilities.

Hindus understand that for most people, simply making a mental resolution is not necessarily effective; the resolution must be acted out in order for it to be vividly "stamped" on the subconscious mind, which will then reorganize its energies to accommodate one's conscious desire. So Prince Hirindra writes his "revised" horoscope each day with sacred turmeric powder on a consecrated wooden board. The planets in his original birth chart are invited to their new positions, then sincerely worshipped so that the new configuration (e.g., Venus in Libra in the 2nd house) is firmly established at all levels of his mind. He says it's his experience that for the next 24 hours, the planets' energies will act as if they actually are in the new sign and house.

Prince Hirindra warns that using this tantric technique has its drawbacks. Every time a planet is shifted from its original natal position, the birth chart becomes unbalanced. If your natal Venus has been shifted out of the 4th house in order to support the 2nd, 2nd house affairs may improve but the 4th house may suffer.

Other planets may be affected as well, as Venus' aspect now changes. Therefore, in rewriting one's natal chart, care must be taken so that the new positions don't inadvertently cause more problems than the old ones.

You cannot literally rewrite the horoscope you were born with; it represents the karmic strengths and challenges allotted to you for this lifetime. With your every thought and action, however, you are currently in the process of writing the horoscope you'll be born with in your next incarnation.

People who characteristically behave with anger and selfishness will find these qualities reflected in their next birth chart. If instead, even in the face of adverse circumstances, they act with courage, cheerfulness and concern for others, this good karma will show itself in the improved placements of their natal planets in a future incarnation.

Rx: REARRANGE YOUR PLANETS

Prerequisite: You must have a fairly good understanding of astrology in order to use this upaya wisely. Each day after your morning meditation, redraw your horoscope on a clean sheet of white paper, placing the planets where they'll be most useful for you that day. Keep in mind that karmic balances are still in effect, so when you shift a powerful planet from a good position in your original birth chart, it may weaken the house you've moved it out of. If you move malefics, keep in mind they'll be casting aspects that could cause problems if you're not wise in handling the new placements. Mentally resolve that for the next 24 hours, this will indeed be your horoscope.

GURU'S GRACE

If you have the opportunity to serve a *satguru*, an authentic spiritual master or a true saint, by all means do so. No matter what your karma is, in the presence of a realized master all bets are off. The blessing of a genuine saint can wipe out karmic debts instantly as if they were canceled checks. A guru who abides in continual awareness of the Divine is an unfailing conduit for God's grace, and God's grace is infinite.

Rx: GRACE

Seek out the company of spiritually advanced souls. (Please bear in mind that not everyone who advertises they're an enlightened being really is.) Serve them with devotion and humility.

Part 4
What Is, Was, And Will Be

A person is born again to experience the consequences
of actions performed in previous births.
Some of these consequences are reaped in the afterlife.
But others can only be experienced
in a physical body in this physical world.

Prashna Marga 1.33

Listen carefully. The essence of the human soul is will.
Whatever you will to happen will happen,
in this life or the next.
Therefore direct your will carefully.

Chandogya Upanishad 3.14.1

20

Astrology in the City of Light: The Eternal Tradition

The streets are so narrow, if I stretch out my arms I can touch the buildings on both sides with my fingertips. It's impossible for cars to get through, so I'm obliged to pitch my luggage over my shoulder and carry it myself. Several times I push up against the wall so a cow can squeeze past. I'm making my way through the labyrinth of the old quarter of Benares, "the city of light," hoping to learn more about Jyotish, the science of light.

Benares is the oldest continuously inhabited city on Earth. It was already ancient when the Veda was composed over 5000 years ago, and then as now tradition says it was a gathering place for saints, pandits and astrologers. I always make a point to visit Benares Hindu University, the largest residential university in Asia. At the beginning of the 21st century astrology made a hesitant comeback in some Western universities (after an absence of centuries), disguised as "cultural astronomy." At BHU you never had to apologize for studying astrology; here the ancient and venerable language of the stars has always been a valued part of the curriculum.

I'm staying at the Trailinga Swami ashram, named after a famous yogi who would escape from the crowds by meditating under the surface of the Ganges for hours at a time. This isn't as unlikely as it sounds: I've more than once observed yogis sitting without breathing. Breath retention is one of the disciplines of yoga practice, designed to promote intense concentration.

There's not a stick of furniture in my room at the ashram. I had expected this and roll my sleeping bag out on the concrete floor. You've got to be seriously committed if you want to study astrology in modern India. Want to run your astrology program? Forget about plugging your computer into an outlet even if you can find one; here electricity comes and goes erratically like lightning. The pandits here don't bother with calling up tens of thousands of astrological principles on a computer. They memorize them.

From the ashram it's a short walk to Pancha Ganga Ghat, where Hindus have been coming to bathe in the purifying waters of the Ganges since time began. I climb down steep, slippery stone steps to the river, and hire a boatman to row me along the spectacular river front. It's impossible to convey how beautiful Benares is in the morning as that radiant god the brahmins call Lord Surya rises over the city. We in the West call him the Sun, irreverently mistaking this shining Divine Being for a big ball of gas. Here natives are out by the thousands, immersing themselves in the Ganges and offering handfuls of sacred water to Lord Surya as they chant the Gayatri, his holy mantra. This city feels like paradise to me. Indeed our word paradise comes from India. It's from *para desha,* Sanskrit for "the supreme land."

Great Buddhist masters taught here for centuries, but there's hardly a trace of them now. Ferocious Muslim rulers laid the city to waste, but it rose again like Lord Surya. One force alone endures in this timeless city: *Sanatana Dharma,* the eternal tradition of India. Al Biruni, the great Muslim scholar who studied in India a thousand years ago, was thoroughly versed in Islam, Judaism and Christianity. He wrote that while these religions seem dramatically different on the outside, their mystical core (Sufism, Kabbalah and Gnosticism) is remarkably similar to Hinduism. Religions come and go but their living essence, the Sanatana Dharma, goes on and on.

Hidden Connections

I can tell you exactly what the saints and intellectuals who lived in this city four, five thousand years ago were teaching. I can do this because India's lineages of yogis and scholars, more than in any other culture on earth, have painstakingly preserved their ancient wisdom. They taught then as now, "This entire universe is Pure Intelligence. It was projected from Pure Intelligence. It is animated by Pure Intelligence. It will merge back into Pure Intelligence. Therefore meditate on that Pure Intelligence." *(Chandogya Upanishad 3.14.1.)*

What does this have to do with astrology? Everything. Because once you understand what these sages are saying then, finally, you will understand why astrology works.

The angular relations between the Earth and the Sun cause the seasons. The angular relations between the Earth and the Moon cause the tides. But the angles between the Sun and Saturn don't make you have issues with authority figures. The angles between the Moon and Venus don't make you a sucker for romance. Yet an experienced jyotishi here in Benares can glance at your horoscope and tell instantly that you can't hold onto a job because you can't stand to be bossed by other people, or that you continually fall in and out of love. If the planets don't cause this, how can the relations between them describe your life so accurately?

The sages say this whole universe is woven together out of the fabric of consciousness. Everything in the cosmos—every atom, every burst of energy, every thought—is intimately related to every other thing like a blanket knit from a single strand of yarn. When Indra, chief of the gods, cast his net over all existence, each segment of the net reflected his own face. *Yat pinde tad brahmande,* "As appears here below, so it appears above." Patterns appearing in the sky simultaneously manifest on Earth. In this cosmology, the motions of the planets don't "cause" events in our lives, they merely reflect the same pattern being projected at that moment in the infinite mind of God. God's will unfolds in all dimensions of space at the same time. We and the stars dance to the same melody.

There is no causal connection between events in the sky and in our lives. but there is often a profound symbolic connection. This fundamental principle, which Carl Jung called synchronicity, is not only the reason why astrology works, but all other forms of divination as well, from palmistry to tea leaves to Tarot cards. The link is not in time and space but in the consciousness of God.

Your conscious mind functions more or less rationally, instinctively following the dictates of logic. If you set fire to your house it will burn down, and you won't have anywhere to live. Your subconscious mind, however, is not affected by the laws of causality at all. If you set fire to your home in your imagination, in a split second with the flick of your will, the house is rebuilt and you can move back in. This sounds like a trivial point, but the yogis say that after death when the body and logical mind associated with it dissolve, our consciousness continues to exist in the world of our collective dreams. So understanding the nature of the mental world is important if we want our transition into an after-death state to be smooth.

That astral world functions not according to the laws of logic, but according to the laws of symbols. Just try reasoning with your subconscious mind. It doesn't work. But the subconscious responds to symbols, and thinks to itself in fantasies and dreams. It doesn't use reasonable thoughts, but meaningful images. The Cosmic Mind (called *Mahat,* "the great one" by the yogis) also thinks and acts symbolically. Why does ritual magic work? Because the objects we offer in our pujas symbolically relate to ideas in the Cosmic Mind. When we symbolically align our will with the cosmic intelligence, magic happens. Our individual minds were, after all, projected from Mahat. We are part of that vast inner network and can consciously work with its subtle connecting links.

In the *Yoga Vasishtha* Sarasvati, the goddess of wisdom, explains, "Consciousness, mind and space: these are not three different things. Each of these is all pervading. The true intelligence inside you, the awareness buried beneath the everyday rambling of your mind, pervades all of space. All living things are connected through this network of intelligence. It is the basis of telepathy, precognition, astrology, and the other occult powers.

"There is a part of your mind which dwells within this Divine Intelligence. Yogis call it the unconfined body. It is everywhere and its powers are unlimited. It is the Supreme Divine Awareness itself."

Everything in the universe is tied to everything else in a way that is inherently meaningful. So the position of the planets at our birth meaningfully reflects our character and destiny. But so does everything else. Here in Benares your astrologer isn't just looking at your birth chart. He or she is also paying attention to what people are calling out in the street as you ask your questions, the part of your body you unconsciously touch as you speak, the color of your clothes and other apparently insignificant incidentals loaded with meaning for someone trained in reading the signs. *Nimitta,* or the study of omens, is an important part of an astrological reading in India, because it is exquisitely sensitive to movements of the Cosmic Intelligence.

In the *Brihat Samhita,* Varaha Mihira (the most famous astrologer in the court of the celebrated emperor Vikram Aditya) explains how astrologers use this tool. If a client is asking who has stolen an article of hers, the astrologer watches to see where she next unconsciously touches herself. If she touches the top part of her arm, the thief is someone in her family, if the bottom portion of her arm, it's an outsider. If she motions to her heart, her husband is the culprit, if her fingertips graze her thumb, it's her daughter. The astrologer may make a judgment based on the appearance of the clouds, the type of bird which sudden soars past the window and the direction in which it's flying, or what sort of person walks by outside and what she's carrying.

Varaha Mihira is as well known here in Benares, some 2000 years after his death, as he was during his lifetime. The story of the legendary astrologer is worth retelling.

The Master Astrologer

Satyavati and her husband, a brahmin couple who lived near the city of Ujjain here in north India, were in their fifties and still had no children. Their birth charts showed *aputhrya dosha,* the inability to have children, but they had tremendous faith in their ability to change their fate through intense spiritual practice. As the years passed, they worshipped Lord Surya, the Sun, with intense feeling. Finally, even as old age dawned, the couple was blessed with a beautiful son they named Mihira, an epithet of the Sun.

Mihira was deeply spiritual, devoting most of his time to spiritual practice and to the study of astrology. Even as a teenager his reputation as an astrologer was formidable. People said he had *vak siddhi,* "spiritual power in his words"; most everything he predicted came true.

One day as he was performing his evening ablutions in the river, two merchants shouted at him from the bank. "Hey you, people here say you're a great astrologer. Tell us how much money we're going to make on this trip."

Still standing in the water, Mihira mentally calculated the position of the planets, then answered evenly. "Neither of you is a merchant. One of you is a king and the other is his advisor. You are in disguise because you don't want your subjects to know about your romantic escapades."

Mihira went on to describe a number of illegitimate births which had occurred in the royal family, information no one outside a small circle in the court could possibly have known.

However, it wasn't just any king standing at the river bank. It was Vikram Aditya, destined to become one of the great emperors of Indian history, whose empire would extend from Afghanistan to Burma. Vikram Aditya knew a man with a valuable skill when he saw one. He immediately invited Mihira to the capital to become his court astrologer.

Vikram Aditya's court was one of the most illustrious in history, including some of the greatest artists, intellectuals, scientists, engineers and astrologers of all time. When one of the emperor's sons was born, the astrologers were summoned to offer their predictions. The news was disturbing: they unanimously agreed the boy would die in his 18th year. Vikram Aditya was not pleased to hear this, and demanded to know more details about exactly how the death was supposed to occur and what could be done to prevent it.

While all the astrologers saw the problem, only Mihira was skilled enough to specify the exact day the boy would die and that he would be killed by a boar. Mihira explained that while most streams of destiny can be altered to some degree, this was a case of fixed karma. Nothing could prevent the boy from perishing that day. "We'll see about that!" the emperor roared.

Eighteen years later, Vikram Aditya had not forgotten the ominous prediction. On the fated day, he locked his son in the top floor of his castle with a group of his closest friends to protect him. On every floor the emperor stationed dozens of armed guards to ensure that no boar—or any wild animal or other threat of any kind—could get near his son.

As the appointed hour neared, the prince, perhaps feeling a bit anxious in spite of the elaborate precautions, stepped outside onto the balcony for a breath of fresh air. He died instantly. His skull was split open by a metal emblem which at that precise moment, in the heavy winds, had shaken loose from a royal standard posted on the roof. The emblem was of the Hindu avatar Varaha, God in the shape of a boar. Within days all India knew the story, and from that day to this, our master astrologer would be known as Varaha Mihira.

How did Mihira make the prediction? No doubt he knew that, according to the sage Parashara, in the Cosmic Mind boars are related to

Rahu, the Moon's North Node. Due to his intense spiritual practices, Mihira had developed a yogic skill called *divya drishti,* "divine vision." This gave him the ability to look at how Rahu was afflicting the prince's chart and instantly sort through the thousands of different things Rahu signifies. A subtle set of interlinking possibilities flashed through his mind till the correct connection was made intuitively: death would be caused by a boar.

The Twinkle in God's Eye

Because the universe was created out of consciousness, because our world is actually a picture in God's awareness, the cosmos operates more like a mind than a material mechanism. Just as apparently unrelated images can be closely linked in our subconscious mind, so particular substances—like boars and the Moon's North Node—are linked in the mind of God. Understanding these links and knowing how to work meaningfully with them is called tantra in India.

We in the West believe that billions of years ago there was a Big Bang, spewing matter out across the cosmos. Very gradually organic compounds evolved, then organic life, and finally consciousness itself, culminating in ourselves, the most conscious beings of all. Hindu belief is almost exactly the opposite. In their view consciousness came first. A vast cosmic intelligence they call Brahma, the creator god, first conceived the idea of the universe and then projected it out of awareness itself. Mind first, then matter.

We in the West distinguish between mental images, which we call myths and fantasies, and outer events which we call real. Indians run the inner and outer worlds together into a perfectly integrated whole. Because of this, they live in sacred time. They perceive life everywhere, even in earth and air and water and fire. They worship God's presence everywhere they see it, in the divine forces outside themselves and the divine forces inside themselves.

Hindus speak of three worlds. The first, our waking reality, is governed by the law of karma. Every thought and action, every fluctuation in the field of energy, causes an equal and commensurate reaction. Understanding how to skillfully make our way through this net of karma is the purpose of Vedic astrology. Transcending the bondage of karma altogether is the purpose of yoga.

The second world isn't physical but you can still see and hear it. This world is made up of *tanmatras* (subtle elements) and operates according to the laws of symbology. Because of these laws, we can propitiate a planet in the sky that represents anger, and inside ourselves anger suddenly subsides.

The third world is formless. It's beyond vision and sound yet it's intensely real. This is the world of pure conceptual awareness where Plato located his *Ideas.* It operates according to the laws of pure understanding. Its contents are the seeds of all manifest existence.

Beyond these three worlds is *turiya,* "that fourth." It is what it is. Without moving, it moves everything. Without knowing, it knows everything. Its operant principle is grace.

Because of grace, every moment in life is auspicious. Every moment is propitious for invoking the presence of the divine. Every moment is the perfect moment to enter into the condition of enlightened understanding.

Jyotish reveals that time is sacred. Its sanctity emanates from the timeless center of creation. "At the core of our being Truth shines—like a thousand suns," says the Veda.

The electricity goes out again, plunging this entire section of Benares into darkness. What a pleasure it is, sitting here on the roof of the Trailinga Swami ashram on a beautiful, clear evening, staring up at the planets and stars, gazing deep into the unfathomable vastness of the mind of God.

21

The Gnostic Sky: Jesus and Jyotish

The Pharisees didn't especially care for Jesus. His biting criticism of their lifestyle was a continual source of acute embarrassment. Finally, one day they approached him and demanded, "If you're really a prophet sent from God, show us a sign from heaven."

Jesus answered, "If the sky is red in the evening, you say the weather will be fair. If the sky is red in the morning, you say it will storm today. You know how to interpret the appearance of the sky, but you can't interpret the signs of the times. You will have no sign but this: the sign of Jonah." (Matthew 16:1-4.)

The sign of Jonah is, of course, a large fish (the prophet Jonah was swallowed by a whale). Jesus was referring to the sign of Pisces and was putting the Pharisees on notice that the recent precession of the Vernal Point into Pisces signaled that a new age was beginning, and that the prophet of that new era stood before them. Jesus was scolding the Pharisees for their inability to recognize the astrological importance of the Age of Pisces, for not being able to "interpret the signs of the times."

Both the Old and the New Testaments open with powerful statements about the validity of astrology. When God creates the planets and stars he says, "Let them be for signs." When Jesus is born, "wise men from the East," who fortunately hadn't heard that good Christians aren't supposed to practice astrology, saw a star signalling the birth of a great soul and set out for Jerusalem to find him.

Fortunately, those of us who want to find Jesus today have more means to do so than at almost any other time in history. Since the discoveries of the Dead Sea Scrolls in Palestine and the Nag Hammadi library in Egypt, as well as of a missing portion of the Gospel of Mark, biblical studies have taken enormous strides forward; we now understand more about Jesus and the early Christian community than scholars have for at least 1600 years.

You would think that priests and pastors everywhere would be enthusiastically educating their congregations about the many exciting findings regarding the early Church which have recently come to light. Instead, a pall of silence hangs over the topic. I'm completely amazed at how even when news outlets like *Time, Newsweek* or public television produce a feature on these new discoveries, the most important findings are discretely omitted. My own teachers at one of the most prestigious seminaries in the country—leading Christian theologians—would be open about this exciting new material with graduate students like me, but in front of their congregations or with the news media, suddenly they became very cagey, censoring their sentences carefully.

The cause for the cover-up is that much of what scholars have recently learned about the early Christians dramatically contradicts what many of us were taught as children in Sunday school. Numerous ancient documents, for example, attest that the disciples Jesus valued most were not the twelve male disciples we usually think of, but his women devotees. These are the kinds of surprises many conservative Christians are not eager to learn about.

Another shock these ancient manuscripts provided was the extraordinary importance some groups of early Christians gave to the planets. In some of their texts the signs of the zodiac are mentioned on nearly every page. There exists strong, though highly controversial, evidence that Jesus himself was acquainted with the power of astrology and that he taught his disciples ways of working with the stars that are still used in countries like India and Tibet to this day. Find that hard to believe? Here are the facts.

The Nazarenes

In southern Iraq, scholars discovered a remarkable sect called the Mandeans who have carefully preserved the religious practices of their ancestors for over 2,000 years. These Semitic people are the only authentic Gnostic sect known to have survived from pre-Christian times.

The reason this group is of such compelling interest to scholars becomes clear when you learn their ancient name. These are the last of the Nazarenes (*nasuraiyi,* literally "guardians of spiritual knowledge"). According to their sacred history, they are the descendants of the mysterious sect into which Jesus Christ was initiated by John the Baptist on the banks of the River Jordan. To this day, the Nazarenes honor John the Baptist as one of the many great prophets of their ancient tradition, and still practice the rite of baptism just as John performed it two millennia ago.

But the Nazarenes are not only known for their elaborate baptisms; they are also recognized as skilled astrologers who from antiquity have passed on their mystical knowledge of the heavens. They possess an enormous mystical literature (which they are not especially happy to share with inquisitive Westerners), including what they claim are actual discourses by John the Baptist himself. Among the works they have preserved in clay, lead, leather or more recently on paper, is the *Sfar Malwashi,* "The Book of the Signs of the Zodiac," one of their primary sources for calculating horoscopes in the ancient manner. As in India, the astrologer's role begins at birth: newborns are taken to the local seer who carefully chooses a name for the infant based on astrological factors.

Could the Nazarenes have been the astrologers mentioned in the Bible who sought out the infant Jesus after detecting a star signalling the birth of a new Jewish king? These "wise men" left expensive gifts with Mary and Joseph, perhaps to help pay for Jesus's travels and education. Maybe they even guided his training until his formal initiation by John the Baptist, a leader of their sect. Throughout the Gospels, Jesus is continually referred to as "the Nazarene."

Surprising fragments of Nazarene teachings on astrology appear in a quotation attributed to Jesus in an early Christian manuscript found at Nag Hammadi. But before we take a look at it, let's see what the Nazarenes had to say about the planets.

Nazarene Astrology

The Nazarenes, like most Gnostic sects, believe that light and darkness, good and evil, are continually at war. This world was produced by an evil creator god, and in it he traps pure souls from the divine world of light. The creator's chief ministers in the enslavement of human souls are the twelve signs of the zodiac, the seven planets, and Ruha, an evil spirit constantly seeking to put out the light.

Obviously, we are not dealing with 21st century humanistic astrology here. The astrology of the Semitic people of Jesus' time was highly mystical, not psychological as it is today, and had a very dark edge. The planets imprisoned the soul with chains of fate, ensuring suffering and death for everyone trapped in this grim, unjust world. When you consider the poverty, continual warfare, and horrendous political brutality (roads were often lined with crucified prisoners) to which many of the people of the first century were exposed, it's not hard to understand how the Gnostics of Palestine and Syria developed such a bleak view.

The Nazarenes, like most mystical sects of the time, including many early Christians, believed in reincarnation, so there was no escape from the destiny outlined for them by the planets until the Day of Judgment, when the earth and the planets themselves would be destroyed by fire. No escape, that is, without *manda*, "divine knowledge," the living experience that we are divine souls whose true home is in the World of Light, beyond the grip of the planetary forces.

To help the deceased find his or her way back to the realm of light, Nazarenes conduct a six-week long ritual following death. Souls are believed to wander for 42 days after leaving their bodies, after which they may be reincarnated on earth or liberated into pure light. Or, if they are irredeemably evil, they may pass into a hell-like state or even be annihilated.

After death, the soul must pass through seven gates, each guarded by one of the classical planets (the Sun, Moon, and Mercury through Saturn). As it confronts each planetary spirit in turn, the soul is called to account for how it used that planetary energy during its lifetime. If, for example, a person has used his martian drive or mercurial intellect in a self-serving or malicious manner, he remains in the grip of that planet's negative power, and is punished appropriately. One of the Nazarene hymns describes this harrowing process:

> My time on earth had ended. I departed
> but the seven planets shut the gates to heaven,
> trying to block my way.
> Those wicked spirits conspired,

"Let's prevent him from reaching the divine light,
and keep him in our power forever."
But I raised the level of my awareness
to the plane of everlasting life.
In my heart I knew I had lived a pure life.
I had become conscious of my Higher Self.
It opened the gates to the highest heaven,
and drove away the planetary spirits.
It clothed me in light
and I shone more brightly than all the lights in the world!

"May your throne in heaven be prepared for you, just as it was when you dwelt there before incarnating on earth, and may the seven planets be powerless before you," runs a Nazarene blessing.

Just as in the *Egyptian Book of the Dead* and the *Tibetan Book of the Dead,* the after-death states are carefully described to the Nazarene. She is provided with secret knowledge and sacred mantras that help her pass fearlessly through the after-death experience. Many Nazarene texts warn that if we don't purify ourselves during our time on Earth, we will not be able to maintain our presence of mind after death, and therefore will not be able to control our destiny. Instead of merging into the light, we will lose contact with our Higher Self, and the planets will set our course for us.

Jesus on the Planetary Powers

In India and Central Asia, spiritual masters sometimes conceal sacred texts, whether in caves, underground or in hidden passageways in temples. These *termas,* as they are called, are gifts for future generations, time capsules full of magic and insight for the people who find them centuries or even millennia later.

About 1700 years ago, an early Christian community in Egypt left just such a gift to posterity. Then in 1945, peasants from the area near Nag Hammadi, half-way up the Nile, discovered several jars filled with these ancient manuscripts hidden in caves in the chalk cliffs near their homes. Scholars later determined these texts had originally been authored in the second and third centuries or earlier, offering an invaluable glimpse into the minds of some of the earliest Christians. Whole new Gospels were discovered, with many new stories about Jesus's life, the authenticity of which scholars will no doubt be debating till kingdom come.

These texts contain some astonishingly modern sounding material; it's amazing to think these manuscripts were written so long ago. Several of them reveal that some early Christians, like feminists today, seriously questioned the legitimacy of the patriarchal god of the Old Testament, and turned back to the ancient Jewish goddess Sophia for inspiration. Other texts show a deep familiarity with Egyptian religion and absolutely amazing similarities to the yogic tradition of India.

One of the Nag Hammadi texts, called *The First Apocalypse of James,* purports to be a dialogue between Jesus and his brother James regarding the soul's experience after death. For any astrologer who's wrestled with the question of the extent to which we're controlled by the destiny drawn in our birth charts, and the extent to which we are free beings, Jesus's advice on how to deal with the power of the planets will resonate strongly.

At the beginning of the story, James is quaking with fear, knowing he will almost certainly be martyred. But James is more afraid of what will happen after death than of death of itself, so Jesus reveals to him the secret of mastering the archons, the binding powers of the zodiac:

"Behold, I will reveal to you the manner of your redemption. When you undergo the pangs of death, the archons will come to seize you. They are like toll keepers, who try to control your soul by force. When one of them asks you, 'Who are you and where are you from,' answer, 'I am a son and I come from the Father.'

"When one of them says to you, 'What kind of son are you and who is your Father,' answer, 'I am from the Father who existed before the beginning of time, and I was his son before time began.'

"When one of them says to you, 'Why were you sent here,' answer, 'I came from eternity to see the things that exist in Spirit and the things that exist in matter. But the things that exist in matter actually exist in Spirit, because they come from the Mother, and the Mother abides in the Father. I call on the imperishable knowledge that is the Mother [the goddess of wisdom Sophia, who is also Achamoth, the mother of the universe] who abides eternally in the Father.'

"Then the archons will release you and you will be free to ascend to the kingdom of light which is your own light."

Jesus Christ is saying that as long as we remember who we really are, divine spirits who exist beyond time, then the planets and signs—the forces of time itself—have no power over us. As long as we realize that the material universe abides in Spirit, the energies of the universe cannot control us, for we are Spirit. The Bible calls the planets and constellations "authorities and principalities." But the forces of time have no authority over that which exists outside time, our immortal soul. When we ally ourselves with our Higher Self, we can act in perfect freedom, no longer subject to any astrological constraint.

The Vedic Perspective

In *The First Apocalypse of James,* Jesus tells James, "Free yourself from the blind idea that you are merely the casket of flesh in which you are embodied. Then you will reach Him Who Is. Then you will no longer be James; rather you are the One Who Is."

We don't know whether Jesus actually spoke these words, all we know is that some early Christians believed he did. They took great pains to preserve this account for future generations. Living so close to the time of Jesus, they were probably in a better position to know what Jesus really did say than we are today, but this account, like everything else about Jesus, remains controversial. Still, it's amazing to find statements attributed to Jesus that are entirely Vedic in tone, to hear him explicitly say that if we free ourselves from one-pointed identification with the body through contemplation and meditation, then we can directly experience God, and in fact that we already are a part of God, "the One Who Is."

In the yoga tradition, the ultimate purpose for doing spiritual practice is to attain moksha, freedom from the bondage of karma. A perfectly Self-realized saint is called a *jivanmukta*, which means "liberated while still in a body." He or she has mastered the stars, and no longer answers to the dictates of fate. Miracles frequently occur in the presence of liberated souls because the laws of karma are suspended in their presence. Yogis teach that the solar system actually exists within the human psyche, and once we have mastered our own minds we govern our inner planets, rather than being blindly driven by inner complexes associated with them.

According to not only the yogic, but also numerous early Christian and Nazarene texts, the "gates" the soul encounters after death, guarded by the planetary spirits, really exist. The intensely bright light which many survivors of near death experiences report seeing even today is the first gate—the gate of the Sun. If you are pure enough to pass through all seven gates, including the last, dreaded gate of Saturn, you have achieved *moksha*, and are free to travel beyond the confines of this solar system.

For Hindus, however, the planets are not evil spirits who force our fate on us, but timekeepers who signal when the time is ripe for our karma to bear fruit. The planets are just doing their jobs. Vedic astrology doesn't blame the planets for the misfortune life brings. Instead Vedic astrologers call on their clients to look at their attitudes and behavior to see what they can do to purify their imperfections and restore harmony with the planetary energies. While the Western tradition condemned the planets (and ultimately condemned astrology), the living spirit of each planet is honored in the Vedic tradition. While the material world is recognized as only a pale reflection of a divine inner reality, it is still treated with the utmost reverence in the Veda, the Hindu Bible. In India, from the most ancient times till the present day, astrology has been hailed as a divine science, an invaluable tool for those of us still grappling with the karma that our planetary cycles deliver to us. Its purpose is to help us find our way home to God, whom the Gnostic texts again and again call "the Lord of Light." The Sanskrit word Jyotish *(jyotir isha)* literally means "Lord of Light."

Jesus in India

Over the past few decades, there's been increasing speculation that during the "lost years" before he began his public ministry, Jesus visited India. This is based on Muslim legends and a Tibetan text which allegedly described a Jesus-like figure. The evidence is so tenuous that I have to agree with orthodox scholars it's far more likely Jesus received his esoteric training from mystical Jewish groups like the Essenes and Nazarenes, both of whom are directly or indirectly described in the Bible. Yet fascinatingly, there is an early Christian text, *The Acts of Thomas,* which claims that Jesus had a profound interest in India and visited his disciple Thomas there some time after recovering from his crucifixion. Unfortunately, the text doesn't clarify whether this was Jesus's first trip to India.

Whether or not Jesus ever traveled east, recent discoveries such as those at Nag Hammadi reveal that the distance between Eastern and Western mystical traditions and their schools of mystical astrology may not be very far.

22

Fear of Foreknowledge: Are We Ready for the Future?

Traditionally in India only priests, after years of strict self-discipline under the guidance of spiritual mentors, master the ability to read the flow of people's karma and predict their destiny. Today, however, Jyotish is being imported to the West and taught at public conferences to anyone who happens to show up. These people are being exposed to an astrological super-science rooted in the insights of ancient sages, honed by millennia of painstaking observations, and potentially awe-inspiring in its predictive precision.

What will happen when this powerful occult science, one with predictive ability so great we may be able to foretell not only specific events in a person's life but perhaps also the very time of their death, falls into the hands of practitioners not necessarily noted for their spiritual maturity?

It's happened before. At Apollonia in the first century B.C.E., a young man named Agrippa brought a friend—a political aspirant like himself—to see an astrologer named Theogenes. At that time the Greeks and Romans were still quite new to astrology, and used a system derived from the far more ancient Indian and Persian models. Predictions by Western astrologers of the time approached the jyotishis' in accuracy, so soothsayers like Theogenes were quite popular. Theogenes gave Agrippa an upbeat reading, so much so that his friend was reluctant to reveal his own birth data, doubting his destiny could be as favorable as Agrippa's. As he finished calculating the second young man's chart, however,

Theogenes began to tremble. Shaking visibly, the astrologer could hardly speak; he simply threw himself at the young man's feet.

Years later when this young man, whose name was Octavian, established himself as the sole head of the Roman empire and one of the most powerful human beings on earth, this remarkable encounter with Theogenes was not far from his mind. Octavian, better known as Caesar Augustus, published his horoscope in an edict so that everyone could see, as Theogenes had, that he had been ordained from birth to rule the empire. Octavian had his Moon sign, Capricorn, stamped on the coins minted during his reign as a continual reminder to his subjects of his star-sealed ascendancy.

It did not take Octavian long to realize the consequences of letting the astrological genie out of the bottle. Any advanced astrologer who had the emperor's birth time could also calculate, in theory at least, his time of death. In 11 C.E. Octavian passed a law forbidding astrologers to predict anyone's demise, especially his.

Incredibly, by 20 C.E., Emperor Tiberius had an astrological Gestapo in place. Its job was to ferret out horoscopes of promising young men to discover which of them posed the most serious threat to the emperor. Tiberius could then have rivals with particularly strong charts slain at his leisure. Emperor Caraculla also employed vast numbers of astrologers in his "star hunt" for potential traitors. I'm not kidding; these events are historically documented.

Imagine the situation. Within topmost political circles, astrologers wielded enormous power. In fact, astrologers were implicated in the debacle of 69 C.E., during the course of which single year a succession of four emperors fleetingly ruled the land, egged on by astrologers who saw their imperial destiny in their horoscopes. One of these monarchs, Vitellius, had had enough of the machinations of astrologers and banned them wholesale from Rome. In response, the astrologers banded together and posted a decree predicting Vitellius' imminent death. Furious, Vitellius sent his soldiers into the streets to kill every astrologer they could find. Dead or alive, the astrologers had the last laugh: as per their prediction, Vitellius was found dead three months later.

By the year 296 C.E., an empire-wide ban on the practice of astrology was in force. The astrologers had brought it on themselves, ignoring all rules of ethics, selling their sacred knowledge to the highest bidder. In cahoots with tyrants and would-be emperors, many of them helped target hapless victims, misled the public and desecrated their sacred art.

The Romans could legislate against astrology but there was no way they could stop its practice. It was somewhat like the situation today: scientists and educators can rail against astrology from sunrise to moonset, but the fact remains people are much less interested in what's "scientific" than in what actually works, and in their experience astrology works. The information it provides is often useful and insightful, so now as then people ignore the authorities and continue analyzing their horoscopes.

Astrology faced a far more serious challenge after Emperor Constantine nominally converted to Christianity and the full brunt of Catholic theology was brought to bear against it. Fascinatingly, the clergy inveighed against astrology not because it didn't work, but because it did. Christian theologians were in no position to claim that astrology was false; practically the very first thing the Old Testament says is that God placed the stars in the sky "for signs" (Genesis 1:14), and practically the first thing the New Testament says is that it was astrology which led the "wise men" to Jesus' manger (Matthew 2:1-12). Since in several places the Bible made such a strong case for astrology's validity, priests attacking the science had to be careful not to shoot themselves in the feet by seeming to contradict the Bible.

What so disturbed the clergy was the fear that if "everything is written in the stars," where was the freedom for our own choice to accept Christ and attain heaven, or reject Christ and burn forever in hell? The position of the church became that even if the stars held the message of our destiny, that message was not for us to read. Foreknowledge was forbidden, dangerous, reserved for God himself and perhaps the angels.

More laws were drafted against astrology; more sermons inveighed against its use. Despite these full-scale attacks, we know that sophisticated astrological predictive techniques continued to be practiced in medieval Europe with considerable success. Generations of royal families continued to employ court astrologers not because the diviners were con artists, but because their predictions were often accurate. The famous Italian astrologer Luca Gaurica correctly foresaw the death of the Duc de Bourbon in 1527, as well as the circumstances of French King Henri II's violent end in July 1559, for example. Gaurica's descriptions of upcoming events easily rivaled those of the best Vedic astrologers today both in specificity of detail and precision of timing.

Throughout the entire Piscean Age, astrology, and divination in general, have been condemned by Western legal and religious authorities. For the past three hundred years, astrology has been held under the gun by scientists who claim it can't work and that its practitioners are defrauding the public. For the 1700 years before that, astrology was banned because it did work, and the consequences of unscrupulous application of its power were genuinely disturbing. For that matter, the consequences of even its legitimate and ethical use were unsettling to those whose theology it challenged. During Roman times, slaves were strictly prohibited from casting the charts of their masters. The wealthy and powerful had no illusions about the threat astrology presented to their dominance if their slaves could use it against them. They also recognized what a powerful tool it offered them in their quest for even greater self-aggrandizement, if they could use it against others themselves. Anyone who doubts that in our own more "enlightened" times astrology would be used by the avaricious to cultivate political power, with potentially disastrous consequences for society at large, need look no further than Ronald Reagan.

What will happen when the movers and shakers of our own corrupt civilization acquire tools similar to those ancient astrologers like Theogenes used? Remember, it's happened before.

It's not too early for the astrological community to begin thinking seriously about the major ethical dilemmas we will be facing in the new millennium. Will astrologers be the light bringers of the era? Or will we, like too many unscrupulous lawyers and businessmen today, eagerly exchange the well-being of society for big cars, big houses and big bucks?

To place this issue in wider perspective, let me briefly describe how this situation was handled in India. While recent social upheavals have altered the way astrology is taught today especially in urban India, traditionally the powerful predictive techniques of Vedic astrology were carefully protected by its practitioners, who consisted largely of the priestly caste and spiritual renunciates. To this day, most astrologers in village India will not part with their secrets for any amount of money. It is safe to guess that similar safeguards prevailed in ancient Babylonia and Egypt, as well as among the advanced astrologers of the ancient Americas.

I would also like to point out that the serious problems which confronted both the Roman empire and later Christianized Europe arose in part because in the West astrology became divorced from its spiritual context. In India, the stars were invariably seen against the limitless backdrop of Spirit. While astrology was condemned by the religious establishment in the West, in India it has always been hailed as the very "eyes" of the Vedic spiritual tradition. Astrology allows us to peer into the future. When we see an obstacle ahead of us in the road we can plan a detour. Indian religion sees foreknowledge as useful and good; Western religion sees it as evil and threatening.

In ancient Greece, fate was thought to be capriciously apportioned by whimsical gods. In South Asia, where belief in reincarnation has always been pervasive, it was understood that we create our own destiny, which then plays out over the course of our lifetimes. Consider how a Vedic astrologer would approach the Greek myth of Oedipus. Oedipus was told it was his destiny to kill his father and sleep with his mother. The Indian would say that, because of his casual attitude toward killing and sexuality in previous lives, Oedipus needed to learn two very important lessons: not to take the life of any other human being, and to respect all women as if they were his mother. Oedipus was given the tools—the prediction of his possible future—to correct his life course. Hot-headedness and lust, however, prevailed: Oedipus angrily slew an older man who refused to get out of his way in the road, and leapt into bed with a wealthy older woman, not realizing they were his parents. The Western perspective is that Oedipus was a tragic victim of fate. From a Vedic point of view, Oedipus could easily have avoided killing his father and sleeping with his mother if he had made wise use of the foreknowledge he was granted.

Will we make wise use of foreknowledge? Today we astrologers use our art to help clients succeed in business. Perhaps tomorrow we will help political parties select unscrupulous candidates who are running the most promising planetary cycles during an election. Maybe we'll advise legislators on the most favorable day to push for passage of a destructive new law. Perhaps we will use the birth data of their opponents to point out hidden character flaws and weak transits during which media attacks may prove particularly effective. In India, high ranking politicians often conceal their birth data or give out false birth times because they recognize how much damage a skilled but unscrupulous astrologer can do. Is there an ethical limit to the types of astrological services we'll offer our clients? Or like the astrologers of ancient Rome, will we provide the best advice possible to our clients, regardless of how they intend to use it?

I asked Ammachi, one of India's greatest living saints, what she thought of the advent of Jyotish in the West. "It is a good thing because so many people can be helped," she said. "But at the same time it has a dark side. When a powerful predictive system falls into the hands of a materialistic culture, the potential for abuse is enormous.

"Jyotish must not be practiced with impure motivation. Astrologers concerned only with making money or gaining fame will not succeed. This is because it is not possible to do Vedic astrology properly without tapas (spiritual self-discipline). Real astrology lies beyond the calculations. It is done through the *dhi.*" *Dhi* is the subtlest portion of the intellect, the thin film of human awareness that separates Shiva (God) from *jiva* (the soul). When *dhi* is purified, one's intuition becomes transparent and the light of divine knowledge can shine undistortedly into the field of our consciousness.

Those of us watching the recent dramatic developments in our field recognize a sea-change coming for Western astrology. A confluence of factors, including the rediscovery of our Greek astrological heritage and the current galvanizing encounter with Vedic astrological adepts, is putting extremely powerful predictive techniques back in our hands. In India, this knowledge was traditionally guarded with fanatic zeal. Because of the democratic nature of our society, however, this newfound ancient science will be available here to anyone who cares to exploit it.

It's happened before. This time, we'd better use it wisely.

AFTER WORDS

If you're interested in learning more about Vedic astrology, you're in luck. When I first started studying there was very little digestible information available in English. In the past few years, however, there's been an explosion of fine books on the subject. Here are my favorites:

Ancient Hindu Astrology for the Modern Western Astrologer by James Braha
Astrology of the Seers by David Frawley
The Betz Ephemeris 1940-2040 by Martha Betz and Keith Betz
Dots of Destiny by Richard Houck
Elements of Astrology by K.S. Charak
The Greatness of Saturn by Robert Svoboda
How to Practice Vedic Astrology: A Beginner's Guide by Andrew Bloomfield
How to Read Your Horoscope by Tom Hopke (Nalini Kantadas)
Light on Life: An Introduction to the Astrology of India by Hart deFouw and Robert Svoboda
Nakshatras by Dennis Harness, Ph.D.
Predictive Astrology of the Hindus by Pandit Gopesh Kumar Ojha
Yogas in Astrology by Dr. K.S. Charak

Since I'm shameless enough to toot my own horn, let me suggest two other books which might be of interest. If you'd like to explore the cultural matrix out of which Vedic astrology emerged, consider picking up my book *The Complete Idiot's Guide to Hinduism.* (Yes, I'm the complete idiot who's trying to guide people to understand Hinduism.) If you're new to Eastern spiritual practices and would like to learn more about hatha yoga and meditation, you might check out another of my books, *Alpha Teach Yourself Yoga.* All my books are available at Amazon.com.

The American College of Vedic Astrology is a wonderful resource for finding a Vedic astrologer in your area, connecting with other people interested in Jyotish, or signing up for seminars. You can check out their website at www.VedicAstrology.org. For some of the best classes in Vedic astrology being offered, log on to www. VedicVidyaInstitute.com.

A few last words of advice. Vedic astrology is not a casual subject. It will acquaint you with the potentials of your life course, but also with your weaknesses, crises you will need to face, and finally with your mortality. My most difficult challenges, including both my husband's cancer and my own, were clearly keyed into both our charts. Working with these realities has deeply impressed on me the truth of karma and reincarnation, and the fact that life here on the planet Earth is, from beginning to end, a spiritual education. The most important lesson I've drawn is that, whatever the stars may say, we need to move forward with courage and faith, caring for each other unselfishly, and continually deepening our connection with Spirit.

I wish you the very best in your spiritual adventure.

About the Author

Linda Johnsen, M.S., is Vedic Astrology Editor for *The Mountain Astrologer* magazine and Contributing Editor for *Yoga International.* She is author of the award-winning *Daughters of the Goddess: The Women Saints of India.* Her other books include *The Living Goddess: Reclaiming the Tradition of the Mother of the Universe, Teach Yourself Yoga in 24 Hours, The Complete Idiot's Guide to Hinduism, Meditation is Boring: Putting Life in Your Spiritual Practice* and *Alpha Teach Yourself Yoga.* Her essays on Hindu astrology and Eastern spirituality have appeared in numerous magazines and anthologies including *Hindu Astrology Lessons.* Linda has a Master's degree in Eastern Studies.

Yes International Publishers

Yes International Publishers was founded by Swami Rama of the Himalayas and his assistant, Theresa King, while they hiked the mountains of Nepal in 1984. They had both started the Himalayan Institute Press in 1972 and wished for another publishing house to share the teachings of the yogis, the scientists, and the mystics with the world.

Yes International publishes books, audios and videos in wellness, yoga, spirituality, mysticism, and personal development. Many of our books have won national awards for their superior content and artistic display of ideas and principles and are published internationally.

By Justin O'Brien, Ph.D. (Swami Jaidev Bharati)
Walking with a Himalayan Master: An American's Odyssey
The Wellness Tree: A Dynamic Program for Creating Opimal Wellness
A Meeting of Mystic Paths: Christianity and Yoga
Mirrors for Men: Personal Reflections
Running and Breathing

By Theresa King
The Spiral Path: Explorations into Women's Spirituality
The Divine Mosaic: Women's Images of the Sacred Other

By Swami Veda Bharati
The Light of Ten Thousand Suns
Subtler than the Subtle: The Upanishad of the White Horse

By Linda Johnsen
Daughters of the Goddess: The Women Saints of India
The Living Goddess: Reclaiming the Mother of the Universe Tradition
A Thousand Suns: Designing your Future with Vedic Astrology

By Charles Bates
Pigs Eat Wolves: Going into Partnership with Your Dark Side
Ransoming the Mind: The Integration of Yoga and Modern Therapy